Dying by the Sword

Dying by the Sword

The Militarization of US Foreign Policy

MONICA DUFFY TOFT AND SIDITA KUSHI

OXFORD
UNIVERSITY PRESS

OXFORD
UNIVERSITY PRESS

Oxford University Press is a department of the University of Oxford. It furthers
the University's objective of excellence in research, scholarship, and education
by publishing worldwide. Oxford is a registered trade mark of Oxford University
Press in the UK and certain other countries.

Published in the United States of America by Oxford University Press
198 Madison Avenue, New York, NY 10016, United States of America.

Library of Congress Cataloging-in-Publication Data
Names: Toft, Monica Duffy, author. | Kushi, Sidita, author.
Title: Dying by the sword : the militarization of US foreign policy /
Monica Duffy Toft and Sidita Kushi.
Description: New York, NY : Oxford University Press, [2023] |
Includes index.
Identifiers: LCCN 2022058408 (print) | LCCN 2022058409 (ebook) |
ISBN 9780197581438 (hardback) | ISBN 9780197581445 (epub)
Subjects: LCSH: Intervention (International law) | Conflict management—United States—History. |
Militarism—United States—History. | United States—Foreign relations.
Classification: LCC JZ6368.T63 2023 (print) | LCC JZ6368 (ebook) |
DDC 303.6/90973—dc23/eng/20230111
LC record available at https://lccn.loc.gov/2022058408
LC ebook record available at https://lccn.loc.gov/2022058409

DOI: 10.1093/oso/9780197581438.001.0001

Printed by Sheridan Books, Inc., United States of America

Monica Duffy Toft dedicates this book to her parents, Joan and William Duffy, for their guidance and strength.
Sidita Kushi dedicates this first book to her immigrant parents, Edmond and Shpresa Kushi, for their love and bravery.

Contents

Preface: The Provenance of "Dying by the Sword"

Then said Jesus unto him, Put up again thy sword into his place: for all they that take the sword shall perish with the sword.

Matthew 26:52, King James Version

In the garden of Gethsemane, immediately after Jesus was betrayed by Judas, Peter attacked one of the Roman soldiers sent there to take Jesus away. Jesus quickly rebuked Peter and admonished him to sheathe his sword. Jesus then gives the reason for his request, which also serves as a warning, that "all they that take the sword shall perish by the sword."

"Dying by the Sword" connects two important ideas. The first is that violence begets violence or, if you choose to use violence then you are more likely to sustain a violent response. It is also a warning to Peter to not act rashly or recklessly. Some damage can be undone: taking an object of value from someone can be compensated for by its return; and insulting or hurting someone verbally can be compensated for by a genuine apology. But the harm that swords can do is harder to undo.

As our book will document, the United States' overreliance on the use of force—living by the sword—has arguably made the United States, and indeed the world, less safe and less prosperous. At a time when a combined human effort to stave off climate disaster is greatly needed, the great peoples of Iran, China, Russia, and the United States, to cite but a few, seem more divided than ever, and more apt to regard each other as lethal enemies approaching an inevitable armed conflict rather than as potential allies in a much greater struggle.

In essence, the proverb flowing from Jesus's lips to Peter's ears remains as relevant as ever. And a return to US leadership by foreign policy circumspection rather than intervention would be very much in keeping with Jesus's admonition and counsel. It will likely take decades to realize, but deescalation of armed violence—and more importantly, the underlying principle represented: that the sword is the most effective means of achieving all desired ends—remains the world's only hope of surviving the intersecting challenges that we now face as a species.

Thanks to our international security colleagues at STTL for their help in narrowing down the title choices!

The Meaning Behind the Cover Image

The cover image of our book further reflects its underlying theme. Rather than raising a torch to represent enlightenment and the path to liberty, a proud Statue of Liberty, the international symbol of a freedom-loving, well-intentioned United States, wields a sword, high into the air, as envisioned by Franz Kafka in his work *Amerika*. This image also resonates strongly with the authors, two women in the field of international security, one of them a first-generation immigrant herself and the other a native of New York, who happened to dress as the Statue of Liberty in her homecoming parade during her senior year of high school, and shortly thereafter raised her right hand to support and defend the Constitution of the United States as a 17-year old private (E-1) in the U.S. Army..

Acknowledgments

This book would not have been possible without the steadfast work and support of the wonderful team at the Center for Strategic Studies (CSS) at Tufts University's Fletcher School. That team includes postdoctoral fellows, PhD fellows, and our large team of research assistants. We thank Nils Hägerdal, who directed the final year of the Military Intervention Project (MIP) and produced a completed data set of US military interventions from 1776 to 2019, and also contributed to case study analysis and summaries.

We are also grateful to past and present CSS postdoctoral fellows Karim Elkady, Benjamin Denison, Stephen Moncrief, and Aroop Mukharjee for their research support on MIP; as well as their insightful reviews of chapter drafts. Thanks as well to past and present CSS Research Fellows Lima Ahmad, Neha Ansari, Zoltan Feher and David Kampf, who each supported this book via their case study research and literature notes.

We thank past and present CSS program coordinators Anna Ronell and Polina Beliakova for their wide range of support for the Center's research initiatives, budgets, and vision, among other contributions.

We should add that in the several years of rigorous research it took to produce the MIP data set and case studies, a superb team of research assistants at the Fletcher School of Law and Diplomacy were instrumental in researching cases, doing background historical research, and updating components of our data set. We are grateful for our RA leaders and researchers Bryan Cassella, Mario Zampaglione, Dylan Farley, Andrew Hogan, and Emily Kennelly who trained and supervised other RAs on dataset coding and entry as well as completed case study research and writing. We thank the rest of our amazing RA team for their hard work, including our senior RAs Daniel Creamer, Jacqueline Faselt, Moriah Graham, Daniel Morton, and Nate Dobbin, as well as Samuel Carletta, Emilio Contreras, David Folsom, Ian Franckling, Camille Freestone, Becki Glawe, Michael Gradus, Sam Green, Nicholas Guarnaccia, Chelsea Hanlon, Madeleine Herr, Grady Jacobsen, Alex Kersten, Abby Kukura, Jack Lashendock, Rachael Lew, Claire McGillem, Meagan Reid, Stefan Shover, Carson Thal, Michael Vandergriff, and Cassandra Zavislak. We're also very grateful for Rachel Goretsky's editing and formatting of our manuscript as it reached its final stage.

We would like to thank the Charles Koch Foundation for its generous funding of our MIP data set and the many activities of the Center for Strategic Studies, from which this book is derived.

We're grateful also to our manuscript reviewers for their insightful feedback, which made this book stronger and better. We're also thankful for our Oxford University Press editor David McBride for his expertise and support through every step of this journey; as well as Kevin Eagan for his editorial guidance and Hemalatha Arumugam and Sarah Ebel for their patient and sound management of our manuscript.

Lastly, we owe so much to our respective families for their love and support through this long and challenging journey. Monica Duffy Toft would especially like to thank her husband Ivan Arreguín-Toft and their children Sam and Ingrid for their support as she started working on this book; and for helping to provide the time, patience, and space needed to finish it.

Sidita Kushi would especially like to thank her parents, Edmond and Shpresa Kushi, for their abundant love, wisdom, and sacrifices. They risked it all in a foreign land for the sake of their children, and it was their bravery and hard work that made it possible for the author to pursue her intellectual dreams. Sidita Kushi would also like to thank her sister Odeta for her constant support and lifelong friendship like no other. Lastly, she is grateful for her husband Iliya, who patiently endured the author's writing process and supplied a healthy dose of distraction.

Introduction

War and Diplomacy in US Foreign Policy

"5,000 troops to Colombia" was ominously scribbled on an innocuous yellow pad in January 2019, showing just how much contemporary US foreign policy is defined by military interventions. The note's author was then-US National Security Advisor John Bolton, who sought to resolve the ongoing presidential crisis in Venezuela by immediately deploying American armed forces abroad.[1] Diplomacy was out, a show of military force was in. Swords over wealth and words was the order of the day. With no ambassador in Venezuela since 2010, American diplomacy was handicapped from the start. While the crisis ended with no US deployment this time, Bolton's note illustrates how readily US political leaders push for immediate military "solutions" to burgeoning international dilemmas. What is worse, these dynamics were and are not unique to Venezuela. This "force-first" mentality reverberates through most contemporary US foreign policy choices. And despite President Joseph Biden's stated commitment to increase the State Department's budget to reengage the world and repair our alliances, funding remains far less than that of the Department of Defense. Yes, Russia's war in Ukraine reinforces the notion that the risk of major interstate war remains, which we do not deny. But two key questions follow: was Russia's slowly escalating belligerency inevitable? And second, does a force-first foreign policy generally result in an escalatory spiral? If history is any guide, the devolution of diplomacy will get worse as the primacy of military statecraft continues to take pride of place.

A critical aspect of our engagement overseas is through ambassadors, who are the president's eyes and ears on the ground in both friendly and unfriendly places. US presidents traditionally reward some generous campaign donors with political ambassadorial appointments. The percentage of such political appointees hovered around 30 percent in the past, with 70 percent of the posts still reserved for career diplomats—diplomats who possess years of hard-earned on-the-ground cultural and practical experience. Under the

Dying by the Sword. Monica Duffy Toft and Sidita Kushi, Oxford University Press. © Oxford University Press 2023.
DOI: 10.1093/oso/9780197581438.003.0001

Donald J. Trump administration, that trend was nearly reversed. What's more, the Department of State lost 12 percent of its employees in the foreign affairs division under Trump, and the diplomats that remained had to fight to remain part of the policymaking process.[2] Increasingly, US foreign policy is now in the hands of inexperienced political appointees in the executive branch.

While President Biden promised to "elevate diplomacy as the premier tool of our global engagement," and "re-empower the finest diplomatic corps in the world," it remains to be seen whether the path dependencies of American diplomacy since the year 2000 will budge, as they will also require a dramatic rebalancing of federal budgets and priorities for many years to come.[3] As of February 2022, Biden has appointed 87 ambassadors, and over half of them are political appointees; continuing the trends of the Trump administration; albeit to a lesser degree.[4]

US diplomacy is experiencing a fundamental shift, one a long time in the making but escalating rapidly in our contemporary era. It is moving away from the era of hard-fought negotiations among career diplomats to an age of kinetic diplomacy—diplomacy by armed force, removed from the in-depth local knowledge garnered by traditional diplomats. What does this shift mean for the future of US foreign policy? Can past patterns offer clues as to the evolution of kinetic diplomacy and its most urgent consequences? By tracing US foreign policy through different eras with a combination of historical narratives, theoretical perspectives, and data-driven empirical analysis, this book identifies both key trends and lessons for contemporary politics.

The Argument

Throughout its history as a global actor, the United States has taken on many roles. It evolved from a relatively isolationist state to a hesitant intervenor to a global policeman and defender of the liberal world order. But in the past two decades, it has often and quickly escalated to the use of force abroad, with strong domestic and international backlash. In survey after survey, if you ask the global public, America is seen as a bigger threat to global peace and prosperity than China and Russia (prior to Russia's invasion of Ukraine).[5] These perceptions may arise from trigger-happy US foreign policy, characterized by an overreliance on force, with minimal support for diplomatic efforts and few consistent national strategies. Relying on military force is hardly a new means to project power abroad. Indeed, factions of more hawkish political elites often contend with more restrained voices and ideologies. In other words, the impulse to be more forceful always existed across every era of US foreign policymaking, but structural forces and historical events sometimes serve to mute or embolden this impulse.

For instance, for an entire decade after Vietnam, the US military's reputation suffered, and few Americans trusted in the use of force abroad. After Ronald Reagan vowed to rehabilitate the US military, and after two equivocal US victories in Grenada and Panama, the US military regained its image as an effective institution, and gained the respect of US public opinion. Yet at the same time, as political scientist Ivan Arreguín-Toft has shown,[6] great powers—even superpowers like the Soviet Union—were losing wars against, on paper, much weaker adversaries more often than winning them. Highly tuned to this problem, the Department of Defense adopted the Weinberger Doctrine as a hedge against joining the toll of losses in unconventional wars. It wasn't to last, largely due to the American habit of fetishizing new technology which, along with traditional US exceptionalism, invariably appears to invalidate the hard-won lessons of past military failures.

In *Humane,* for example, Samuel Moyn tells the story of how the United States has succeeded in reimagining armed combat as a consistent, first-line tool of foreign policy, instead of as an imperfect tool of last resort, or as a prelude to quagmire (think Afghanistan, 2001–2022). Examining over a century of history, he reflects on how the availability of precision weaponry and the path dependencies of safeguarding the US national image led us to the contemporary era of "forever wars," perhaps minimizing some of the violence but perpetuating US dominion globally.[7] Historically, attempts to decrease the friendly costs of war (i.e., our own casualties) only serves to make war a more palatable tool of foreign policy; as in the case of the United States' post-9/11 drone warfare programs, which present a sanitized image of modern warfare and separate that image from the everyday lives of both American citizens and policymakers.

In recent decades, domestic structures and international events strengthened the American impulse towards forcefulness to unprecedented levels. Such factors include but are not limited to the aftermath of a US "unipolar moment" in which, following the end of the containment doctrine against the Soviet Union, national interests expanded to include human rights promotion, democratization, drug interdiction, and other non-trivial but nonvital geopolitical interests. US militarism also found fertile ground in rising defense spending even after the end of the Cold War, propelled partially by growing power of "the Iron Triangle:" the confluence of interest of congressional committees, US federal agencies, and special interest groups and defense industry lobbyists.[8] In fact, according to OpenSecrets, a non-profit that measures money flows within the Iron Triangle, between 1998 and 2021, the defense sector led by corporations such as Raytheon, Lockheed Martin, and Boeing was one of top-ranked spenders on lobbying the US government.[9]

Not only is the frequency of US military intervention increasing, but the level of US hostility is rising, the nature of US interventions is shifting, and its aims are escalating. In fact, our data reveal the United States hasn't had a year without at least one newly started military intervention since 1974. According to our research, the United States has undertaken almost 400 international military interventions since 1776, with more than half of them occurring after World War II. What's more, the United States waged 29 percent of these interventions in the post–Cold War era and they were more intense.[10] With recent interventions in Afghanistan, Iraq, and Libya, as well as weaponized drone campaigns in Pakistan, Yemen, and beyond, the widespread global concern about America's role in the world we and others have highlighted should not be surprising.

As its experience in and exit from Afghanistan attest (now standing as longest US war by far, as Figure AI.1 reveals), assessing the success of US military interventions is a fraught endeavor as well.[11] On one hand, in most of its contemporary missions, the United States overwhelmed other states with its military power and won a good number of short-term victories. On the other, in these same missions, the United States often failed to achieve long-term goals: a problem known colloquially as "losing the peace." Its lack of diplomatic engagement often inflames insurgencies and ignites civil wars in the wake of swift military victories. Therefore, worst of all, the United States is increasing its use of force abroad at a time when the resort to arms is, at a minimum, unlikely to advance US interests and, in fact, increasingly likely to prove counterproductive; such as in urban warfare and counterinsurgency operations.[12]

We describe current US foreign policy as kinetic diplomacy, which supplanted the traditional statecraft trifecta of diplomacy, trade and aid, and war as a last resort. As traditional diplomacy withers away and political elites gut the US Department of State, military interventions—including shadowy special operation missions, drone strikes, and "gray zone warfare" efforts—grow at unsustainable rates; as do the quantity and quality of US adversaries.

By means of an historical and data-driven review of the dominant foreign policy trends from the nation's founding in 1776 until today, we contend the United States has become addicted to military intervention. Each individual crisis appears to demand a military response, but a short-term respite then results in an even bigger problem later, which again seems to beg of an armed response, and so on and on: violence begets violence. Unlike the past, where force was a last resort, the United States now pursues a whack-a-mole security policy—much more reactionary than deliberate, lacking clear national strategic goals. We trace different eras of US foreign policy, marked by changing US strategic objectives. In the 1700s, the key US strategic goal was independence from Britain. The 1800s involved national expansion and the conquest of the Great Frontier, while warding off European powers. The United States emerged from relative isolation in the early 1900s to focus on the so-called war to end all wars, then shifted to defeating the Axis powers decades later. During the Cold War, the United States relied on the strategy of containment to prevent World War III, deterring a great power rival while promoting democracy, free trade, and the establishment of international institutions. By the 1990s, the United States aimed to establish itself as the leader of a New World Order through multilateral cooperation, the further enmeshment and institutionalization of Western norms, and a relatively balanced arsenal of foreign policy tools. In the post-9/11 era, US strategic goals shifted to preventive war: a global war on terror, which propelled the country down the path toward kinetic diplomacy.

Dying by the Sword dedicates a chapter to each defining era of US foreign policy, introducing historical narratives and compelling patterns from the Military Intervention Project (MIP) along the way. Each chapter highlights how the United States used and balanced primary tools of statecraft—diplomacy, trade, and war—to achieve its objectives. The book concludes with a warning that if the United States does not abandon its addiction to force-first, kinetic diplomacy, it will do permanent damage to its vital national interests; including its diplomatic corps, economic influence, and international reputation. It will be doomed to more, more costly, and counterproductive wars. And it will spell disaster for America's domestic and international stability.

These trends matter. Policymakers and the broader public need direct knowledge and access to a clear accounting of the patterns, outcomes, and

net effects of US militarism across time. After all, the descent into kinetic diplomacy directly impacts US domestic policy. Money spent on foreign wars
means money diverted away from economic development, health care, pan-
demic response, social welfare, education, infrastructure, job creation, and
other critical domestic public goods. Beyond this, a more kinetic foreign
policy prompts a higher risk of American casualties abroad, rising national
deficits and debt, and deteriorating international perceptions of US behavior,
which may demoralize long-time allies while increasing the quantity and
quality of US adversaries. US aggression may further legitimate aggression
by other international actors. For instance, the US invasion of Iraq after 9/11
decreased its international legitimacy in matters of human rights and democracy, making it more difficult to uphold international norms of nonaggres-
sion and noninterventionism across the international community at large.[13]
And for Russia, which continues to hold that great power status comes with
privileges not available to other states, acting aggressively abroad underlines
Russian claims that when it employs force abroad it is only acting as any great
power—and in particular, the United States—acts. In other words, ramped-
up US militarism results in increased threats to the US homeland as well as
to the stability of the international community and postwar world order—an
"order," it must be recalled, that was designed to permit openly hostile great
powers to co-exist without risking a species-ending third world war. Kinetic
diplomacy puts all that at risk.

Ultimately, this book aims to provide a concise synthesis of the entire arc
of America's intervention history, offering empirical analysis of the main
trends seen in our unique and comprehensive data set on all US military
interventions. Our analysis shows the United States does not need to restrain
itself from engaging on the world stage fully. Rather, it must rely on a more
extensive array of tools to secure its vital interests and contribute to a more
peaceful world. But we also argue that the impact of decades of force-first,
kinetic diplomacy comes with inertia: a cumulative effect whose most costly
aspects may take years to reverse. It will take skilled and consistent leadership to undo the damage already done by a sometimes necessary, but on balance excessive, resort to violence as a default foreign policy. Moreover, it will
take an educated and alert public to hold its leaders to account in how US
interests are secured and US dollars are spent to secure those interests.

This introduction first offers an outline of the critical turning points,
debates, and tools in US grand strategy and then introduces the book's approach, illustrating how it offers distinct contributions from previous

empirical efforts. Next, the introduction highlights the seven eras of US foreign policy, assessing the country's strategic goals. We also show how current patterns of US foreign policy are detrimental to the future of the country and the world before providing a roadmap for subsequent chapters.

Grand Strategy and the Three Pillars of Statecraft

Generally, the United States interacts with other states in the international system through the use of force, trade, and diplomacy, institutionalized via the departments of defense, commerce, and state, respectively. Of course, there has always been a trade-off between diplomacy and war. As General James Mattis, commander of US Central Command in 2013 said in Congressional testimony, "if [Congress doesn't] fund the State Department fully, then I need to buy more ammunition."[14] But what happens when diplomacy becomes a shell of its former self? What ensues when a grand strategy pillar the United States took for granted for centuries—diplomacy first and war as a last resort—collapses?

Unfortunately, the United States no longer balances its various tools of statecraft as it once did. Its eagerness to rely on military force escalated during the Cold War, mainly because the American public fell for the narrative of domino logic, and the image of an irrational communist enemy bent on world domination. In terms of Soviet, Chinese, and Cuban foreign policy, this narrative was not entirely false. But it wasn't policy but the dehumanization of the 'other' that ultimately led to a habit of leading with armed force. If its enemies were monsters that could not be reasoned with, then why bother even attempting to sway them from their path of destruction through bargaining and diplomacy? Better to beat them into submission.

But this widely held assumption of irrationality is far removed from realities on the ground. Even the most fervent communist rebels or leaders have tangible, strategic goals, such as national independence or increasing their resource capabilities; goals the United States could have engaged through shrewd diplomacy and economic statecraft. At least during the Cold War and in the immediate post–Cold War period, this assumed irrationality mainly applied to communist leadership and was restrained by the grand strategy of containment.

The 9/11 attacks, however, shattered any lingering nuance for good. The aftermath of the terrorist attacks—attacks organized and led by self-proclaimed religious actors undeterred even by the certainty of their own physical destruction—emboldened those political leaders who, in their bid to promote greater US military involvement, would depict enemies as irrational haters and their populations as bad people. Once this narrative takes hold, diplomacy is off the table as there is a refusal to negotiate with evil people, especially terrorists. Only brute force remains as an option. The George W. Bush administration took it a step further by identifying preventive wars as a tool of grand strategy. The logic is to kill evil, irrational enemies abroad before they have a chance to attack at home.

This is how kinetic diplomacy became enshrined in the US political psyche. Fueled by narratives of irrational, evil enemies, kinetic diplomacy grows in parallel with shrinking diplomatic capacity and bloated defense budgets, egged on by powerful interest groups within the Iron Triangle. The more force is resorted to, the more it has to be resorted to, and the United States ends up in a permanent state of war; a state of war which acts to abridge civil liberties and due process, stunts economic growth and starves infrastructure maintenance, and even suppresses gender equity (an environment of pervasive threat acts as a tax on women's leadership and full participation in the nation's economic, political, and social life).

To clarify, kinetic diplomacy is not the same as coercive diplomacy.[15] In the case of coercive diplomacy, a state relies on a combination of diplomatic channels to threaten a costly escalation unless the target countries comply.[16] In kinetic diplomacy, a state immediately turns to predominantly stealthy military resources, such as drone warfare, special operations, and covert missions, to violently coerce a rival in an attempt to prevent a costly escalation. In a word: it attempts to achieve its goals by killing. Unfortunately, even the best trained special operations forces can only accomplish so much without the aid of traditional diplomatic support, economic levers, or better intelligence. And intelligence comes in two main types: short-term, battlefield and operational intelligence; and long-term, cultural, linguistic, and historical intelligence. Military might only goes so far without both types of intelligence, and without the other basic tools of modern statecraft.

Hampered by an overreliance on force, the United States is also struggling to craft a new grand strategy that will help guide its national security and foreign policies into the future. While the concept of grand strategy is naturally fluid and frequently a subject of academic debate, we can generally define it as the highest-order vision that molds a state's foreign policy ends and means and as the overarching approach to national security—one that applies both to wartime and peacetime.[17] Thus, grand strategy demands the prioritization of interests, consensus formation on threats and opportunities, and contingency plans for changing circumstances. Moreover, grand strategy must leverage and organize all instruments of statecraft, such as war, trade, aid, and diplomacy, toward the pursuit of national interest and power.

As subsequent chapters illustrate, the United States relied on at least one or two grand strategic visions across different eras to formulate and achieve critical objectives. If we consider the contemporary era, there are competing visions for what the United States should try to achieve, from isolation to deep engagement, as outlined in Table I.1.

These contemporary debates and schools of thought on what America's strategy is or should be focus on the country's proper role in the international system in the wake of the Soviet Union's collapse. Scholars and policymakers alike continue to debate whether the United States should remain leader of the "free" world, continue some sort of engagement but in a more restrained manner, or pull back from existing commitments and focus its energy at home (isolationism).

Modern-day strategies differ from those pursued during the Cold War, which featured the United States counterbalancing the Soviet Union. It was a robust Department of State that shepherded the United States to its superpower status in the post–World War II era. Under the guidance of personalities such as George C. Marshall, the secretary of state beginning in 1947, the United States continued to safeguard the vital connection between diplomatic power and military effectiveness. It reinforced the expectation that civilian officials always outranked generals in policy decisions, as witnessed when President Harry S. Truman fired General Douglas MacArthur over MacArthur's insistence on continuing to seek a decisive victory in North Korea in 1951, despite contradictory administrative directives.[18]

Thanks to another diplomat, George F. Kennan, deputy chief of mission in Moscow, the United States successfully navigated the Cold War era as well. In his "Long Telegram" and subsequent "X Article" in *Foreign Affairs,* Kennan helped temper US military responses to its primary threat, the Soviet Union.[19] Kennan declared that an all-out military option would fail because the United States had already demobilized in Europe while a large number of Soviet troops remained within rapid striking distance of Paris and the rest of Western Europe. Most importantly, Kennan reminded the American public and its elites that while the Soviet Union held to an expansionist revolutionary ideology, it still behaved in pragmatic, self-interested ways

Table I.1 Summary of Contemporary US Grand Strategies

Grand Strategy	Main Themes
Neo-Isolationism[a]	US must distance itself from international politics to safeguard its security. Since there are no threats to the homeland, the US does not need to intervene abroad. <ul><li>US is not responsible for maintaining world order;</li><li>Economic growth driven by private sector;</li><li>US should not seek to spread its values abroad;</li><li>Policies: Withdraw from NATO, end US military presence abroad, and defocus from nuclear proliferation.</li></ul>
Restraint[b]/ Offshore Balancing[c]	US must avoid involving itself in security affairs unless another state is seeking to establish hegemony in three strategic regions: Western Europe, Northeast Asia, and the Persian Gulf. <ul><li>Retrench from current extensive global role and from maintenance of "US-led international order;"</li><li>No forward posture of US forces;</li><li>Military should be used rarely, only with clear goals;</li><li>Rely on deterrent power of nuclear weapons;</li><li>Maintain a relatively open trade system;</li><li>Policies: Withdraw from NATO and withdraw US forces from Europe, withdraw from the Gulf to the lowest level possible, and maintain enough US presence in Asia to balance with allies against China.</li></ul>
Selective Engagement[d]	US should only intervene in regions that directly affect its security, typically powers with significant industrial, economic, and military potential, as per realism. This is a compromise between restraint and liberal hegemony. <ul><li>Focus on relationship with Europe, East Asia, and the Persian Gulf;</li><li>Forward posture of US forces;</li><li>Main goals:</li><li>Prevent war between great powers;</li><li>Prevent the rise of adversarial regional hegemons;</li><li>Prevent nuclear proliferation;</li><li>Preserve access to oil supplies;</li><li>Pursue "liberal values" of free trade, democracy, human rights, only when they do not harm primary security interests;</li><li>Policies: Maintain existing formal and informal alliances and maintain forward posture in key regions, but withdraw US forces from other regions.</li></ul>
Collective Security[e]	US should promote the growth of democratic governments and international institutions to prevent conflict and mitigate the security dilemma, as per (neo)liberal institutionalism. <ul><li>Collective security applied to humanitarian crises;</li><li>Usage of force allowed via humanitarian interventions;</li><li>Policies: Build and maintain international institutions, prevent nuclear proliferation, stop regional conflict, and stop humanitarian atrocities across borders.</li></ul>

Table I.1 Continued

Grand Strategy	Main Themes
Liberal Hegemony[f] Primacy/ Deep Engagement	US must become/remain the world hegemon to maintain the international liberal order to ensure peace. It must sometimes rely on force to spread liberal values and institutions. • Maintain unrivaled military power and preserve unipolar distribution of power; • Forward posture of US forces; • Create and maintain extensive level of permanent alliance commitments worldwide; • Biggest threats stem from failed states, rogue states, and illiberal states; • Policies: Pursue nuclear nonproliferation, bolster US military to Cold War levels, support democratization and free trade, wage regime change wars.

[a] Barry R. Posen and Andrew L. Ross, "Competing Visions for U.S. Grand Strategy," *International Security* 21, no. 3 (Winter 1996-1997): 5–53, doi:10.2307/2539272.

[b] Barry R. Posen, *Restraint: A New Foundation for U.S. Grand Strategy*, Cornell Studies in Security Affairs (Ithaca, NY: Cornell University Press, 2014); Eugene Gholz, Darryl G. Press, and Harvey M. Sapolsky, "Come Home, America: The Strategy of Restraint in the Face of Temptation," *International Security*, 21, no. 4 (2017):5–48.

[c] John J. Mearsheimer and Stephen M. Walt, "The Case for Offshore Balancing," *Foreign Affairs*, (July/ August 2016); Christopher Layne, "The U.S. Foreign Policy Establishment and Grand Strategy: How American Elites Obstruct Strategic Adjustment," *International Politics*, 54, no. 3 (2017): 260–275; Christopher Layne, "From Preponderance to Offshore Balancing," *International Security*, 22, no. 1 (Summer 1997): 86–124; John J. Mearsheimer, *The Great Delusion: Liberal Dreams and International Realities* (New Haven, CT: Yale University Press, 2018).

[d] Robert J. Art, "Geopolitics Updated: The Strategy of Selective Engagement," *International Security*, 23, no. 3 (Winter 1998–1999): 79–113, doi:10.2307/2539339; Robert J. *Art, A Grand Strategy for America* (Ithaca, NY: Cornell University Press, 2004).

[e] Rodger Payne, "Cooperative Security: Grand Strategy Meets Critical Theory?" *Millennium*, 40, no. 3 (2012): 605–624, doi: 10.1177/0305829812441733; Charles A. Kupchan and Clifford A. Kupchan, "The Promise of Collective Security," *International Security* 20, no. 1 (1995): 52–61; Michael Mihalka, "Cooperative Security in the 21st Century," *Connections* 4, no. 4 (Winter 2005): 113–122.

[f] Stephen G. Brooks, John Ikenberry, and William C. Wohlforth, "Don't Come Home, America: The Case against Retrenchment," *International Security* 37, no. 3 (2012): 7–51; Stephen Brooks, John Ikenberry, and William Wohlforth, "Lean Forward: In Defense of American Engagement," *Foreign Affairs* 92, no. 1 (2013): 130–142, 137; John G. Ikenberry, *Liberal Leviathan: The Origins, Crisis, and Transformation of the American World Order* (Princeton, NJ: Princeton University Press, 2011); Joseph S. Nye, *The Future of Power* (New York: Pacific Affairs, 2011); Robert Kagan, *The World America Made* (New York: Alfred Knopf, 2012); Stephen G. Brooks and William Wolhforth, *America Abroad: The United States' Global Role in the 21st Century* (New York: Oxford University Press, 2016).

internationally. Thus, just like any other rational actor, the Soviets could be incentivized against aggression and expansion through a policy now known as containment. This route emphasized the need to prevent the Soviet Union from subverting other governments while promoting the appeal of the rule of law, free speech, free and fair elections, and market capitalism across the world. Through this diplomatic route—consistent with its "City Upon a Hill" roots, the United States avoided direct military confrontation with another great power, sparing the lives of countless troops and civilians.

At this time, President Truman and his administration also knew that the US public would not support another major war unless enemies directly threatened American soil. But over time, hawkish factions grew. Proponents of a "rollback" strategy wanted to deploy all US national resources to vanquish the "evil empire" of the Soviet Union and its satellite dictatorships and to "roll back" the Soviet occupation of Eastern Europe. The hawks' stance was an ideological, moral, even religious one, with endless confidence in US military might. Across the decades, they continued to push for a more aggressive, militarized US foreign policy, even amid the clear successes of containment. They awaited their chance to redirect foreign policy. In fact, these dissenting voices would eventually alter the very meaning of Kennan's containment strategy. The afterlife of Kennan's containment strategy would encompass a more expansive militarized policy that led to a disastrous US military intervention in Vietnam's civil war.[20]

Each of these grand strategies serves as an ideal type; describing (and in some cases advocating for) different levels of action and engagement and different policy responses using different tools of statecraft depending on the international environment. Alongside empirical and historical evidence, we use these perspectives and other theoretical premises to help explain patterns of US foreign policy and military interventions and predict future trajectories. The book also considers the merits and limitations of each grand strategy across the eras, focusing particularly on the more contemporary debates between restrainers (intellectual descendants of containment advocates) and deep engagers (intellectual descendants of rollback advocates).

To understand when, why, and how the United States relied on military force, it's also worth recognizing the two most important institutions guiding Washington's national security and foreign policy. The historical trajectories of the Department of State and the Department of Defense are therefore key parts of the story.

The influence of the State Department in the making of US foreign policy and grand strategy has fluctuated throughout the past 200-plus years since its inception. "Until World War II, the State Department was the major organization responsible for foreign affairs," with elite politicians and even future presidents serving as secretary of state, including Thomas Jefferson, James Madison, James Monroe, John Quincy Adams, Martin Van Buren, and James Buchanan.[21]

As the United States grew into a great power and its international relationships expanded, the management of foreign affairs necessitated the involvement of other departments and agencies. Hence, as advances in communications technologies such as railroads, steamships, aircraft, and radio made the world effectively smaller and, more importantly, dramatically compressed time for deliberation and collaboration, the Department of State waned in overall influence in foreign policymaking.[22] At the dawn of the Cold War, newly appointed secretary of state George Marshall sought to strengthen the department's capabilities and influence, asking George Kennan to set up the Policy Planning Staff.[23] Throughout the Cold War and in the post–Cold War period, "operational demands (putting out fires) and the inherent tension between useful specificity and diplomatic generality have made the exercise of policy planning in the Department of State a perennial problem. This situation has tended to shift much of the weight of policy planning to the NSC [National Security Council] staff and the DoD [Department of Defense]."[24]

The State Department has not been able to avoid a significant loss of influence over the past several decades, which is directly connected to the rise of military interventionism in US foreign policy, among other factors such as a growing bureaucracy and a more interconnected global economy.[25] An increase in US power and greater reliance on force as a tool of foreign policy also brings the Department of Defense to the forefront of foreign policymaking—a political dynamic that the military itself initially resisted, and which became painfully obvious to the general public after 9/11.

The Department of Defense did not initially dominate decision making in the same way it does today. As with the State Department, it was the emergence of the United States in the mid-twentieth century as a great power that brought about structural changes in the executive agencies responsible for defense. It was during World War II that the current headquarters of the department, the Pentagon, was built: "At the time of its construction in 1941–43, President Franklin D. Roosevelt and most of the government and the public believed that the building was a response to temporary circumstances and that it would not be required for the military after the war when conditions would return to normalcy. But the memory of the surprise attack on Pearl Harbor led most Americans and their leaders to share the belief that US security would from now on demand constant vigilance and constant readiness. As such the post-World War II world never returned to what Americans regarded as normalcy."[26]

US demobilization following the end of World War II and the dawning of the Cold War led to serious restructuring in the defense establishment. Since 1947, a series of defense reorganization acts have significantly strengthened the role of the secretary of defense as well as further centralized the department toward greater efficiency and responsiveness.[27] The balance between military and civilian leaders within the department has also shifted throughout the history of the Pentagon, with ongoing public debates about how best to separate politics and the military.

The Approach of the Book

Our book provides a unique, powerful blend of original data-driven analysis and a narrative history of US foreign policy as it relates to the use of armed force abroad. And though our core focus remains illuminating the empirical record, our analysis remains framed by theoretical insight. Each chapter includes a range of aggregated patterns of US intervention from our Military Intervention Project (MIP); providing data on essential trends across time and place, as well as more nuanced historical discussions on crucial political events across the eras. Below we detail our two-pronged approach to analyzing US military interventions and foreign policy and graphically show how it differs from currently existing sources and methods.

The Military Intervention Project

The Military Intervention Project (MIP) is a comprehensive data set of all US military interventions since the country's founding. It also measures potential drivers of military intervention as well as the domestic and international costs of US military involvements, encompassing over 200 different unique variables.[28]

Military interventions include the threat, display, or direct usage of force by the United States against another state or foreign actor/territory, including over 100 American Indian nations. We, however, present the frontier war and drone warfare data separately from "traditional" US interventions. We reduce a wider universe of potential means of advancing US national interests to three main categories: (1) military intervention; (2) economic trade and aid; and (3) diplomacy and soft power (e.g., Hollywood). Diplomacy is an example of the United States relying on nonviolent tools of statecraft in advancing its foreign policy.

In comparison to the most robust existing data sets of US military intervention, MIP more than doubles the universe of cases, integrates a range of military intervention definitions, expands the timeline of analysis, and offers more transparency and nuanced analysis through supplemental case narratives of every intervention.[29]

MIP thus offers empirical measures of all instances of US military intervention from 1776 until 2019, alongside all the significant drivers and consequences of these interventions. For a more in-depth scope of analysis, historical case study narratives of every mission complement the aggregated data set. By relying on a broad historical lens of US military interventions, this research also speaks to long-term trends, dramatic changes, and lasting costs and benefits to domestic and international politics. By including a range of literature-relevant definitions of US military intervention, MIP can assess empirical results across these definitions and their corresponding data sets.[30]

Not only does MIP greatly expand the universe and variables on US military interventions, but it also offers the gold standard for case documentation via its written case studies of each instance of US military intervention, confirmed by at least three scholarly sources. This distinct method of approach allows MIP to add more cases to its universe, edit missing or otherwise incorrect data from other sources, remove certain cases from the definition of US military intervention, and incorporate more nuanced variable measurements. Ultimately, these MIP distinctions also produce distinct new patterns of US military intervention, which are vital to theoretical debates and contemporary policy discussions.

To better show the advances in MIP, we briefly compare important patterns of US military interventions arising from the current leading data set on military interventions, the Militarized Interstate Disputes (MID).[31] We chose MID because it is the most comparable to MIP, includes the best documentation, and is the most widely used by scholars. Nevertheless, as will become apparent, MIP and MID do not agree on a host of patterns, from the number of interventions to the targets and the nature of those interventions.

Figure I.1 compares US military interventions captured by MIP and MID across all eras.[32] Our data set contains a total of 392 cases of US military intervention from 1776 until 2019 that have been confirmed by case study analysis and at least three scholarly sources. This number does not include the Frontier Wars or drone warfare universes. In this process, MIP removed

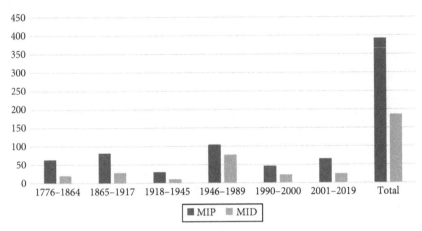

Figure I.1. MIP-MID Comparative Graph of US Interventions by Era, 1776–2019

Citation: The Militarized Intrastate Disputes (MID) codebook and data set are found here: Glenn Palmer, Vito D'Orazio, Michael Kenwick, and Matthew Lane, "The Mid4 Dataset, 2002–2010: Procedures, Coding Rules and Description," *Conflict Management and Peace Science* 32 (2015): 222–242; Zeev Maoz, Paul L. Johnson, Jasper Kaplan, Fiona Ogunkoya, and Aaron Shreve, "The Dyadic Militarized Interstate Disputes (MIDs) Dataset Version 3.0: Logic, Characteristics, and Comparisons to Alternative Datasets," *Journal of Conflict Resolution*, (2018), doi: http://journals.sagepub.com/doi/full/10.1177/0022002718784158.

178 uncertain cases that were found in other existing data sets but could not be confirmed as a US military intervention by our in-depth case study analysis (our complete case study narratives are available upon request). MID contained 134 of these removed cases, but 52 of them were already correctly marked by MID as characterized by zero US hostility, meaning that the United States did not respond to another country's military usage of force toward them. Therefore only 82 MID cases were removed from MIP due to the inability to confirm a US threat of force, display of force, or usage of force. In other words, out of the 268 total MID cases of US intervention with some level of hostility, MIP was only able to confirm 186 of them. Even with its many removed cases, MIP contains about 200 more cases of intervention than MID.

It also becomes immediately evident that MID reports most of its interventions for the Cold War period and underreports for all other periods, relative to MIP. Both data sets report the Cold War era (1946–1989) as the most militaristically active for the United States, with the 1868–1917 era following close behind. But MID and MIP disagree beyond these rankings. MIP reveals the post-9/11 era, running from 2001 to 2019, to be the third most active for US interventions. MID patterns prompt the opposite conclusion, with the United States seemingly decreasing its frequency of interventions from 1990 onward. Overall, however, MIP offers many more cases to the universe of US military interventions, which allows it to capture cycles of US interventions that have gradually increased in frequency across time, especially in the 1980s and beyond. MID, on the other hand, reveals no such drastic cyclical patterns over time.

In addition, MID reports more US interventions against European state targets relative to other regions of the world, as shown in Figure I.2. According to MIP, the United States has undertaken 34 percent of its interventions against countries in Latin America and the Caribbean, 23 percent in East Asia and Pacific, 14 percent in the Middle East and North Africa, and only 13 percent in Europe and Central Asia. Moreover, while MIP shows that over 9 percent of US interventions have occurred in Sub-Saharan Africa, MID barely registers any activity within these target regions. In other words,

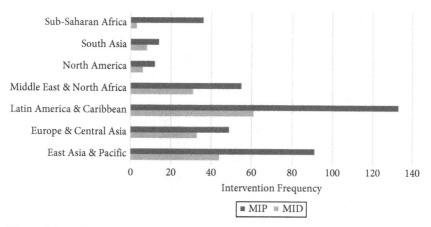

Figure I.2. MIP-MID Comparative Graph of US Interventions by Region, 1776–2019

Citation: The Militarized Intrastate Disputes (MID) codebook and data set are found here: Glenn Palmer, Vito D'Orazio, Michael Kenwick, and Matthew Lane, "The Mid4 Dataset, 2002–2010: Procedures, Coding Rules and Description," *Conflict Management and Peace Science* 32 (2015): 222–242; Zeev Maoz, Paul L. Johnson, Jasper Kaplan, Fiona Ogunkoya, and Aaron Shreve, "The Dyadic Militarized Interstate Disputes (MIDs) Dataset Version 3.0: Logic, Characteristics, and Comparisons to Alternative Datasets," *Journal of Conflict Resolution*, (2018). doi: http://journ als.sagepub.com/doi/full/10.1177/0022002718784158. The Military Intervention Project (MID) introductory article, dataset, and codebook are found here: Sidita Kushi and Monica Duffy Toft, "Introducing the Military Intervention Project Dataset on US Military Interventions, 1776–2019," *Journal of Conflict Resolution* (2022). doi: 10.1177/00220027221117546.

MID does not capture one of the most important regional trends that arose in the 1990s and 2000s.

MID's data set seems to include more European targets of intervention, which corresponds with its Cold War focus. When including the unconfirmed cases of intervention collected by MID ($n = 82$), we see an even stronger focus on interventions against countries in Europe and Central Asia and countries in Latin America.

Following MID's example, MIP also rates the United States' intervention on a scale from 1 to 5, from the lowest level of (1) no militarized action to (2) the threat of force, (3) display of force, (4) use of force, and, finally, (5) war. As shown in Figure I.3, MIP illustrates a far higher number of instances in which the United States relied on the use of force than MID—over two times more often. Within MIP, almost half of the coded US military interventions included the direct usage of force abroad (41 percent of the cases), and over half of them (52 percent) have included displays of force.

These brief comparisons across time, region, and hostility levels between our new data set and the most comprehensive existing data set on US military interventions, reveal discrepancies in historical patterns of US intervention, ones that hold essential policy implications. By applying our MIP

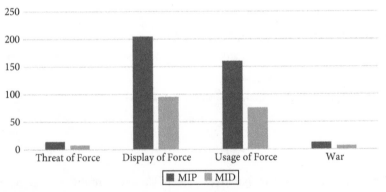

Figure I.3. MIP-MID Comparative Graph of High Hostility Levels, 1776–2019
Citation: The Militarized Intrastate Disputes (MID) codebook and data set are found here: Glenn Palmer, Vito D'Orazio, Michael Kenwick, and Matthew Lane, "The Mid4 Dataset, 2002–2010: Procedures, Coding Rules and Description," *Conflict Management and Peace Science* 32 (2015): 222–242; Zeev Maoz, Paul L. Johnson, Jasper Kaplan, Fiona Ogunkoya, and Aaron Shreve, "The Dyadic Militarized Interstate Disputes (MIDs) Dataset Version 3.0: Logic, Characteristics, and Comparisons to Alternative Datasets," *Journal of Conflict Resolution*, (2018). doi: http://journ als.sagepub.com/doi/full/10.1177/0022002718784158. The Military Intervention Project (MID) introductory article, dataset, and codebook are found here: Sidita Kushi and Monica Duffy Toft, "Introducing the Military Intervention Project Dataset on US Military Interventions, 1776–2019," *Journal of Conflict Resolution* (2022). doi: 10.1177/00220027221117546.

data set, our book presents brand-new empirical, historical, and theoretical contributions to the discussion on US military interventionism.

Historical Analysis by Era

But MIP is not the only innovation of this book. While MIP allows us to grasp the broader pattern of US interventionism across centuries, our parallel historical analysis enables us to trace the progression of pivotal events and elite decision-making in the country over key foreign policy issues. In other words, the historical case studies can tell the stories behind the numbers, especially the ones of great transition from one trend to another, of ideas and motivations that guided the leadership at the time, and of cultural or historical events that shifted the tides. We rely on our collection of almost 400 case studies of US military intervention to begin this journey, supplementing it with historiography, archival evidence, and other primary sources. Each chapter traces several key historical events and the military, economic, and diplomatic reactions to these events across each distinct era, often through the eyes of prominent statesmen and policymakers.

The Landscape of US Military Intervention

Overall, our MIP data and case analysis reveal the United States increased its use of armed force abroad since the end of World War II, throughout the Cold War, and continuing into the post-9/11 era. This is shown in Figure I.4.

From the 1970s to the 1980s, the number of new US interventions doubled and continued to rise until 2010. However, what is striking is that although the 2010–2019 decade indicates a decline in the number of new interventions, this figure does not account for interventions that continued—the long wars—that began earlier, including Afghanistan and Iraq.

Over these periods, the United States grew to prefer the direct use of force over threats or displays of force, increasing its hostility levels while its target states decreased theirs in response. Along the way, the regions of interest changed as well. Furthermore, Defense Department spending has substantively outpaced expenditures by the State Department. For instance, even at its highest, Department of State (DOS) outlays are about 5 percent of Department of Defense (DOD) total outlays.

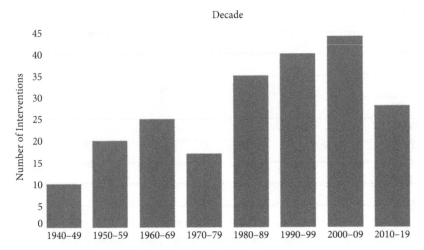

Figure I.4. US Military Interventions by Decade, 1940–2019

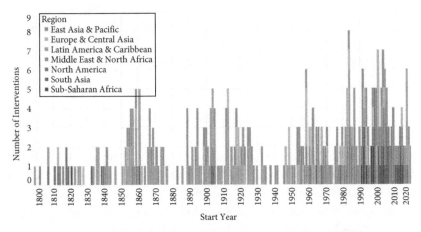

Figure I.5. US Military Interventions by Year and Region, 1776–2019

Figure I.5 shows that US interventions have taken a cyclical pattern over time, increasing with each cycle. According to this time-series view, the United States' last year without a new military intervention was in 1974. Prior to that, it was 1952.

Regional trends shifted over the years too. Up until World War II, the United States frequently intervened in Latin America and Europe, which stills account for nearly 50 percent of total US interventions as per Figure I.6.

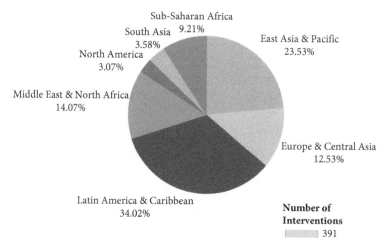

Figure I.6. US Interventions by Region, 1776–2019

Beginning in the 1950s and increasing by the 1980s, the United States moved into the Middle East and North America (MENA), and by the 1990s, it doubled down on MENA and directed its focus to Sub-Saharan Africa and South Asia as well. More recent US interventions are increasingly targeting the MENA region and Sub-Saharan Africa, especially in the post–Cold War era. In a short amount of time, these interventions now make up almost a quarter of total US military interventions across the centuries (Figure I.6). Figure I.7 further showcases this regional shift across the eras. The regional expansion of the usage of force parallels America's rise from a regional hegemon to a global hegemon.

Figures I.8 and I.9 further refine these patterns by distinguishing between hostility levels during US interventions.[33] Figure I.8 shows that the United States generally preferred displays of force and usage of force over the threat of force and interstate war. However, this pattern does not hold across all periods, as shown in Figure I.9.

Figure I.9 reveals the usage of force has grown as a proportion of all interventions across the eras. Interestingly, the post-9/11 era, running from 2001 to 2019, appears to be the third-most active for US interventions of relatively higher hostility levels. In this era, threats of force are absent, while instances of the active use of force are overwhelmingly commonplace. Since 2000 alone, the United States engaged in thirty interventions at level 4 or 5. Arguably, the post–Cold War era produced fewer great power conflicts and

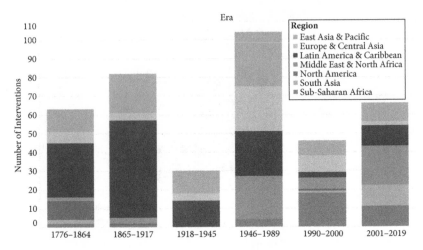

Figure I.7. US Military Interventions by Era and Region, 1776–2019

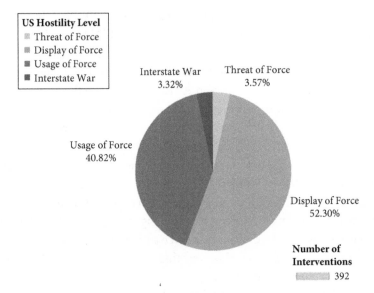

Figure I.8. US High Hostility Levels, 1776–2019

instances in which to defend vital US interests, yet US military interventions continue at high rates and higher hostilities. Thus, this militaristic pattern persists during a time of relative peace, one of arguably fewer direct threats to the US homeland and security.

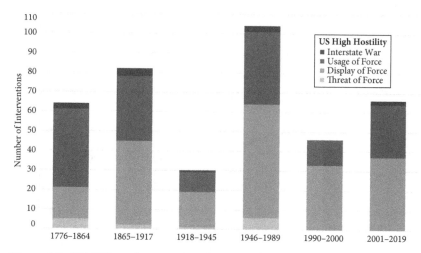

Figure I.9. US Military Interventions by Era and Hostility Levels, 1776–2019

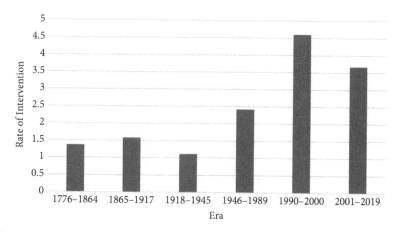

Figure I.10. US Military Intervention Rates across the Eras, 1776–2019

Figure I.10 graphs the rate of US military interventions across these same eras. Since each era consists of a different number of years, we see the increase in US military interventions more clearly by calculating the rate of intervention by year within each era.

Between 1776 and the end of World War II, the United States intervened about once a year. During the Cold War, the United States intervened at a much higher rate per year, but it wasn't until the end of the Cold War that the United States substantially increased its rate of intervention to 4.6 per year.

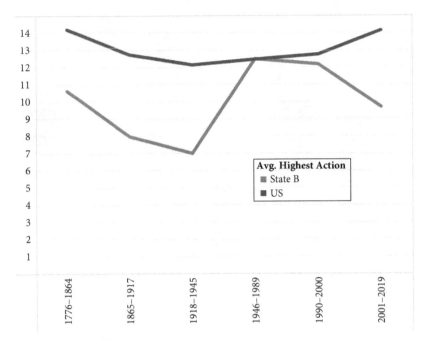

Figure I.11. Highest Military Action by United States versus State B across the Eras, 1776–2019

The pattern of increased US hostilities becomes more evident when we compare the highest levels of military hostility by the United States to the target state in a conflict year. In Figure I.11, we graph comparative hostilities between the United States and State B through the measurement of the highest military action taken by each side during the year of the dispute, a category that breaks down the more general hostility levels we introduced above.[34]

The measure of 1 equates to no military action, while 14 (the highest in the graph of era averages but not in the full sample of interventions) denotes a border violation by the US usage of force. In between, the measure 7 represents a show of troops, 9 a show of ships, 10 denotes an alert show of force, and 12 denotes a military mobilization in the show of force broader category. Higher military actions such as clashes (18), raids (19), and interstate wars (23) exist across the spectrum of US interventions as future chapters reveal, but they are not average measures across the eras.

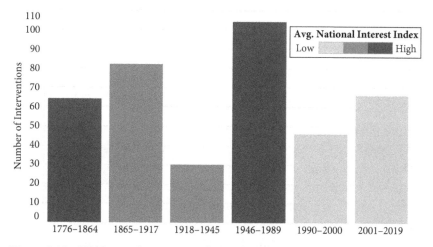

Figure I.12. US National Interests and Intervention Patterns, 1776–2019

While target states dramatically decreased their levels of hostility after the Cold War related to disputes with the United States, the United States escalated hostilities well into the post–Cold War era. Figure I.11 thus reveals a widening gap of military actions between the United States and State B, especially since 2000.

MIP also measures national interest-related factors from 1776 to 2019. Figure I.12 uses the same US intervention frequencies from above as a backdrop for the measurement of US national interests across the eras. We apply a National Interests Index that adds up separate measures on contiguity, colonial history, alliances, and natural resources.[35]

The United States involved itself in military conflicts with high national interests until the 1860s, usually fought to preserve the new nation and expand its domestic territory and sphere of influence. National interests dipped in the next eras during the time of the Banana Wars and Mexican Revolution, but then spiked during the Cold War alongside intervention frequency. In the post–Cold War, the United States intervened in pursuit of less vital national interests as US geopolitical rivalries and vital threats to homeland security faded. Thus, the post–Cold War era saw the United States wield its military might toward more missions of democratization, human rights enforcement through humanitarian interventions, and third-party interventions in internal domestic crises across the world.

Unfortunately, this means that the United States experienced higher intervention rates even when lower levels of national interest were at stake. These patterns do not bode well for aspirations toward a prudent, rational, and optimized foreign policy and doctrine on the usage of force. It also counts as a serious criticism of US global leadership; which suffers from increasingly easy claims of US foreign policy double-standards and hypocrisy. Moreover, it might explain why increasingly, the rest of the world sees the United States as a threat.[36]

The militarization of US foreign policy is also seen in the patterns of Department of Defense (DOD) outlays relative to the Department of State (DOS) and intervention frequencies across the years in Figure I.13.

These figures show that the proportion of DOD outlays and interventions have increased dramatically since 2001, with slightly lower DOD outlays beginning in 2013. DOS outlays on their own have also increased, yet DOS spending, even at its peak, remains only 5.5 percent of total DOD spending. Further, while US military expenditures experience cycles of growth and waning, their exponential rise in the post–Cold War, especially in the early 2000s, is swift, severe, and the highest level of expenditures yet for the country, despite the lack of an existential security threat.

In the chapters to come, we will break down these trends and contextualize them using an array of primary sources and historical analysis.

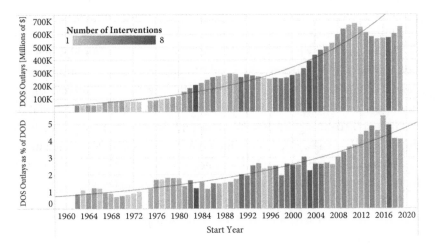

Figure I.13. DOD and DOS Outlays related to Interventions, 1960–2019

Citation: Office of Management and Budget. *Historical Tables.* https://www.whitehouse.gov/omb/historical-tables.

Chapter Overview

The chapters that follow focus on distinct eras of US foreign policy. We categorize eras by significant historical and geopolitical events that shaped US military aspirations and capabilities.

The period of 1776 to 1864 sees the United States rise above its colonial dependency and isolationist beginnings to become a regional power, expanding its territory through the bloody Frontier Wars and land purchases, warding off European ambitions in the Western hemisphere through the Monroe Doctrine, and surviving the Civil War. Next, 1865 to 1917 denotes the pre–World War I era, with the United States transforming into an imperialist power in Latin America and protecting its commercial interests abroad, such as through the open-door policy in China. The era of 1918 to 1945 marks the post–World War I through World War II period, as the United States emerges from the Great Depression and political isolation to come to the defense of its European allies. The post–World War II Cold War era from 1946 to 1989 marks the height of US military, political, economic, and cultural power as it balances against its Soviet rival.

As the victor of the Cold War, the United States experiences its "unipolar moment" from 1990 to 2000, marked by the pre-9/11 foreign policy priorities of liberal leadership through humanitarian military interventions, democratization, and free trade. Finally, the period from 2001 to the present is defined by the Global War on Terror and the rise of kinetic diplomacy.

Chapter 1. America the Expander, 1776–1864

Until the War of 1812, the United States was a weak, isolated actor, with little presence on the international stage as it struggled for legitimacy and respect among traditional European powers. The United States undertook very few military interventions in the form of colonial proxy wars within North America against its European rivals and engaged in some more distant skirmishes such as the Barbary Wars.

But between 1813 and 1864, America's objectives changed to conquering the Great Frontier. Much of its foreign policy consisted of waging the frontier wars against over 100 different North American Indian nations. Throughout this period, the United States grew in military and economic power but confined its power projections within its continental-wide neighborhood, with some key exceptions in the Pacific. Yet the United States was far from an isolationist power.

Chapter 2. America the Western Hegemon, 1864–1917

By this era, the United States had solidified and enlarged its statehood, expanded its power within North America, enforced its sphere of influence in Latin America, and even defended itself against North African Barbary pirates. As it neared the completion of its forceful Manifest Destiny from the East to the West of the continent, the United States battled over 100 Native American nations for territorial conquest and displaced and killed an astounding number of people during these Frontier Wars.

In the aftermath of this internal colonization in the late 1800s and early 1900s—experienced by indigenous Americans more as a genocide—the United States vied for regional power within its neighborhood, now extending fully to Latin America and the Caribbean, and several islands in the South Pacific. We trace how the once imperialized United States becomes the imperialist, highlighting key events including the Spanish-American War, Mexican Revolution, Banana Wars, and the Philippine-American War. The United States expanded its sphere of influence beyond its neighborhood and reaches the heights of regional hegemony as it progressed through the late 1800s and into the 1900s. Thus, in this pre–World War I era, the United States was as a growing imperialist power across Latin America and the Pacific, while restraining European powers from economic and political gains in the continent.

Chapter 3. America the Hesitant Helper, 1918–1941

Judging by the momentum of the previous era, we would expect the United States to increase its international involvement into the next era by expanding its imperialist ambitions beyond Latin America and generally making its mark in more strident ways internationally. That was not America's path between the two world wars. Instead, this chapter highlights stark reversals in US foreign policy in the pre–World War II era, moving from its previously imperialist ambitions to isolationist tendencies, and then finally to becoming a hesitant helper of its European allies. America's isolationist streak arose from dire domestic economic conditions, which then spread like wildfire across the Atlantic. American political and economic isolationism fanned the flames of rising fascist movements around the world, which ultimately dragged a reluctant United States from its political hibernation.

This era concluded with the United States extending its tools of war, trade, and diplomacy far beyond its neighborhood to punish Monarchist Germany in World War I; and to rescue China and Europe to end a second world conflagration in World War II; a conflagration marked by mass murder and rape against civilians in Poland, the Balkans, the Soviet Union, Korea, and China. Across the western world, this era propelled the isolationist United States from that of an emergency ally to that of an often-benign great power, ready to act on the world stage. Key historical events and issues included interventions in Central America and the Far East, the global economic crisis, isolationism, and the rise of fascism, as well as World War II.

Chapter 4. America the "Leader of the Free World," 1946–1989

The United States emerged from World War II as a hero to its European allies and as a superpower, generally unharmed by the devastation of the war. In fact, World War II emboldened US industrial production, military advancements, and the promotion of American values, beliefs, and institutions worldwide. The Cold War era featured the United States as one of two superpowers in a new bipolar world order.

During this time, the United States' greatest objective was to deter Soviet expansion, whether it be territorial, militaristic, economic, or ideological. Foreign policy specialists and leaders came to a shaky consensus on how to deal with the Soviet threat: containment, which demanded high diplomatic engagement alongside selective military involvement. As political elites broadened interpretations of the strategy of containment, another policy alternate lingered in the background, rollback. The persistent proponents of rollback pushed for greater US militaristic commitment to completely "roll back" new Soviet territorial gains in Europe and political influence around the globe. While muted for part of the Cold War, the rollback camp never disappeared. Its proponents pushed the policy of containment toward more belligerent ends and shaped pivotal US foreign policy decisions in the future.

Despite its aggressive rivalry with the Soviet Union, the United States was still perceived as a strategic and restrained actor on the world stage, standing for the sought-after principles of democracy, human rights, and market freedoms. Major historical events during the Cold War included the occupation of Europe and Japan, Chinese civil war, Korean War, interventions and coups against leftist governments in Latin America, the Vietnam War, détente, the oil crisis, Afghanistan operations, and more.

Chapter 5. America the Unipolar Hegemon, 1990–2000

As the victor of the Cold War, the United States emerged as the liberal world hegemon and unipolar power in the 1990s. But the United States also lost its sense of purpose with the fall of the Soviet Union, as it was no longer driven by a clear rivalry and acute security challenges. The post–Cold War era required a reorientation of US grand strategy and the identification of new and less threatening national interests to pursue, which proved challenging.

The United States pursued self-proclaimed good intentions (albeit selectively applied and often disastrous) like democratization, human rights promotion, and free-market expansion, as seen in its humanitarian military interventions, regime change efforts, multilateral missions, and free trade deals. Despite its increasing influence and power in this era, the United States continued to rely on diplomacy and trade as pillars of its foreign policy, on top of its multilateral militarism.

The George H. W. Bush administration dealt with the collapse of the Soviet Union effectively and supported Germany's reunification afterward in 1990. America's first big military intervention in the 1990s, the overthrow of Saddam Hussein during the Gulf War of 1990–1991, was a success and denoted the zenith of America's military power and influence. Unfortunately, despite its pinnacle of power and international respect garnered during this time, US leadership floundered in identifying a new coherent grand strategy in the post–Cold War era and applying it consistently and effectively across political crises, including the interventions in the Middle East, humanitarian responses (or lack thereof) in Somalia, Haiti, and Rwanda, and the Balkan interventions.

In a sense, US grand strategy became the victim of the corollary of Weinberger and Powell Doctrine: if military intervention was only legitimate against other states capable of directly harming the United States, that only made the world safe for dictators and mass murderers, ranging from Pol Pot in Cambodia, to Rwanda's *Interhamwe*, to Serbia's Slobodan Milosevic in the Balkans. As Richard Falk, a US foreign policy practitioner, put it, the United States in this period faced a painful dilemma: standing idly by was intolerable, yet a permanent victory via military intervention remained impossible.[37]

Chapter 6. America the Unleashed, 2001–present

The post-9/11 era ushered the most significant US foreign policy reorientation from "diplomacy first, and force as a last resort," to "military force first." This period saw the rise of its defense budget and special operations and the waning of State Department funds, influence, and diplomatic capacity—a hallmark of kinetic diplomacy. The September 2002 National Security Strategy formalized the "Bush Doctrine," considering terrorists as hostile states, particularly fearing that Islamist movements could one day get their hands on nuclear weapons.[38] Due to such threat perceptions, the Bush Doctrine also pushed preventative wars and unilateral practices of rampant militarism.[39]

During this era, the United States overestimated the capabilities of its military superiority, disregarding other tools of statecraft. This often meant that the United States embarked on military missions that garnered early successes but then failed to consolidate effective post-war strategies and gain local and ally support. This chapter also includes a section tracking the evolution of US military technology such as drone warfare.

Chapter 7. Conclusion

The last chapter traces the path toward kinetic diplomacy and evaluates trends and implications for the future of US power, prosperity, and international security. It summarizes the empirical and historical journey and provides a list of policy and theoretical recommendations for the future.

* * *

The next chapter begins our journey into US foreign policy and the use of force with the beginnings of the nation itself. The United States emerged as a new state with little ambition and few resources. It was a critical period for the country as it began its westward movement and sought to establish itself economically, diplomatically, and militarily.

Notes

1. Monica Duffy Toft, "America Now Solves Problems with Troops, Not Diplomats," *The Conversation*, October 3, 2019, https://theconversation.com/america-now-solves-problems-with-troops-not-diplomats-120956.
2. Jack Corrigan and Government Executive, "The Hollowing-Out of the State Department Continues," *The Atlantic,* February 11, 2018, https://www.theatlantic.com/international/archive/2018/02/tillerson-trump-state-foreign-service/553034/.
3. "Foreign Policy and American Leadership Plan," Biden-Harris Democrats Website, https://joebiden.com/americanleadership/.
4. "Ambassadors Appointed by Joe Biden," Ballotpedia, 2022, https://ballotpedia.org/Ambassadors_appointed_by_Joe_Biden; Daniel Strauss, "Biden's Political Appointments for Ambassador Posts Rile Career Diplomats," *The Guardian,* July 31, 2021,https://www.theguardian.com/us-news/2021/jul/31/biden-political-appointments-ambassador-posts.
5. These figures were collected prior to Russia's invasion of Ukraine. We expect these trends to change in the aftermath of Russia's aggression. Global Attitudes and Trends, Pew Research Center, February 10, 2019, https://www.pewresearch.org/global/2019/02/10/climate-change-still-seen-as-the-top-global-threat-but-cyberattacks-a-rising-concern/#changing-threats-in-a-changing-world.
6. Ivan Arreguín-Toft, *How the Weak Wars: A Theory of Asymmetric Conflict* (Cambridge: Cambridge University Press, 2005).
7. Samuel Moyn, *Humane: How the United States Abandoned Peace and Reinvented War* (New York: Farrar, Straus and Giroux, 2021).
8. Gordon, Adams, *The Iron Triangle: The Politics of Defense Contracting* (New York: Council on Economic Priorities, 1981).
9. See ranking here: https://www.opensecrets.org/federal-lobbying/ranked-sectors?cycle=a . See specific corporate actors here: https://www.opensecrets.org/federal-lobbying/top-spenders.
10. This data arises from the findings of the Military Intervention Project (MIP) undertaken at the Center for Strategic Studies (CSS). For more details, see MIP Research. 2019. The Center for Strategic Studies, https://sites.tufts.edu/css/mip-research/.
11. Craig Whitlock, "The Afghanistan Papers: At War with the Truth." *The Washington Post*, December 9, 2019, https://www.washingtonpost.com/graphics/2019/investigations/afghanistan-papers/afghanistan-war-confidential-documents/.
12. Ivan Arreguín-Toft, *How the Weak Win Wars* (Cambridge: Cambridge University Press, 2005) and John Spencer, "The Eight Rules of Urban Warfare and Why We Must Work to Change Them," *Modern War Institute at West Point*, January 12, 2021. https://mwi.usma.edu/the-eight-rules-of-urban-warfare-and-why-we-must-work-to-change-them/#:~:text=While%20the%20complex%20physical%20terrain,engage%2Dat%2Ddistance%20capabilities.

13. Michael E. Becker, Matthew S. Cohen, Sidita Kushi & Ian P. McManus, "Reviving the Russian empire: The Crimean Intervention through a Neoclassical Realist Lens," *European Security* 25, no. 1 (2016): 112–133.

14. Richard Sisk, "Mattis Heads into Marathon Tussle with Congress on Defense Budget," *Military.co, June 12, 2017,* https://www.military.com/daily-news/2017/06/12/mattis-heads-marathon-tussle-congress-defense-budge.html.

15. Monica Toft, "The Dangerous Rise of Kinetic Diplomacy," *War on the Rocks*, May 14, 2008, https://warontherocks.com/2018/05/the-dangerous-rise-of-kinetic-diplomacy/.

16. In one of the classical works on coercive diplomacy, Alexander George defines it as "to back one's demand on an adversary with a threat of punishment for noncompliance that he will consider credible and potent enough to persuade him to comply with the demand." Alexander George, *Forceful Persuasion: Coercive Diplomacy as an Alternative to War* (Washington, DC: Endowment of the United States Institute of Peace, 1991), 4.

17. For definitions of grand strategy, see Thomas P. Cavanna, "U.S. Grand Strategy," *Oxford Research Encyclopedia, American History* (New York: Oxford University Press, 2019); Walter A. McDougall, "Can the United States Do Grand Strategy?" *Foreign Policy Research Institute*, April 13, 2010, https://www.fpri.org/article/2010/04/can-the-united-states-do-grand-strategy/; David Edelstein and Ronald Krebs, "Delusions of Grand Strategy: The Problem with Washington's Planning Obsession," *Foreign Affairs* 94, no. 65 (2015): 109–116; Lukas Milevski, *The Evolution of Grand Strategic Thought* (Oxford: Oxford University Press, 2016); Hal Brands, *What Good is Grand Strategy: Power and Purpose in American Statecraft from Harry S. Truman to George W. Bush* (Ithaca, NY: Cornell University Press, 2014), 3; Robert J. Art, *A Grand Strategy for America* (Ithaca, NY: Cornell University Press, 2003), 1; Paul Kennedy, "Grand Strategy in War and Peace: Toward a Broader Definition," in *Grand Strategies in War and Peace,* edited by Paul M. Kennedy (New Haven: Yale University Press, 1992), 4; Barry R. Posen, *Restraint. A New Foundation for U.S. Grand Strategy* (Ithaca, NY: Cornell University Press, 2014), 13.

18. Monica Duffy Toft, Fewer Diplomats, More Armed Force Defines U.S. Leadership Today," *The Conversation*, March 28, 2018, https://theconversation.com/fewer-diplomats-more-armed-force-defines-us-leadership-today-92890.

19. George F. Kennan, "Telegram, George Kennan to James Byrnes [Long Telegram]," Harry S. Truman Administration File, Elsey Papers, February 22, 1946; George F. Kennan, "The Source of Soviet Conduct ['X Article']," *Foreign Affairs*, July 1947, https://www.foreignaffairs.com/articles/russian-federation/1947-07-01/sources-soviet-conduct.

20. Thomas P. Cavanna, "U.S. Grand Strategy," *Oxford Research Encyclopedia, American History* (New York: Oxford University Press, 2019), doi: 10.1093/acrefore/9780199329175.013.721.

21. Jerel Rosati and Scott de Witt, "The Department of State," in *Routledge Handbook of American Foreign Policy,* edited by Stephen W. Hook and Christopher M. Jones (New York: Routledge, 2012), 179.

22. Jerel Rosati and Scott de Witt, "The Department of State," 179–180.
23. Wilson D. Miscamble, *George F. Kennan and the Making of American Foreign Policy, 1947–1950.* (Princeton, NJ: Princeton University Press, 1992), 5.
24. Amos A. Jordan, William J. Taylor, Jr., Michael J. Meese, and Suzanne C. Nielsen, *American National Security*, Sixth Edition (Baltimore, MD: Johns Hopkins University Press, 2009), 90.
25. Rosati and de Witt, "The Department of State," 179–180.
26. Historical Office, Office of the Secretary of Defense, *Pentagon History*, adapted from *The Pentagon: The First Fifty Years*, https://history.defense.gov/DOD-History/Penta gon/History/.
27. Jordan et al., *American National Security*, 91.
28. The data set and most of the analysis that follows are first introduced in, Sidita Kushi and Monica Duffy Toft. "Introducing the Military Intervention Project Dataset on US Military Interventions, 1776–2019," *Journal of Conflict Resolution (2022)*. doi: 10.1177/00220027221117546.
29. Our data set codebook and appendix are available upon request.
30. MIP's unit of analysis is a US military intervention within a target country, with start and end dates. Taking inspiration from MID's definition, MIP's broadest definition of US intervention encompasses united instances of international conflict or potential conflict outside of normal peacetime activities in which the purposeful threat, display, or use of military force by official US government channels is explicitly directed toward the government, official representatives, official forces, property, or territory of another state actor. See: Douglas M. Gibler, *International Conflicts, 1816-2010: Militarized Interstate Dispute Narratives* (Landham, MD: Rowman & Littlefield, 2018).
31. The Militarized Intrastate Disputes (MID) codebook and data set are found here: Glenn Palmer, Vito D'Orazio, Michael Kenwick, and Matthew Lane, "The Mid4 Dataset, 2002–2010: Procedures, Coding Rules and Description," *Conflict Management and Peace Science*, 32 (2015): 222–42; Zeev Maoz, Paul L. Johnson, Jasper Kaplan, Fiona Ogunkoya, and Aaron Shreve, "The Dyadic Militarized Interstate Disputes (MIDs) Dataset Version 3.0: Logic, Characteristics, and Comparisons to Alternative Datasets," *Journal of Conflict Resolution*, (2018), doi: http://journals.sage pub.com/doi/full/10.1177/0022002718784158.
32. It is important to note, however, that MID includes other international state actors within its intervention universe, but we only use the subsample of US interventions. Additionally, the MID sample of interventions only include those up to the year 2010.
33. It is important to note, however, that not all of MIP's intervention cases have confirmed levels of hostility, thus, some measures are coded as "unclear."
34. Please refer to the MIP codebook for full coding on Highest Actions. We have generally adapted this measure from the Militarized Intrastate Disputes (MID) codebook and data set.
35. According to realist scholars, geopolitical national interests drive trends of military interventions. This literature equates national interest to the maintenance and global expansion of geopolitical influence, a favorable distribution of power, often by relying

on former colonial relationships; and the pursuit of political interests within a region. See Alex J. Bellamy and Paul D. Williams, "Who's Keeping the Peace? Regionalization and Contemporary Operations," *International Security* 29, no. 4 (2005): 157–195; Michael Gilligan and Steven J. Stedman, "Where Do the Peacekeepers Go?" *International Studies Review* 5, no. 4 (2003): 37–54; Richard Perkins and Eric Neumayer, "Extra-territorial Interventions in Conflict Spaces: Explaining the Geographies of Post-Cold War Peacekeeping," *Political Geography* 27, no. 8 (2008): 895–914; Refer to the Appendix for details on the measurements for the National Interests Index.

36. Attitudes and Trends, *Pew Research Center,* February 10, 2019, https://www.pewresea rch.org/global/2019/02/10/climate-change-still-seen-as-the-top-global-threat-but-cyberattacks-a-rising-concern/#changing-threats-in-a-changing-world.

37. Richard N. Falk, "Hard Choices and Tragic Dilemmas," *The Nation* 257, no. 21 (1993), p. 757.

38. John L. Gaddis, *Surprise, Security, and the American Experience* (Cambridge, MA: Harvard University Press, 2004), 30–31.

39. Andrew J. Bacevich, *American Empire: The Realities and Consequences of U.S. Diplomacy* (Cambridge, MA: Harvard University Press, 2002); Michael Mann, *Incoherent Empire* (London and New York: Verso, 2002).

Introduction Appendix

Table AI.1 Top Ten US Military Interventions with the Most Troops Deployed, 1776–2019

Intervention	Start Year	US Troops Deployed
World War II	1941	16,000,000
World War I	1917	4,700,000
Vietnam War	1964	2,594,000
Korean War	1950	1,789,000
Operation Desert Storm	1991	532,000
War of 1812	1812	468,000
Spanish-American War	1898	290,000
NPT Threats (North Korea)	1993	200,000
Operation Iraqi Freedom	2003	170,000
Berlin Crisis	1961	148,000

Table AI.2 Top Ten US Military Interventions with most Battle Fatalities, 1776–2019

Intervention	Start Year	US Battle Fatalities
World War II	1941	291,557
Vietnam War	1964	58,000
World War I	1917	53,402
Korean War	1950	34,000
War of 1812	1812	4,999
Operation Iraqi Freedom	2003	4,491
The Philippine-American War	1899	4,200
War in Afghanistan	2001	2,372
Mexican-American War	1846	1,733
Laos Civil War	1962	728

Source: The Military Intervention Project. Sidita Kushi and Monica Duffy Toft, "Introducing the Military Intervention Project Dataset on US Military Interventions, 1776–2019," *Journal of Conflict Resolution* (2022). doi: 10.1177/00220027221117546.

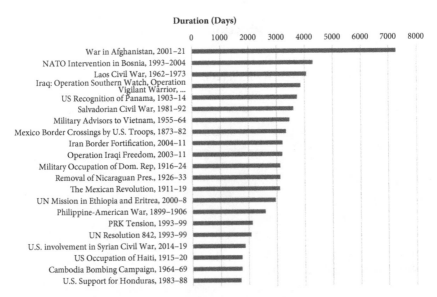

Figure AI.1 Top 20 Longest US Military Interventions in Days, 1776–2019 (Including War in Afghanistan ending in 2021)

1

America the Expander

The conquest of the earth, which mostly means the taking it away from those who have a different complexion or slightly flatter noses than ourselves, is not a pretty thing when you look into it too much. What redeems it is the idea only.

Joseph Conrad, *Heart of Darkness*

The United States started as an agricultural nation of thirteen colonies and 2.4 million people. Yet the 1860 census revealed the population stood at over 31 million—of which nearly four million were slaves—in thirty-three states and ten organized territories.[1] This early expansion, both in population and territory occurred partially via repeated military operations waged against American Indian foreign nations and many "filibuster"[2] military actions within Latin America, all while the young country attempted to evade involvement in Old World politics. The United States' early expansionism was driven by the powerful ideology of Manifest Destiny as well as domestic interests in maintaining the corrosive institution of slavery. By the American Civil War, the United States was quickly moving toward industrialization, which allowed the North to triumph over the South.

This chapter traces the beginnings of the United States as a sovereign state from 1776 to 1864. Until the War of 1812, the United States was a relatively weak, actor, with little presence on the international stage. It still struggled for legitimacy and respect with European great powers. The United States undertook few military interventions in the form of colonial proxy wars within North America against its European rivals and naval battles against quarrelsome pirates. Instead of military might, the United States initially relied more on threats and shows of force as well as diplomatic strategies to guard its new sovereignty and interests. The sword remain sheathed.

Dying by the Sword. Monica Duffy Toft and Sidita Kushi, Oxford University Press. © Oxford University Press 2023.
DOI: 10.1093/oso/9780197581438.003.0002

This changed after the War of 1812. From 1813 to 1864, US objectives changed to that of conquering the Great Frontier. Hence, much of its foreign policy consisted of waging asymmetrical Frontier Wars against over 100 different indigenous North American Indian nations. Legally, the US Constitution empowered Congress to "regulate commerce with foreign nations, and among the several States, and with the Indian tribes," making the wars against American Indian nations the overwhelming legacy of US foreign policy in its first era of existence.[3] Throughout this period, the United States grew in military and economic power, concentrating first on the continent and then across the Western hemisphere. Thus, by the end of this first era, the United States had moved speedily away from its isolationist foreign policy beginnings.[4]

The first section of the chapter offers a historical synthesis of the United States' first grand strategy. It also highlights the centrality of the Frontier Wars as part of the country's expansionist foreign policy. The second part examines the nation's earliest militarism and foreign policymaking outside of the continent. Part three delves into the grand strategy of US expansionism outside of the continent until 1864, while part four relays key historical events from 1812 to 1864 that helped to shape US foreign policy into the next era. The last part of the chapter analyzes America's journey from a weak, relatively isolated power to a regional player in the international system.

America's Beginnings and the Frontier Wars

America's First Grand Strategy, 1776–1812

"For we must consider that we shall be as a city upon a hill. The eyes of all people are upon us. So that if we shall deal falsely with our God in this work we have undertaken . . . we shall be made a story and a by-word through the world."[5] As echoed by Puritan leader John Winthrop's words from 1630, America has always seen its journey as exceptional and sought to become an inspiring exemplar for the rest of the world to praise and emulate. Yet the history of US grand strategy and foreign policy reveals a duality: from its earliest days, America has been a crusader and a conqueror. As Robert Kagan writes, "That self-image, with its yearning for some imagined lost innocence, hardly matches the record of our behavior stretching back to the nation's founding. We should recall that our 'city upon a hill' was an expansionist power from the moment the first pilgrim set foot on the continent and that it never stopped expanding, territorially, commercially, culturally, and geopolitically over the next four centuries."[6] In other words, the US impulse toward expansion via military might is not unique to the modern era, but this expansionist impulse has been moderated to varying degrees across the eras by power and economic limitations as well as other tools of foreign policy. The United States' diplomatic engagements during this early era, in lieu of direct warfare in many cases, bought the country the time to grow, strengthen, and ultimately rival and outmatch the power of its European competitors.

In its first century, while the United States sought to isolate itself from European politics, it still wanted to aggressively expand within North America. When the thirteen colonies announced their freedom from British rule in the Declaration of Independence on July 4, 1776, the new country's first grand strategy focused on two objectives: realizing its independence from Britain and expanding its territory across the continent. Both objectives required the use of diplomacy and force. For the first objective, the colonies fought the Revolutionary War against the British crown, finally achieving independence in 1783. While the Americans needed to enlist France's help during the war, they were careful to steer clear of French-British rivalry through shrewd diplomacy.

Henry Kissinger argued, "Since no European country was capable of posing an actual threat so long as it had to contend with rivals, the Founding Fathers showed themselves quite ready to manipulate the despised balance of power when it suited their needs."[7] During this time, a slew of conflicts in Europe between France, Britain, and Spain prompted President George Washington to declare American neutrality. Several diplomatic negotiations resulting in the Jay Treaty with Britain (1794) and the Pinckney Treaty with Spain (1795) successfully preserved the country's neutrality and allowed it time to mature, consolidate, and strengthen itself for the future.

In the aftermath of the Revolutionary War, the United States had several unresolved disputes with Britain. Among them were contentions over unfair tariffs, restrictions on maritime trade, and the British occupation of northern forts that they had agreed to vacate.[8] These latent tensions reached a boiling point as the French Revolution started, sparking a war between France and Britain in 1793. US political elites were divided on which side to support. Secretary of State Thomas Jefferson supported the French, while Secretary of the Treasury Alexander Hamilton supported Britain. In the end, President Washington sent Chief Justice John Jay to negotiate a peace treaty with Britain to avoid another war and to increase trade between the two countries. But Jay lacked leverage. His only bargaining chip was the threat to remain neutral and defend against seizures of goods with military force.[9] Unfortunately, Hamilton lost even this leverage when he independently contacted Britain and assured them the United States would not maintain a neutral status. This failure to present a united front cost the United States significantly during negotiations.

With this unfavorable starting position, the United States was unable to demand much from the British. Britain agreed to withdraw from their posts in northwestern America as well as to a new commercial treaty between the two countries.[10] The consequences of the Jay Treaty went beyond those few concessions, however. France came to resent the treaty, seeing it as a betrayal of the United States' trade deal with France, which would ultimately devolve into an undeclared war.[11] Moreover, the Jay Treaty left several issues unresolved with Britain that spilled over into the War of 1812. Domestically, the agreement was met with outrage and criticism from the public and Jeffersonian politicians alike.[12] Despite such long-term consequences, however, this act of diplomacy prevented a war with Britain at a time when the United States was vulnerable, and most importantly, it afforded the United States more time to unite domestically and build up its strength.

Shortly after, in 1795, US foreign policy elites embarked upon a similar, albeit more successful diplomatic effort with Spain, negotiating the Treaty of San Lorenzo—also known as Pinckney's Treaty. Spurred by its faltering position, the need to end the war against the French, and the fear of a possible US-British alliance in the aftermath of Jay's negotiations, Spain finally came to the negotiating table. The United States occupied a dominant position in these negotiations, and it was able to reject Spain's demands of a US-Spanish alliance and push for the removal of duties on trade while still gaining all desired concessions from Spain. The final treaty resolved territorial disputes between the two countries and gave US ships the right to free navigation of the Mississippi River and duty-free transport through the port of New Orleans, both of which were still under Spanish control.[13] Perhaps more important for the future, the treaty further encouraged US westward expansionism and the fulfillment of Manifest Destiny, or the belief in a God-given right of white US citizens to expand their power across the continent.

As Washington uttered in his farewell address in 1796, his young country was determined to avoid permanent alliances and minimize political connections with other countries.[14] Thus, the United States relied on selective military force alongside diplomacy and economic statecraft to advance American territorial expansion. A range of treaties after 1794 resolved the border issues with Canada and Florida in the United States' favor, bolstered American trade by opening the Mississippi River, and established American commercial influence in the British West Indies.[15]

Still, diplomatic statecraft could not prevent the United States from falling into conflict with the Old World for long. Just before the turn of the nineteenth century, the young American Republic engaged in its first major conflict since the Revolutionary War. The 1798–1800 Quasi-War was an undeclared war waged with Revolutionary France, making it the second longest war of the era at 1,260 cumulative days. Often referred to as America's first limited war, the Quasi-War was almost exclusively fought on the high seas, in the Gulf of Mexico, and off the Eastern Coast of the United States by naval and privateer forces on both sides.[16]

Following the execution of Maximilien Robespierre during the height of the French Revolution, the Directory—the ruling body of the French state at the time—declared war on Great Britain, Austria, Prussia, and the Netherlands, all monarchal empires. In response to the French declaration of war, the British seized islands in the Caribbean under French control. Livid, the Directory protested to the Americans that they were obligated under the 1778 Treaty of Alliance to help defend French holdings in the Caribbean. In addition to American inaction in the Caribbean, the French were also incensed at American policy toward the British outlined by the Jay Treaty, especially regarding British privateers' exclusive rights to American ports, a right that was previously granted exclusively to France. The Jay Treaty prevented the United States from trading war material with Britain's adversaries, which now included Revolutionary France. In response to these policies, the French began attacking American merchant ships in the Atlantic Ocean and the Caribbean Sea, particularly around the island of St. Domingue. The United States was helpless. It did not have an official Navy and relied on a shabby set of revenue cutters to defend against French aggression.[17]

Hoping to avoid war, President Adams dispatched a team to France to negotiate peace. But the French rebuked America's diplomatic gesture, demanding the United States provide the Directory with money, loans, and an apology. When the Americans refused and attempted to leave, the XYZ Affair ensued. The Directory threatened that if the Americans departed France, the French Navy would begin an unconditional war against US merchants.

Unwilling to take such a chance, the American delegation left Eldridge Gerry behind. In hindsight, however, it likely would have backfired on the French if they followed through on the threat, as it would have drawn the United States and Great Britain closer together.[18]

As the situation with France became more fraught and with diplomacy no longer an option, Congress suspended all political ties, trade, and diplomatic exchanges with the revolutionary state. Then it passed "An Act to Further Protect the Commerce of the United States" in July 1798, officially beginning the Quasi-War. This legislation allowed American merchants and warships of the nascent Navy to seize armed French ships anywhere in the world to protect American commerce.[19] Despite France's aggression, Congress opted against a formal declaration of war, instead choosing to steer the United States into a gray area of conflict. More importantly for American military lore, the most well-known land battle at Puerto Plata Harbor (Dominican Republic) represents the first deployment of US Marines on foreign soil.[20]

Following several coups against the Directory, Napoleon Bonaparte ascended to the French throne. The Adams administration, acting against hawkish Senators led by Alexander Hamilton, negotiated with the Napoleon court to bring an end to the war. Following the hard-won peace in 1800, the Franco-American alliance was officially severed.[21] Additionally, at the war's end, the United States chose not to disband its Navy as it had done following the American Revolution. The conclusion of the Quasi-War thus saw the establishment of the United States' first peacetime Navy, which further distanced the United States from its isolationist beginnings.[22]

Expanding the Frontier

The early 1800s saw the United States strengthen its military power and use it alongside diplomatic carrots and sticks for both defense and territorial expansion across the great frontier. The crown jewel of early American diplomatic expansionism was President Thomas Jefferson's Louisiana Purchase of 1803, "which brought to the young country a huge, undefined territory west of the Mississippi River from France along with the claims to Spanish territory in Florida and Texas—the foundation from which to develop into a great power."[23] While Jefferson focused on domestic priorities and avoided alliances with foreign powers like previous American presidents, the Louisiana Purchase more than doubled the country's territory and thus its power potential. European powers did nothing to stop the United States from growing at the time, as they were distracted by the ongoing Napoleonic Wars. In fact, the conflicts raging in Europe boded well for US growth with economic pressures compelling the French and Spanish to sell Louisiana and Florida territories.

Despite its inward focus, the United States used its growing power for even greater territorial expansion through the Frontier Wars and its forays into more distant parts of the region. Contrary to its diplomacy-first stance with European powers, the United States' grand strategy in the New World was expansionary and militaristic. From 1768 through 1889, the United States engaged in "943 actions in twelve separate campaigns and numerous local incidents."[24] The American settlers fought several wars with Native Americans (American Indians), a pattern that would last for 100 years. Though Native American tribes fought on both sides of the Revolutionary War, over 10,000 Native Americans joined the British forces. The prominent Iroquois Nation was destroyed by the war, as its Six Nations tribes supported opposite sides.[25]

Data on the Frontier Wars, 1776–1890

The United States devoted much of its military power in the 1800s to waging war against American Indian nations and expanding itself westward via military interventionism. As Figure 1.1 showcases, while the late 1700s and early 1800s saw the United States involved in twenty conflicts a year against the American Indian nations in the East, by the mid-1800s the United States was up to fifty conflicts a year in the East and the Plains.

The peak of US military engagements occurred in 1865 with the United States fighting almost 150 conflicts across the Plains and the West. These increases relate to the legacy of Jackson's Indian Removal Act as well as the Western land grabs and Gold Rush after the Mexican War. Thus, the United States fought a small portion of American Indian nations in the East from 1776 until 1815, intensified these fights and expanded into the Plains by 1850, and then significantly increased military conquest across the Plains and the West by the next decade.

Figure 1.2 shows that most of these Frontier Wars occurred in modern-day Texas, Arizona, California, and Oregon.

Although most conflicts happened west of the Mississippi, that the East experienced the highest casualties per conflict, with modern-day Pennsylvania

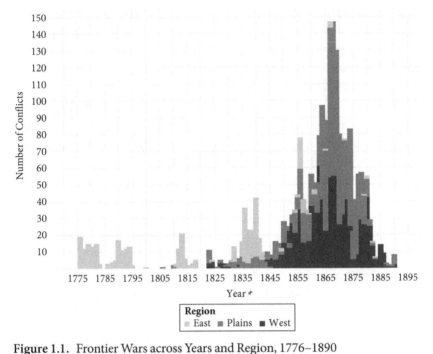

Figure 1.1. Frontier Wars across Years and Region, 1776–1890

Citation: The source for the data on American Indian Wars is from Jeffrey A. Friedman. "Using Power Laws to Estimate Conflict Size," *Journal of Conflict Resolution* 59, no. 7 (2015): 1216–1241. We thank him for sharing his full data set with us.

experiencing an average of 403 fatalities per conflict (compared to twenty casualties per conflict in Texas). The grave consequences of the Frontier Wars therefore resonated across regions and nations, whether in the number of conflicts or deaths.

The pervasive racism of identifying Native Americans as "savages," Manifest Destiny, and the aggressive westward expansion exacted horrible human casualties on the Native American tribes. Figure 1.3 quantifies the devastating human impact of the US Frontier Wars had on over 100 individual American Indian nations.

American Indian nations incurred most of the battle casualties during the Frontier Wars, with thousands of lives lost. The Creek, Comanche, and Santee Sioux suffered the most deaths.

Perhaps no event better captures the mid-nineteenth century shift in US-Indian policy or the cost Manifest Destiny than the forced removal of the Cherokee Nation from its traditional homeland in 1838 and 1839.[26] The

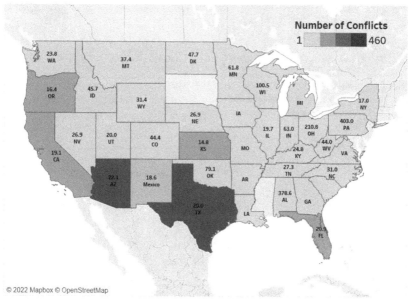

NOTE: Color shows Number of Conflicts. Numbers show average Casualties per conflict.

Figure 1.2. Map of Frontier Wars and their Average Recorded Casualties, 1776–1890

Citation: Jeffrey A. Friedman. "Using Power Laws to Estimate Conflict Size," *Journal of Conflict Resolution* 59, no. 7 (2015): 1216–1241.

forced removal of Native Americans and the Frontier Wars displaced indigenous populations and amounted to social, cultural, and political destruction. James Fenimore Cooper sums up this experience of devastation and erasure in *The Last of the Mohicans*: "My day has been too long. In the morning I saw the sons of the Unamis happy and strong; and yet, before the sun has come, have I lived to see the last warrior of the wise race of the Mohicans."[27]

America's Expansion Beyond the Continent

Beyond the Frontier Wars, the United States also began to exert some power outside of the continent during the early years of its statehood, most clearly during its involvement in the Haitian Revolution and the more distant Barbary Wars. These stand as notable events during a time of limited regional involvement for the United States. Importantly, they showcase the United

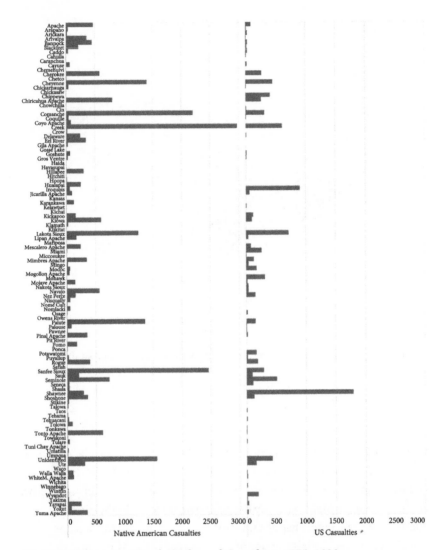

Figure 1.3. Frontier Wars by Tribe and Casualties, 1776–1890

Citation: Jeffrey A. Friedman. "Using Power Laws to Estimate Conflict Size," *Journal of Conflict Resolution* 59, no. 7 (2015): 1216–1241.

States' rising naval power and some of its first international political conflict as an independent country.

The Haitian Revolution

As the United States actively fought off hundreds of American Indian nationals within the continent, political developments in its backyard rendered isolationism unfeasible. The French Caribbean colony Saint-Domingue erupted into open revolt in August 1791 as the predominantly African slave population sought to achieve the same *liberté, égalité,* and *fraternité* promised by the French Revolution. The Haitian revolutionaries defeated their plantation masters by 1793 but didn't throw off the yoke of European oppression until 1804, by which time they had defeated successive British, Spanish, and French interventions.[28]

The United States wavered on the Haitian Revolution, with some factions supporting the revolutionaries and others eager to thwart them. While it did not intervene militarily in Haitian affairs, the Washington administration provided substantial economic support to white planters, and later administrations would pursue policies that seriously handicapped the development of the Haitian economy.

George Washington's administration provided $726,000 over twenty-two months in 1792–1793 to the white planters fighting the Haitian rebels.[29] Washington wrote in a letter to French minister Jean Baptiste de Ternant, "The United States are [well-disposed] to render every aid in their power...to quell the alarming insurrection of Negroes."[30] The threat posed by a successful slave revolt in Haiti to the white planter class in the United States served to unify staunch opponents like Thomas Jefferson and Alexander Hamilton.[31] Although difficult to confirm, it is also thought that a few thousand Americans, predominantly merchants and expatriates in Haiti, fought alongside the white planter class.[32]

President John Adams propelled a brief shift in US policy toward Haiti. Adams preferred a weak, independent Haiti to one dominated by other European powers and found slavery personally distasteful. He was also worried about Haiti choosing to pursue policies akin to state-sponsored piracy instead of formal recognition and trade. Adams sent an envoy to Toussaint Louverture and recognized Haiti's new government early in his administration. In the first instance of American military support for another state, Adams dispatched the USS *Constitution, Boston, Connecticut, General Green,* and *Norfolk* to support Louverture against a British-sponsored revolt.[33]

Haiti's formally declared independence from France on January 1, 1804, marked the first successful revolution since the American Revolution concluded in 1783. Fearful of a slave revolt in the neighborhood and being a slave owner himself, President Thomas Jefferson quickly reversed his predecessor's policy by enacting an embargo against Haiti in 1804. Despite growing trade links between Haiti and the United States, the embargo lasted until 1810 and trade volume did not recover until the 1820s.[34]

The United States did not formally recognize an independent Haiti until 1862, decades after formerly antagonistic European powers like England, France, and Spain. The United States' involvement in the Haitian Revolution helps elucidate internal American political divisions over slavery, European alliances, and colonialism. It also clearly follows a racial pattern of US foreign policy, with the United States remaining on an isolationist footing with white European states but engaging in a range of disputes with nonwhite nations and populations during its early years.

Barbary Wars: Birth of a Navy and Growth of American Power

During its first era, the United States also engaged with nonstate actors further away from its neighborhood, expanding its militaristic forays into international waters. For centuries, the Ottoman Empire and the European nations fought over maritime supremacy, especially in the Mediterranean. Both sides dueled with conventional navies and "state-sponsored maritime marauders known as corsairs," often mislabeled as pirates who worked independently.[35] Arguably the most famous corsairs were the ones from the Barbary States (the Ottoman Regencies of Algiers, Tunis, and Tripoli, along with independent Morocco) who preyed on weaker Atlantic powers in the Mediterranean, including the United States.[36] Barbary corsairs harassed and captured merchants and sailors for ransom or slavery. European nations, like Great Britain and France, paid tribute to the Barbary States for safe passage, seeing the exchange as a win-win situation: the two powers increased their share of Mediterranean trade and North African states did not challenge the superior British or French navies.

After the United States declared independence, its commercial ships lost the protection of the British navy against attacks by the North African raiders. The United States' decision to engage with the Barbary corsairs marked a larger goal to "establish the United States's place in the international order of the day."[37] Though the wars are not remembered as well as other conflicts, they were the first time the United States conducted military operations overseas in a foreign land and they inspired new national pride within the United States.[38]

American engagements with the Barbary privateers differed in their levels of aggression and outcomes. For instance, the Algiers' corsairs were especially aggressive. In 1785, Dey Muhammad of Algiers declared war on the United States and captured several American ships.[39] The financially struggling Confederation government at the time could not raise a Navy or offer tribute to protect US ships.[40] The United States' disputes with Morocco, on the other hand, ended more amicably, and by 1786, Morocco signed a treaty with the United States. By 1794, Congress authorized the construction of the first six ships of the US Navy in response to the Algerian seizures. In 1795, the United States sent diplomats to the African states and settled on a treaty in which the United States agreed to pay tribute, freeing eighty-three American sailors as well.[41]

By the time Thomas Jefferson became president in 1801, America faced another crisis. While the new nation faced economic challenges and struggled with heavy debt, its merchant ships suffered attacks from Barbary pirates once again, with sailors taken hostage.[42] The president attempted to negotiate with the Barbary corsairs several times but to no avail. Eventually, Tripoli declared war on the United States, citing late payments of tribute, marking the First Barbary War, which became the longest lasting war the United States fought during the era (1,490 cumulative days).[43] Several battles on sea and land occurred until the United States won in 1805, occupying Derna. Later in the same year, the United States signed a treaty with Tripoli, where the United States paid $60,000 in ransom for the imprisoned sailors. The treaty, however, did not resolve the issue of corsair raids, which lead to the Second Barbary War.

In 1812, Algiers declared war on the United States and captured American ships as part of an agreement with the British. Once the War of 1812 ended, Congress, as requested by President Madison, authorized the use of force against Algiers in March 1815. After a series of US victories, Algiers surrendered, and the subsequent treaty called for the release of all captives, the end of tributes, and guaranteed shipping rights in the Mediterranean.

With the conclusion of the Second Barbary War, the United States had expanded its influence and commercial interests in the Mediterranean. It had also taken its first step as a military power on the sea by establishing its nascent Navy. These wars marked the first encounter the United States had with Muslim nations.

Data on Expansion beyond the Continent

Until the early 1800s, most US military interventions occurred within North America itself. The revolution in Haiti and the Barbary Wars provided early indications for how the United States might engage beyond the continent.

These early interventions were in the form of small proxy wars against European colonial ambitions, including battles against the United Kingdom of Great Britain and Northern Ireland, Spain, France, and Russia, to secure territories within modern-day Florida, Oregon, New Mexico, among others. The United States also undertook battles in Latin America and the Caribbean against European powers and often in support of white colonists, as in the case of Haiti, where the United States sought to consolidate control beyond its immediate territory.

Driven by the Monroe Doctrine and enabled by European distraction, by the 1830s the United States focused much of its military might against Latin American nations, particularly Mexico and Nicaragua, and even some distant targets in East Asia, such as China and Japan. By 1864, not only had the United States dramatically increased the frequency of military interventions, but it had also expanded its military influence, moving beyond its North American neighborhood and into Latin America, Asia, and Europe. It is

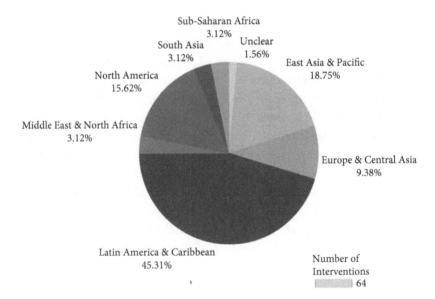

Figure 1.4. US Interventions by Region, 1776–1864

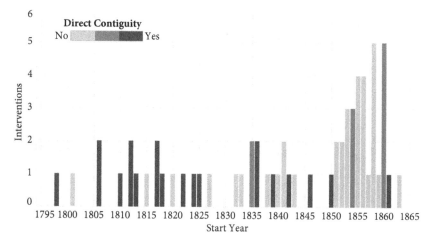

Figure 1.5. US Interventions by Contiguity, 1776–1864

important to note, however, that even at the end of this era of expansion, the United States primarily targeted the Americas.

Indeed, as Figure 1.4 summarizes, out of the sixty-four US military interventions between 1776 and 1864, almost half of them targeted Latin America and the Caribbean, while almost 16 percent of them targeted North America.

More surprising is that approximately 19 percent of the interventions targeted East Asia and the Pacific. In other words, by the end of the era, the United States moved from a position of extreme vulnerability to that of a regional power and growing global power, starting to expand its militaristic forays into the Middle Eastern and North Africa as well as the Pacific. Still, it had yet to reach any significant semblance of international influence by military might.

Figure 1.5 shows the relationship between US interventions and contiguity from 1776 to 1864. We define direct contiguity by the same standards as the Correlates of War (COW) using both land and water borders.[44] The graph only focuses on whether the United States and State B possess direct contiguity, not the degrees of the contiguity.

Until 1825, the United States used the vast majority of its military tools against its direct neighborhood. But since the 1840s, the United States and its targets have rarely been contiguous, denoting the next phase of US expansion beyond neighboring territory and indicating a shift in its capacity to project power.

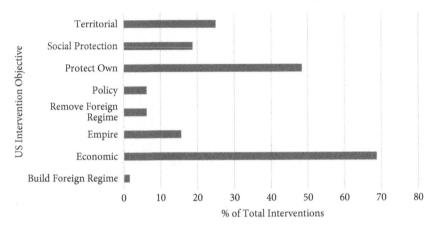

Figure 1.6. US Military Intervention Objectives as Percentage of Total, 1776–1864

By the 1850s, each spike in military interventionism was often followed by periods of deep economic recession.[45] While the causality of the relationship between interventions and economic downturn is not clear, there was a clear economic motivation behind most of the United States' early military interventions when measuring US objectives for intervention. As Figure 1.6 shows, almost 70 percent of the United States' military interventions during this era contained economic objectives (objectives are not mutually exclusive), which appear more frequently than territorial, policy, and all other intervention objectives.[46]

This set of motivations makes it quite clear that maintenance of territorial control, protection of citizens, and economic assets were the key drivers of US actions, indicating a continued period of consolidation of American power.

Analyzing America the Expander, 1812–1864: An Evolving Grand Strategy

History reveals that the idea of Manifest Destiny and the bloody mid-nineteenth century US-Indian policy cannot be separated from the rise of Andrew Jackson and the school of foreign policy he inspired. Although decidedly isolationist when it came to US engagements overseas, he showed little reticence in engaging militarily with the sovereign Native Americans. Before entering politics, Jackson served as a general and led US forces in the

First Seminole War, which resulted in the forced removal of the Seminole tribe, the US annexation of Florida from Spain, and the boundary agreement with Spain on Oregon country (1819). These events gave the United States the momentum to expand to the Caribbean and Pacific Oceans.

Jackson inspired many politicians and movements in the past two centuries. While Jackson shelved the US naval buildup initiated by his predecessors, he supported the Indian Removal Act (1830), which opened more space within the country but did not aggressively expand US territory. In Walter Russell Mead's interpretation, the populist Jacksonian school "believes that the most important goal of the US government in both foreign and domestic policy should be the physical security and the economic well-being of the American people . . . that the United States should not seek out foreign quarrels, but when other nations start wars with the United States," America must win.[47]

The United States was finding creative ways to justify forcefully removing American Indians from their territory and claiming ownership over legitimate, sovereign nations. In his 1831 ruling, *Cherokee Nation v. the State of Georgia*, Chief Justice John Marshall stated that "the Indian territory is admitted to compose a part of the United States," and that the tribes were "domestic dependent nations" and "their relation to the United States resembles that of a ward to his guardian." By the following year, the Supreme Court reversed this and ruled that Indian tribes were sovereign and immune from US state laws. Still, Jackson refused to enforce the decision and gained the signature of a Cherokee chief that agreed to "relocation," even though he did not represent all the Cherokee nation. By 1838, Jackson's attempts succeeded, and his view of American Indian nations as "wards" of the United States dominated policymaking. Under threat from federal troops and the Georgia state militia, the Cherokee tribe was forced to the plains across the Mississippi. Out of a total of 15,000 Cherokees, between 3,000 and 4,000 died on the "Trail of Tears."[48]

Military campaigns and Manifest Destiny decimated most of the American Indian tribes in North America in the 1800s. Perhaps because the Frontier Wars occurred within contemporary US borders, they are not often labeled as what they truly were—US military interventions with extremely destructive humanitarian outcomes.

The United States Expansionism beyond the Continent, 1812–1864

After Manifest Destiny, the second objective of the period's US grand strategy was to stay out of continental European power politics. This was initially advanced by President James Madison and US involvement in Spanish territories in Florida and the Gulf of Mexico in 1810:

> Indeed, Madison's ostensibly innocuous exploit provided the ideological foundation and the diplomatic justification for future annexation of foreign territory, from Spanish Florida in 1818 to nearly all of Mexico in 1848, and ultimately Alaska, Hawaii, and Cuba in the late nineteenth century.[49]

Madison's actions included authorizing US occupation of Spanish Florida territory, partially motivated by the declaration of the West Florida Republic by Americans in the Baton Rogue area. Madison also supported and signed the No Transfer Resolution in 1811,[50] which referred specifically to US-Spain territorial disputes in the Gulf, but also established the principle that European states could not transfer colonies in the Western Hemisphere between themselves.

Madison's policies foreshadowed possibly the most momentous American foreign policy declaration in the nineteenth century, the so-called Monroe Doctrine. The Monroe Doctrine later expanded upon the No Transfer Resolution's warning against European intervention in the United States' sphere of influence: "The reverse side of this policy of American self-restraint was the decision to exclude European power politics from the Western Hemisphere."[51] Announced in 1823, the Monroe Doctrine closed the Western Hemisphere to European interference but opened it to American intervention. The declaration was explicit in stating that the United States would reserve for itself the right to intervene militarily in Central and South America.[52] Although its implementation depended on the British Navy for decades to come, this principle of noninterference was to serve America's continued and undisturbed expansion westward and southward.

It appears that while Jackson, Madison, and Monroe set the scene and crafted the policy tools, two other presidential administrations drove the increase in US interventionism. The Franklin Pierce and James Buchanan administrations expanded the continental United States, sought to take Cuba from Spain, and succeeded in extending US influence to the East, including within China and Japan. During the Pierce administration, the United States also initiated many smaller displays of force in Japan as part of Commodore Matthew C. Perry's expeditions.

Driven partly by rumors of Japan's coal deposits, the United States was interested in opening diplomatic and trade relations for some time. For example, Commodore James Biddle embarked on a diplomatic mission to Japan in 1846 but failed to establish relations.[53] Almost ten years later, Commodore Matthew Perry was sent to Japan with a letter from President Fillmore addressed to the Emperor. The letter asked Japan to open itself up to trade with the United States, while Perry's four warships and 300 armed personnel served as a clear show of force. In February 1854, Perry returned with more ships and negotiated the Kanagawa Treaty, which opened two Japanese ports to American ships. It also contained a most favored nation clause, creating a foundation for future trade, and led to the opening of an American consul in Japan. Due to America's coercion, Japan's isolationist foreign policy largely ended after the Perry expedition.[54]

The United States used force several times within China, Nicaragua, Panama, Fiji, Cuba, and other targets. The Buchanan administration followed in Pierce's footsteps, especially when Ambassador William Walker attempted to take over Nicaragua. The increasing militarism overseas only stopped in the wake of the US Civil War from 1861 to 1865 during Abraham Lincoln's presidency.

To better understand the possible motivations for US engagement, we created a National Interests Index. The index adds up separate measures on contiguity, colonial history, alliances, and natural resources.[55] As Figure 1.7 reveals, the United States first involved itself in military conflicts with high national interests, usually fought to preserve the new nation and expand its domestic territory and sphere of influence.

There is variation in the period up to 1845 between high interests interventions and low national capabilities. It is striking that high national interest interventions declined between 1850 and 1860, while the frequency of interventions increased exponentially. We can also see that US trends of interventionism paralleled another indicator of power and interests, US national material capabilities, measured by the Composite Index of National Capability (CINC).[56] Beginning in the mid-1800s, the more powerful the United States became, the stronger it enforced its foreign policy.

Its growing power also ensured the United States achieved many of its political, military, and policy objectives via its military confrontations. As

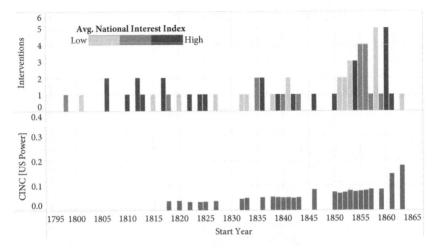

Figure 1.7. US Interventions by National Interests and Capabilities, 1776–1864

Citation: Correlates of War Project. *National Material Capabilities, 1816–2012*. Version 5. http://www.correlatesofwar.org; J. David Singer, "Reconstructing the Correlates of War Dataset on Material Capabilities of States, 1816–1985," *International Interactions*, 14 (1987); 115–132.

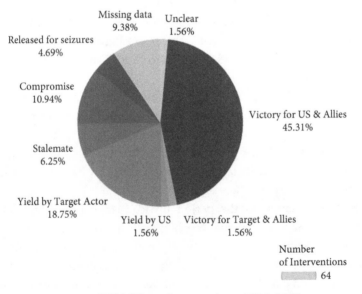

Figure 1.8. Outcomes of US Military Interventions, 1776–1864

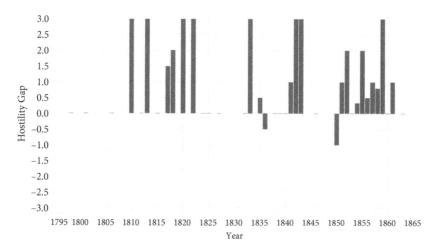

Figure 1.9. United States and State B Hostility Gap, 1776–1864

Figure 1.8 illustrates, during its first era of statehood the United States "won," or achieved its objectives, during almost half of its military disputes outright, and it was able to get target states to yield about 19 percent of the time.

Importantly, the United States only yielded to other states about 2 percent of the time, and target states only won about 2 percent of the time. It is important to note that we define a US win as the United States obtaining their stated objectives during or after the intervention, and a yield as the United States directly giving up on the pursuit of these objectives as related to the target state, and a compromise as involving direct negotiation and incorporation of both the United States' stated objectives and the target state's objectives, to varying degrees. Also, the United States consistently implemented more hostile military responses relative to its target states, as seen in Figure 1.9.

Key Historical Events for America the Expander, 1812–1864

While these aggregated patterns help contextualize and foreshadow US ideas and behavior, it's important to delve deeper into key historical and paradigmatic events that shaped US foreign policy during its first wave of expansionism beyond the continent. We look at the War of 1812, the Mexican-American War, and filibustering in Latin America, which allowed private economic interests to become enmeshed with national politics and American interventions, before exploring lesser-known interventions in the Pacific.

The War of 1812

The War of 1812 is typically eclipsed in popular American memory by definitively victorious conflicts like the Civil War and World War II. In contrast, the War of 1812 presents no clear victor, or even a single, obvious cause. However, the War of 1812 established crucial precedents in the development of US foreign policy, North American geopolitics, and national identity in the United States and Canada. It is also the war with the highest battle fatalities for the United States during this era, followed by the Mexican-American War.[57]

When the United States declared war on Great Britain in June 1812, the most common justification cited was British violations of US maritime rights. These violations began nearly a decade prior, as Great Britain and most of Europe were engulfed in the Napoleonic Wars. Great Britain blockaded France for the duration of the Napoleonic Wars, blocking US trade with one of its closest allies. Furthermore, the British Navy began the practice of impressment, in which British ships would stop merchant vessels and "press" crews into service in the British Navy against their will. While it is likely that some of the sailors pressed into the British Navy were former British sailors, impressment also caught US sailors, inflaming public opinion against the British.[58] Still, scholars doubt whether the violation of maritime rights "either singly or in combination, were *sufficient* causes for war."[59]

The real causes of the War of 1812 (as the eventual peace Treaty of Ghent would hint at) were not solely commerce and neutral rights, but related to western expansion, territorial conquest, and relations with American Indian nations. Previous expansions, including the Louisiana Purchase, could not sate the desire for ever-increasing supplies of land for settlers moving westward out of the original thirteen colonies. Some scholars note the early settlers utilized "wasteful land practices," stripping nutrients from the soil and requiring more land to support the settlers.[60] American citizens tended to look toward the Native American lands west of the Mississippi and British Canada to the north as the best options for acquiring new farmland.[61]

Slavery also impacted the decision to go to war in 1812; many Southern elites favored the annexation of Canada, as they presumed it would make it easier to annex Florida as a slaveholding territory.[62] These divergent regional interests were displayed openly in the vote to authorize war in June 1812. The majority of New England, New York, and New Jersey representatives voted against the war, as they feared open warfare would harm to their cosmopolitan and commercial interests.[63] Regardless, Congress voted to authorize war against the British by a margin of 79 to 49 in the House and 19 to 13 in the Senate, the first and closest margin for a formal declaration of war in US history.

The military consequences of the War of 1812 were almost as unclear as the original motivations. The war was fought primarily in four theaters, including the western or frontier theater where US forces battled against the British-armed Native American forces under Tecumseh, the northern where US forces attempted to invade Canada twice to no avail, the eastern coastal theater where British forces attacked Baltimore and sacked Washington, DC, and the maritime theater where the outnumbered US Navy mostly held its own against the British Navy. There were few decisive victories. The only decisive engagements occurred along the western and southern frontiers, where US forces under the command of future presidents William Henry Harrison and Andrew Jackson scored significant victories against British-allied Native Americans.

Materially, the aftermath of the War of 1812 differed little from the initial conditions. No territory was exchanged, and in many ways the political situation returned to the status quo ante. The United States continued its westward expansion, and Britain continued to utilize its unquestioned naval supremacy. Popular imagination cast the War of 1812 as a victory in the United States and British Canada, where local forces had successfully defended their respective homes from foreign aggression. The War of 1812 also served to "confirm" the existence of the United States to the international community. Twice, the United States fought the greatest military in the world, and twice they defeated them.[64]

The War of 1812 did result in one clear loser—Native Americans. Unifying disparate tribes to counter settler colonialism proved a difficult task, and Tecumseh's death and the subsequent fracturing of his Confederacy left Native Americans divided, weaker, and unable to mount successful efforts to stop the appropriation of their homes. Furthermore, the western tribes were now unable to access the British weapons and resources necessary to even the playing field. The War of 1812 seems to present a decisive moment in the history of Native American peoples when they lost the internal unity necessary to stave off US expansionism.

The Mexican-American War

The Mexican-American War was another conflict that sprung from similar trends of US expansionism. After Texas declared independence from Mexico in 1836 and was annexed by the United States in 1845, Mexico's President Jose Joaquin Herrera severed relations with the United States. US President James K. Polk, however, wanted to continue relations and sent a diplomat to Mexico City to purchase New Mexico and California. US-Mexican relations further soured when the envoy was refused a visit with the Mexican President. Insulted by the snub, Polk stationed troops along the US-Mexican border to provoke an attack from Mexico. When Mexican forces crossed the Rio Grande and attacked the American soldiers, Polk argued to Congress that Mexico had "invaded our territory and shed American blood on American soil," when in reality, the territory was still disputed. Nonetheless, the United States declared war on Mexico on May 1846.[65]

Polk's war plan was originally limited, and he assumed the war would be over quickly.[66] He had three main objectives: defend the Rio Grande boundary, acquire California and New Mexico, and inflict sufficient damage on the Mexican army to ensure a favorable political settlement.[67] But the war proved longer and more involved than expected. Despite American battle victories, the Mexican government mounted a protracted guerrilla campaign and were only forced to the negotiating table after the United States launched the first large-scale amphibious assault operation in its, history, taking Veracruz, the strongest fort in the Western Hemisphere, before continuing to Mexico City.[68]

The war concluded in February 1848 with the Treaty of Guadalupe Hidalgo. The United States received nearly 1 million square miles of territory in what is now New Mexico, Utah, Nevada, Arizona, California, Texas, Washington, western Colorado, and more for $15 million.[69] Historian George Herring noted that the Mexican-American War was the nation's first major military intervention abroad and its first experience with occupying another country.[70]

Filibustering in Latin America

The case of Nicaragua in the mid-1800s also represents an important type of US intervention, involving both formal government action and private military might via the alliance of powerful corporations and filibuster operations. Both the United States and Britain were interested in Nicaragua as a transit route through the isthmus.[71] Specifically for the United States, the country provided a sea route to California amid the Gold Rush. Nicaragua initially welcomed US involvement as a way to counter the colonial ambitions of Britain.[72] In 1849, economic carrots incentivized Nicaragua to sign a contract with Cornelius Vanderbilt, allowing his company to build a canal in the country. This and other business deals, however, was not accepted by the entire local population and in 1853 the United States intervened to settle a dispute between Vanderbilt and local authorities.[73]

By July 1854, the United States had dispatched a naval warship, the USS *Cyane*, to bombard the city of Greytown, which functioned as a trade port and protectorate under the United Kingdom. In addition, a contingent of 200 US Marines was deployed to set fire to the British Consulate in Greytown and the surrounding buildings.[74] The attack was justified as retaliation for the assault and kidnapping of the American minister to Nicaragua, Solon Borland, by the United Kingdom's provincial government, after Borlond interfered with the local arrest of an American citizen.

The destruction of Greytown served a much broader agenda.[75] The United States was seeking to expand its economic and political influence in Latin America and limit the influence of European powers in the Western Hemisphere. Greytown was a strategic point for trade and private commerce between the Eastern and Western United States during the California gold rush, and the United Kingdom's preoccupation with the Crimean War ensured retaliation for taking the port would be nonexistent.[76]

But it wasn't just the US government and corporations that involved themselves in such expansionist ambitions in Latin America. Perhaps no other man encapsulates the dark side of American ideals—Manifest Destiny, exceptionalism, and imperialism—in the nineteenth century better than William Walker. Known as a "filibuster," he sought to establish English-speaking colonies in Mexico and Central America for the sake of spreading Western civilization and to enhance his own personal wealth and power.[77] His filibustering incited several revolts in Central America, but he enjoyed substantial support from the American public seeking to "Americanize"

Central America.[78] His most notable expedition was in Nicaragua in 1855. Liberal and conservative party factions in Nicaragua were embroiled in civil conflicts for years, and the liberal faction eventually requested Walker's assistance with the promise of land and money. Walker agreed and took advantage of the turmoil to bring his own mercenary group. He convinced Vanderbilt's colleagues, Charles Morgan and Cornelius Garrison, to betray Vanderbilt and take over his company.[79] With this support, the liberals won the civil war, and Walker became the commander of the Nicaraguan army. A puppet government was established, which the US government quickly supported. Walker's poor political and military skills, however, soon alienated local supporters and eroded his power, leading to a rebellion to overthrow him.

The "National War" was a costly conflict where Central American countries, Vanderbilt, and the British worked together to end Walker's rule.[80] Finally, the United States intervened and sent the Navy to protect their economic interests and civilian lives. Navy Commander Charles H. Davis negotiated a truce, and Walker was forced to surrender to the Navy in 1857.[81] But Walker was not arrested, and later took a mercenary group back to Nicaragua in an attempt to retake the country. This time, however, US vessels intercepted Walker and compelled him to surrender.[82]

In the end, Nicaragua suffered severe long-term damage from these conflicts, while the United States did not face any long-term consequence for its foreign policy. Walker was, of course, just one of many of filibusterers with private militaries during this era of US expansionism.

Expansion in the Pacific

The era was also marked by lesser-known smaller altercations and military expeditions in the Pacific that were usually undertaken to strengthen America's commercial position with China in the mid-1800s and secure strategic ports in a region of economic interest. Expeditions in Samoa and Fiji are some of the many examples of US military intervention and "filibuster" operations to protect both national and private trade routes and commercial interests. In other words, a country that was set on isolationism had now expanded its interests outside of its own neighborhood.

As the United States sought to expand its influence in the Pacific, Samoa became the first important naval station and harbor for trade in the region. The United States instigated at least three skirmishes with the native population of Samoa during the nineteenth century to assert control,[83] and its forceful presence helped to establish its imperial strength in the Pacific.

Samoa, despite being divided by rival chieftains, signed trade treaties with foreign nations, including the United States in 1838.[84] It was also around this time the United States began the Exploring Expedition to survey the Pacific. After a US sailor was murdered on Upolu (an island of Samoa), Lieutenant William L. Hudson was ordered to arrest the suspect.[85] Arriving with two naval ships, Hudson requested the suspect be handed over, however, the local chief refused. In retaliation, Hudson and his men burned several towns to the ground before leaving, now known as the bombardment of Upolu.[86]

As in Samoa, the United States established connections with natives in Fiji for the sake of maritime trade and colonial expansion. While he is more well-known for exploring Antarctica and his mixed legacy throughout his naval career, Charles Wilkes led the exploring expedition to the Fiji Islands in 1840.[87] Wilkes made arrests, burned down villages and their crops, and demanded provisions for the expedition.[88] Many criticized Wilkes's actions in Fiji, arguing he went too far in the destruction and killing of natives.[89]

After the exploits of Wilkes's punitive expedition, maritime activities remained relatively peaceful. The stability came to an end when the USS *John Adams* was sent to Fiji to seek compensation from the (self-proclaimed) king of Fiji, Cakobau, in 1855.[90] The United States held him responsible for trade damages and arson in the area. After refusing to pay, marines were sent to capture him. Ultimately, Cakobau escaped and avoided paying any alleged debt to the United States.[91] Tensions remained high between Americans and the Fiji locals, and it was perhaps inevitable that another conflict would arise when two American traders were killed in Fiji in 1859.[92] In the ensuing battle, a village was burned and several natives were killed, including two chiefs.[93] The battle was the last major conflict the Navy had with the local population, and it solidified the Fiji Islands as a base for maritime trade in America's empire.

Other US militaristic forays into smaller Pacific islands shared similar motivations, methods, and outcomes. These interventions were critical for establishing the United States as a global strategic actor, and ultimately, by the next era, the US presence was firmly cemented in the Pacific, especially its imperialistic economic relations with Japan and China.

Conclusion and Ties to the Present

Even though the United States achieved independence from Britain in the Revolutionary War and proved itself against distant North African states and privateers, it still preferred an internal political orientation in the early 1800s. But this isolationism was short-lived as America expanded its territory and pursued its interests beyond the continent. The War of 1812, which saw the British occupation and burning of Washington, DC, ended with a peace treaty and no obvious winner in 1815. The war, however, signaled another landmark moment for US power. Although the American military campaign was disastrous, the country survived the conflict and earned the respect of Britain and the world, now widely seen as a legitimate state power. Most importantly, perhaps, the War of 1812 emboldened nationalist sentiments, expansionist ambitions, and a desire to protect the new state against future threats.[94]

Isolation from European power politics and North American territorial expansion remained the guiding objectives of US grand strategy 1812 to 1864, but with different emphases and in changed circumstances. In this period, westward expansion was believed to be the God-willed Manifest Destiny of the new nation: "It is our Manifest Destiny to overspread the continent allotted by Providence for the free development of our yearly multiplying millions."[95] As Walter Prescott Webb describes in *The Great Plains*:

> We see a nation of people coming slowly but persistently through the forests, felling trees, building cabins . . . advancing shoulder to shoulder, pushing the natives westward toward the open country . . . They are nearing the Plains. Then, in the first half of the nineteenth century, we see the advance guard of this moving host of forest homemakers emerge into the new environment, where there are no forests, no logs for cabins. . . . Before them is a wide land infested by a fierce breed of Indians, mounted, ferocious, unconquerable, terrible in their mercilessness. They see a natural barrier made more formidable by a human barrier of untamed savagery.[96]

Although the United States dominated the Western hemisphere and some Pacific hotspots during this first era, its continental expansion nevertheless remained limited. The dispute over slavery drove a wedge between abolitionist states in the north and slave states in the south. Thus, the consolidation of the Union relied on a delicate balance between these two types of states. Yet by December 1845, Polk's annexation of Texas, under the pretext of protecting it from European powers, coupled with the northern states' economic prosperity, altered the political balance, and made the US Civil War all but inevitable.[97]

This first pre–Civil War era of United States foreign policy lasting until 1864 may at first glance appear completely disconnected from present US foreign policy. The United States had yet to achieve its current borders, it avoided foreign alliances, and rarely engaged in military conflict overseas. However, the ideological groundwork for the present American Empire was laid in the early years of US history. The dominant eighteenth- and nineteenth-century concepts like Manifest Destiny, American exceptionalism, and even pervasive racism continue to influence domestic politics and foreign policy in the United States to this day.

The ideology of "American exceptionalism" posits that the United States represents a uniquely moral and righteous nation among the international community. This ideology has been utilized to justify in whole or in part any number of atrocities committed by the United States, both in the 1800s and today. In the 1800s, this ideology supported centuries' long US military interventions against American Indian nations as well as militarism and aggression in Latin America and the Pacific.

The trope of the United States as a divinely inspired nation influenced the imperial expansion of Manifest Destiny and continues to echo in the modern political landscape. President Ronald Reagan invoked the United States' inherent morality against the "Evil Empire" in the waning days of the Cold War, President George W. Bush inveighed against the "Axis of Evil" and explicitly invoked American exceptionalism to argue for unilateral intervention in Iraq, and President Donald Trump's campaign slogan "Make American Great Again" sought the restoration of unapologetic American dominance. Most insidiously, American exceptionalism tends to distort popular conceptions of American history. The contradiction of the world's greatest nation emerging from its revolutionary war to steal native land, enslave millions, and brutally colonize foreign people cannot be resolved, and thus the unflattering aspects of American history are massaged or dismissed from the foreign policy picture as a result.

Early US grand strategy balanced two contradictory impulses between expansion and isolation. The Louisiana Purchase and perpetual territorial against the Native Americans display a desire to expand the territorial reach of the United States. However, strong isolationist tendencies prevented American leadership from establishing meaningful involvement in European or global affairs until the late nineteenth century. Interestingly, this isolationism did not apply to the Western Hemisphere or nonwhite populations in North America. Prior even to the Monroe Doctrine, the United States intervened in the Haitian Revolution and fought multiple skirmishes against Spanish and British forces in Florida. The Monroe Doctrine codified the predominant sentiment among US leadership that the United States would refrain from involvement in European affairs, so long as European powers did not meddle in the US sphere of influence, where the United States took up the role of the colonizer.

Although the magnitude, scope, and tactics of intervention have changed, the United States continues to treat Latin American states as partially sovereign, or sovereign until their policies conflict with US interests. The United States continues to rely on direct military aggression as well as more covert special operations and economic statecraft to support or overthrow foreign regimes, as it did in Haiti, Mexico, Nicaragua, Samoa, and more in the 1800s. These patterns have enveloped the world at large in more recent years, not just the American neighborhood.

Notes

1. Historical census data available at "1860 Census. Population of the United States," US Census Bureau, https://www.census.gov/library/publications/1864/dec/1860a.html.
2. Defined as person engaging in unauthorized warfare against a foreign country.
3. "Indian Treaties and Removal Act of 1830," Office of the Historian: U.S. Department of State, accessed April 1, 2022, https://history.state.gov/milestones/1830-1860/indian-treaties.
4. For a debate on whether the United States was an isolationist power during the 1800s, see Richard W. Maass, *The Picky Eagle: How Democracy and Xenophobia Limited U.S. Territorial Expansion* (Ithaca, NY: Cornell University Press, 2020); Erik Grynaviski, *America's Middlemen: Power at the Edge of Empire* (Cambridge: Cambridge University Press, 2018); and Charles A. Kupchan, *Isolationism: A History of America's Efforts to Shield Itself from the World* (New York: Oxford University Press, 2020).
5. John Winthrop, "A Model of Christian Charity" (also known as "City Upon a Hill"), sermon delivered on board the ship *Arbella*, April 8, 1630, https://history.hanover.edu/texts/winthmod.html.
6. Robert Kagan, "Dangerous Nation," *International Politics* 45 (2008): 404.
7. Henry Kissinger, *Diplomacy* (New York: Simon & Schuster, 1994), 30.

8. "John Jay's Treaty, 1794–95," Office of the Historian, US Department of State, accessed June 29, 2020, https://history.state.gov/milestones/1784-1800/jay-treaty; James Roger Sharp, *American Politics in the Early Republic: The New Nation in Crisis* (New Haven, CT: Yale University Press, 1993), 114–5.

9. "John Jay's Treaty, 1794–95," US Department of State.

10. "Jay Treaty," *Encyclopædia Britannica*, May 14, 2020, https://www.britannica.com/event/Jay-Treaty.

11. "Jay Treaty," *Encyclopædia Britannica*.

12. Amanda C. Demmer, "Trick or Constitutional Treaty? The Jay Treaty and the Quarrel over the Diplomatic Separation of Powers," *Journal of the Early Republic* 35, no. 4 (2015): 584, www.jstor.org/stable/24768869.

13. "Treaty of San Lorenzo, 1795," Office of the Historian, US Department of State, https://history.state.gov/milestones/1784-1800/pickney-treaty.

14. Cavanna, "US Grand Strategy."

15. Kissinger, *Diplomacy*, 31.

16. Alexander DeConde, *The Quasi-War; The Politics and Diplomacy of the Undeclared War with France 1797–1801* (New York: New York Scribner, 1966).

17. Donald R. Hickey, "The Quasi War: America's First Limited War, 1798-1801" *The Northern Mariner/le Marin du Nord*, 18 no. 3–4 (July–October, 2008): 67–77, https://www.cnrs-scrn.org/northern_mariner/vol18/tnm_18_3-4_67-77.pdf.

18. Michael Rak (CPTN, USN), "The Quasi War and the Origins of the Modern Navy and Marine Corps." United States Naval War College, February 10, 2020, https://apps.dtic.mil/sti/pdfs/AD1092634.pdf.

19. *An Act to Authorize the Defence of the Merchant Vessels of the United States Against French Depredations*, U.S. Code (1798), https://avalon.law.yale.edu/18th_century/qw02.asp.

20. DeConde, *The Quasi-War*.

21. Gregory E. Fehlings, "America's First Limited War." *Naval War College Review* 53, no. 3 (Summer, 2000): 1–43. https://digital-commons.usnwc.edu/cgi/viewcontent.cgi?article=2563&context=nwc-review.

22. Rak, "The Quasi War and the Origins of the Modern Navy and Marine Corps."

23. Kissinger, *Diplomacy*, 31.

24. Kori Schake, "Lessons from the Indian Wars," *Policy Review*, no. 177 (2014): 71–79.

25. James D. Drake, and Christopher McKnight Nichols, "Native American Wars," in *The Oxford Encyclopedia of American Military and Diplomatic History*, edited by Paul S. Boyer (Oxford: Oxford University Press, Inc., 2013).

26. Amy H. Sturgis, *The Trail of Tears and Indian Removal* (Westport, CT: Greenwood Press, 2007), xiii.

27. James Fenimore Cooper, *The Last of the Mohicans: A Narrative of 1757* (New York: Open Road Media, 1826, 2014).

28. Arthur Stinchcombe, "Class Conflict and Diplomacy: Haitian Isolation in the 19th-Century World System," *Sociological Perspectives* 37 (1994): 2.

29. Timothy M. Matthewson, "George Washington's Policy Towards the Haitian Revolution," *Diplomatic History* 3 (1979): 321.

30. Matthewson, "George Washington's Policy," 327.

31. Matthewson, "George Washington's Policy," 322.

32. Matthewson, "George Washington's Policy," 325.

33. "John Adams Supports Toussaint Louverture, Horrifies Jefferson," Massachusetts (New England Historical Society, April 22, 2020), https://www.newenglandhistorical society.com/john-adams-supports-toussaint-louverture-horrifies-jefferson/.

34. Tim Matthewson, "Jefferson and the Nonrecognition of Haiti," *Proceedings of the American Philosophical Society* 140 (1996): 35.

35. Elizabeth Huff, "First Barbary War," Monticello, accessed May 2, 2020, https://www. monticello.org/site/research-and-collections/first-barbary-war; "Pirates, Privateers, Corsairs, Buccaneers: What's the Difference?" *Encyclopedia Britannica*, accessed May 3, 2020, https://www.britannica.com/story/pirates-privateers-corsairs-buccaneers-whats-the-difference.

36. "Barbary Wars, 1801–1805 and 1815–1816," Milestones in the History of U.S. Foreign Relations, Office of the Historian, accessed April 30, 2020, https://history.state.gov/ milestones/1801-1829/barbary-wars.

37. Walter Russel Mead, review of *The Barbary Wars: American Independence in the Atlantic World*, by Franklin Lambert, *Foreign Affairs*, May 2005, https://www.foreign affairs.com/reviews/capsule-review/2005-05-01/barbary-wars-american-independe nce-atlantic-world.

38. Mead, review of *The Barbary Wars*.

39. Huff, "First Barbary War," Monticello.

40. "Barbary Wars," Office of the Historian.

41. "Barbary Wars," Office of the Historian.

42. Huff, "First Barbary War," Monticello.

43. See Table 1.1 in the appendix for a list of intervention during this era, including their cumulative durations and fatality levels.

44. Contiguity denotes whether the United States and State B are: Separated by a land or river border; separated by 12 miles of water or less; separated by 24 miles of water or less (but more than 12 miles); separated by 150 miles of water or less (but more than 24 miles); separated by 400 miles of water or less (but more than 150 miles); Correlates of War Project. Direct Contiguity Data, 1816–2016. Version 3.2. http:// correlatesofwar.org.

45. As per the National Bureau of Economic Research (NBER), a recession is defined as "a significant decline in economic activity spread across the economy, lasting more than a few months, normally visible in real GDP, real income, employment, industrial pro-duction, and wholesale-retail sales."

46. For economic objectives, the US attempts to protect economic or resource interests of itself or others in the target region. For the original MIPS objective coding that we heavily rely on, see Sullivan, Patricia and Michael Koch, MIPS Codebook, 2008, https://plsullivan.web.unc.edu/wp-content/uploads/sites/1570/2011/09/MIPS_ codebook_Sullivan.pdf. Refer to the Appendix for comprehensive coding and definitions of the types of intervention objectives. Social protective objectives, for

instance, can be further disaggregated into Socially protective interventions and humanitarian interventions.

47. Walter Russell Mead, *Special Providence: American Foreign Policy and How It Changed the World,* A Century Foundation Book (New York: Alfred A. Knopf, 2001), xvii.

48. "Indian Treaties and Removal Act of 1830," Office of the Historian.

49. William S. Belko, "The Origins of the Monroe Doctrine Revisited: The Madison Administration, the West Florida Revolt, and the No Transfer Policy," *The Florida Historical Quarterly* 90 (2011): 158.

50. Belko, "The Origins of the Monroe Doctrine," 180.

51. Kissinger, *Diplomacy*, 35.

52. Kissinger, *Diplomacy,* 35

53. "The United States and the Opening to Japan, 1853," Department of State, Office of the Historian, accessed September 8, 2020, https://history.state.gov/milestones/1830-1860/opening-to-japan.

54. "Brief Summary of the Perry Expedition to Japan, 1853," US Navy, 1953, accessed September 8, 2020, https://www.history.navy.mil/research/library/online-reading-room/title-list-alphabetically/b/brief-summary-perry-expedition-japan-1853.html.

55. Full codebook is available upon request.

56. The CINC reflects an average of a state's share of the system total of each of the six elements of capabilities in each year, weighting each component equally. The six components are: military expenditures; military personnel; iron and steel production; primary energy consumption; total population; and urban population. The CINC will always range between 0 and 1. "0.0" would indicate that a state had 0% of the total capabilities present in the system in that year, while "1.0" would indicate that the state had 100% of the capabilities in a given year. Sources: Correlates of War Project. (d). *National Material Capabilities, 1816–2012.* Version 5. http://www.correlatesof war.org; J. David Singer, "Reconstructing the Correlates of War Dataset on Material Capabilities of States, 1816-1985," *International Interactions,* 14 (1987): 115–132.

57. See Table 1.1 in the Appendix for a complete list of battle and total fatalities per conflict during this era.

58. J. C. A. Stagg, "James Madison and the Malcontents: The Political Origins of the War of 1812," *The William and Mary Quarterly* (1976): 558.

59. Stagg, "James Madison and the Malcontents." The issues of impressment and blockade were much more relevant prior to 1812, and the British rescinded the Orders in Council shortly before the United States declared war in June 1812. Foreshadowing later communication challenges, the United States did not receive word of the change in British policy until after war had been declared.

60. Warren H. Goodman, "The Origins of the War of 1812: A Survey of Changing Interpretations," *The Mississippi Valley Historical Review* (1941): 5

61. Goodman, "The Origins of the War of 1812," 4.

62. Goodman, "The Origins of the War of 1812," 8.

63. Goodman, "The Origins of the War of 1812," 2.

64. Rachel Hope Cleves et al., "Interchange: The War of 1812," *The Journal of American History* (2012): 4.

65. "Mexican-American War," in *Britannica Academic*, July 21, 2017, https://academic-eb-com.ezproxy.library.tufts.edu/levels/collegiate/article/Mexican-American-War/52384.

66. George C. Herring, *From Colony to Superpower: U.S. Foreign Relations since 1776*, The Oxford History of the United States (New York: Oxford University Press, 2011), 198.

67. K. Jack Bauer, *The Mexican War, 1846–1848* (Lincoln: University of Nebraska Press, 1993), 394.

68. Herring, *From Colony to Superpower*, 201.

69. Miller, Michael C. "Mexican-American War." *Oxford African American Studies Center.* December 1, 2006, accessed August 6, 2020, https://doi.org/10.1093/acref/9780195301731.013.44885.

70. Herring, *From Colony to Superpower,* 201.

71. John A. Booth, *The End and the Beginning: The Nicaraguan Revolution* (Charlottesville, VA: Avalon Publishing, 1982); "Foreign Intervention, 1850–68," retrieved June 20, 2020, http://countrystudies.us/nicaragua/8.htm.

72. Booth, *The End and the Beginning.*

73. Wassim Daghrir, "American Foreign Policy Fiascos: US Policy in Nicaragua as a Case Study," *Advances in Social Science Research* 4, no. 8 (2017): 83, https://www.effatuniversity.edu.sa/English/Research/Publications/Documents/2017-2018/American%20Foreign%20Policy%20Fiascos.pdf.

74. For an exploration of the private interests related to Greytown, see: Will Soper, "Revisiting Nineteenth-century U.S. Interventionism in Central America: Capitalism, Intrigue, and the Obliteration of Greytown., American Nineteenth Century History 18, no. 1 (2017): 19–44.

75. Soper, "Revisiting Nineteenth-century U.S. Interventionism in Central America."

76. Matthew Waxman, "Remembering the Bombardment of Greytown," *Lawfare*, 2019, https://www.lawfareblog.com/remembering-bombardment-greytown.

77. Bill Carey, "Commodore Cornelius Vanderbilt fought war over route through Central America," *Vanderbilt Register,* March 2002.

78. Ralph Lee Woodward, Jr., "Review: William Walker and the history of Nicaragua in the Nineteenth Century," *Latin American Research Review* 15, no. 1 (1980): 237–240.

79. Bill Carey; "Foreign Intervention, 1850–68;" Tim Merill, ed., *Nicaragua: A Country Study* (Washington, DC: GPO for the Library of Congress, 1993).

80. Carey, "Foreign Intervention, 1850–68."

81. Carey, "Foreign Intervention, 1850–68"; "Instances of Use of United States Armed Forces Abroad," 4.

82. Carey, "Foreign Intervention, 1850–68," 4.

83. Barbara Salazar Torreon and Sofia Plagakis, "Instances of Use of United States Armed Forces Abroad, 1798–2017," Congressional Research Service, updated January 13, 2020, https://fas.org/sgp/crs/natsec/R42738.pdf, 3; Stuart Anderson, "'Pacific Destiny' and American Policy in Samoa, 1872–1899," 46, https://core.ac.uk/download/pdf/5014543.pdf.

84. Stuart Anderson, "'Pacific Destiny' and American Policy in Samoa, 1872–1899,"

85. Harry A. Ellsworth, *One Hundred Eighty Landings of United States Marines 1800–1934* (Rockville: Wildside Press, 2011), 145.

86. Barbara Torreon, "Instances of Use of Armed Forces," 3; Harry Ellsworth, *One Hundred Eighty Landings*, 145–146.

87. Antony Adler, "The Capture and Curation of the Cannibal 'Vendovi': Reality and Representation of a Pacific Frontier," *The Journal of Pacific History* 49, no. 3 (2014): 256.

88. Tom Welch, "A Glimpse of History: Vendovi, the Fiji Cannibal Chief of Wilkes' Exploring Expedition," Orcas Issues, published September 27, 2011, https://orcasissues.com/glimpse-of-history-vendovi-the-fiji-cannibal-chief-of-wilkes-exploring-expedition/; Adler, "The Capture and Curation of the Cannibal," 268; "Fiji Islands," Naval History and Heritage Command, accessed June 14, 2020, https://www.history.navy.mil/our-collections/art/exhibits/exploration-and-technology/alfred-agate-collection/1840/fiji-islands.html.

89. Adler, "The Capture and Curation of the Cannibal," 271–272.

90. "This Day in Naval History—Sept. 12," Published July 24, 2002, https://www.navy.mil/submit/display.asp?story_id=2784.

91. "This Day in Naval History—Sept. 12."

92. "Irregular Warfare and the Vandalia expedition in Fiji, 1859," Naval History Blog, published October 9, 2010, https://www.navalhistory.org/2010/10/09/irregular-warfare-and-the-vandalia-expedition-in-fiji-1859.

93. "Irregular Warfare and the Vandalia expedition in Fiji, 1859."

94. Jasper M. Trautsch, "The Causes of the War of 1812: 200 Years of Debate," *Journal of Military History* 77 (January 2013): 275–278.

95. John L. O'Sullivan, "Annexation," *United States Magazine and Democratic Review* 17, no. 1 (July-August 1845): 5–11.

96. Walter Prescott Webb, *The Great Plains* (Lincoln: University of Nebraska Press, 1931, 1981), 140–141.

97. Cavanna, "US Grand Strategy," 3.

Chapter 1 Appendix

Table A1.1 List of US Military Interventions with Duration and Fatalities, 1776–1964

Year	Name	Duration (Days)	US Battle Deaths	State B Battle Deaths	Avg. Total Battle Deaths	US Total Deaths	State B Total Deaths
1798	Quasi War	1260	40	102	81	40	113
1801	First Barbary War	1490	0	0	0	0	0
1806	Arrest of Pike's Expedition	30	0	0	0	10	0
1806	Gulf of Mexico Pirates	Unclear	Unclear	Unclear	Unclear	Unclear	Unclear
1810	Annexation of West Florida	4	0	0	0	0	0
1812	War of 1812	975	4999	4258	4555	8666	6556
1812	Patriot War	780	—	—	—	—	—
1813	Occupation of West Florida	30	0	0	0	0	0
1815	Second Barbary War	290	0	0	0	0	0
1817	Amelia Island Affair	1	0	0	0	0	0
1817	First Seminole War	468	47	101	148	47	101
1818	Oregon Territory claims	2	0	0	0	0	0
1820	African Slave Trade Mission	1095	Unclear	Unclear	Unclear	Unclear	Unclear
1822	Landings to Suppress Piracy in Cuba	1012	0	73	73	0	73
1824	Fajardo Affair	14	0	0	0	0	0
1825	Piracy Battle in Cuba	1	0	8	8	0	8
1827	Anti-Piracy Operations in the Cyclades	73	1	85	86	1	85
1832	First Sumatran Expedition	3	2	210	212	2	210
1833	Protect Interests in Argentina	16	0	0	0	0	0

Year	Event						
1835	Protect Consulate in Callao & Lima	362	0	0	0	0	0
1835	Ingham Incident	1	0	0	0	0	0
1836	General Urrea Incident	180	0	0	0	0	0
1836	General Gaines in Nacogdoches	258	0	0	0	0	0
1838	Second Sumatran Expedition	9	0	0	0	0	0
1839	Aroostook War (Pork and Beans War)	34	0	0	0	0	0
1840	Fiji punitive expedition	14	2	7	9	2	7
1841	Battle of Drummond's Island	4	1	12	13	1	12
1841	Retaliation for treaty abrogation	1	0	0	0	1	0
1842	Capture of Monterey	3	0	0	0	0	0
1843	Protect Americans in Canton	—	0	0	0	0	1
1846	Mexican–American War	648	1733	5000	6733	13283	9000
1850	The Cardenas Expedition	193	0	10	36	0	10
1851	Jaffa Massacre Deployment	30	0	0	0	0	0
1851	Freeing US merchant ship	24	0	0	0	0	0
1852	Buenos Aires Protection	437	0	0	0	0	0
1852	Lobos Islands Affair	70	0	0	0	0	0
1853	Perry Expedition	355	0	0	0	0	0
1853	Koszta/Smyrna Affair	1	0	0	0	0	0
1853	Burning of San Juan Del Norte	491	0	0	0	0	0
1854	Battle of Muddy Flat	72	4	Unclear	4	4	Unclear
1854	The Black Warrior Affair	40	0	0	0	0	0
1854	Bombardment of Greytown	1	0	0	0	0	0
1855	Anti-Piracy in Shanghai & Ty-ho Bay	79	5	0	509	5	0
1855	Fiji Punitive Expedition	52	1	10	11	1	10

(continued)

Table A1.1 Continued

Year	Name	Duration (Days)	US Battle Deaths	State B Battle Deaths	Avg. Total Battle Deaths	US Total Deaths	State B Total Deaths
1855	Protection of Foreign Nationals in Montevideo	6	0	0	0	0	0
1855	Callahan's Raid	6	0	0	0	0	0
1856	Battle of the Barrier Forts	46	6	375	381	6	375
1856	1st Military Intervention in Panama	4	0	0	0	0	0
1856	Isthmus Mail Tax	109	0	0	0	0	0
1856	Show of Force in Gulf of Mexico	22	0	0	0	0	0
1857	William Walker's Surrender	42	0	0	0	0	0
1858	Fiji punitive expedition	10	0	100	100	0	100
1858	Response Jaffa Riots	30	0	0	0	0	0
1858	Landing During Instability in Uruguay	26	0	0	0	0	0
1858	Paraguay Expedition	253	0	0	0	0	0
1858	Forgotten Crisis of 1858	121	0	0	0	0	0
1859	Landing at Shanghai During Unrest	3	0	0	0	0	0
1860	Colombian Revolution Intervention	12	0	0	0	0	0
1860	Border Incursion, Pursue Juan Cortina	60	1	30	31	1	30
1860	Battle of Anton Lizardo	1	1	Unclear	Unclear	1	Unclear
1860	Mexican War of Reform	1	0	0	0	0	0
1860	Kisembo Unrest	3	0	Unclear	Unclear	0	Unclear
1861	Trent Affair	50	0	0	0	0	0
1863	Shimonoseki Campaign	425	5	42	47	5	42

2

America the Western Hegemon

We are provincials no longer. The tragic events of the thirty months of
vital turmoil through which we have just passed have made us citizens
of the world. There can be no turning back. Our own fortunes as a na-
tion are involved whether we would have it so or not.[1]

Woodrow Wilson, March 5, 1917

During the first era of US foreign policy before the American Civil War, the
United States solidified its statehood while staying largely out of European
affairs, enlarged the size of its contiguous territory, established and enforced
its growing sphere of influence in Latin America, often through private filibuster missions, and defended itself against North African Barbary pirates.
The United States battled over 100 Native American nations for territorial
conquest and displaced and killed an astounding number of people in the
Frontier Wars to attain its supposed Manifest Destiny to stretch its unequiv-
ocal control from coast to coast across the continent. And its regional power
extended fully to Latin America and the Caribbean and several islands in the
South Pacific.

In this chapter, we trace how the once-imperialized United States became the imperialist. Relying once again on historical narratives and data
patterns from the Military Intervention Project, we highlight key events in
US foreign policy from 1865 to 1917, the pre–World War I era. As the United
States progressed through the late 1800s and into the 1900s, it expanded its
sphere of influence beyond its neighborhood and reached the heights of regional hegemony. Thus, the United States was a growing imperialist power
across Latin America and the Pacific while it continued to restrain European
powers from economic and political gains on the continent during the pre–
World War II era.

The first section of the chapter synthesizes the grand strategy trends and
debates of the era through both narratives and data snapshots. Next, we

Dying by the Sword. Monica Duffy Toft and Sidita Kushi, Oxford University Press. © Oxford University Press 2023.
DOI: 10.1093/oso/9780197581438.003.0003

introduce data-driven patterns and graphics of US military interventionism that contextualize the subsequent historical narratives, including the most critical, World War I. Finally, the chapter places the era within a broader historical perspective and discusses the parallels and contradictions relative to contemporary US foreign policy.

American Grand Strategy and Power, 1865–1917

Relative Isolationism, 1865–1898

Despite the staggering death toll of up to 750,000 and destruction brought on by the American Civil War, the United States emerged from the rubble in 1865 as a strong, industrial nation determined to forge its own path and steer clear of messy European politics.[2] In 1867, the United States almost doubled its territory via its purchase of Alaska from Russia, and coupled with the surge of technological innovations and an influx of immigrants, the United States was roaring down the path of industrialization and urbanization. Yet it was not ready to shift its grand strategic focus from internal to external expansion just yet. Instead, in the period between 1865 and 1898, the United States chose relative isolationism as its new grand strategic posture. Fareed Zakaria aptly writes, "While America emerged from the Civil War as a powerful industrial state, unquestionably one of the three or four richest nations in the world, its foreign policy was marked by a persistent reluctance to involve itself abroad."[3]

During this era, beneath the surface of this temporary isolationism, the direction of American grand strategy was shifting from internal expansion within the continent to external expansion across the Western Hemisphere and parts of the Pacific. Perhaps most importantly, US territorial expansion was no longer the primary goal—it was replaced by exploiting and protecting its growing commercial interests abroad.[4]

Western Hegemony, 1898–1914

By 1898, the previously missing condition for broader American expansionism—sufficient state power—had been achieved, ushering in the beginnings of the modern American state.[5] In the 1890s, the executive branch bypassed or coerced Congress to end previous isolationist policies in favor of greater international involvement and imperialism. Thus, expansion in the Western Hemisphere, and relatedly, the removal of European influence from the region became the new grand strategy of the United States. This new grand strategy of imperialist expansion rested on the Monroe Doctrine of 1823, which dramatically broadened the scope of what marked American affairs and interests.[6] The United States' isolationist front also fractured in the aftermath of the economic depression of the mid-1890s, which led to mounting pressures by corporate industries to open new markets abroad, such as the open-door policy in China.

Ironically, the economic downturns of the late-1800s occurred as a consequence of the high economic productivity brought by the industrial revolution. The US production rate greatly outstripped the amount people in the United States could consume at the time. In other words, supply greatly outpaced demand. Following two severe economic recessions, US leaders were more determined than ever to find new foreign markets to absorb excess domestic production. In fact, it was this emphasis on international markets that prompted a buildup of US naval power to protect American commercial shipping and economic interests overseas. Arguably, corporate interests spearheaded the United States' new strategy to protect its markets from other great powers and expand into new markets.[7]

Figure 2.1 highlights the post-1890s increase in militarism. While commercial interests and economic benefits largely drove many US foreign policy choices and interventions during this era, the sheer quantity of recessions from 1865 to 1917 obscures potential trends.

An indispensable tool for the implementation of America's new grand strategy of economic imperialism was a battleship navy. Naval historian and strategist Alfred Thayer Mahan developed the policy, and Secretary of the Navy Benjamin Tracy lobbied for it in Congress, arguing "that a strong offense was the best defense."[8] Mahan feared that without greater expansionism, the US economy would not be able to absorb the large amounts of commercial and industrial products that it was producing. Mahan believed the government was responsible for ensuring access to new international markets by procuring three things: a merchant navy to carry American goods abroad, a battleship navy to deter or coerce rival states or pirates, and a large network of naval bases to facilitate the distribution of fuel, supplies, and communications.

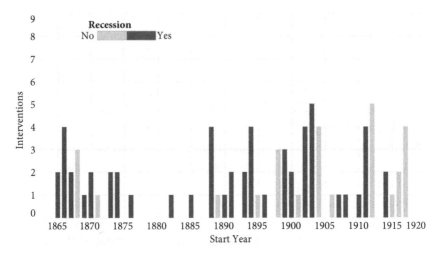

Figure 2.1. US Interventions and Patterns of Economic Recession, 1865–1917

Citation: "US Business Cycle Expansions and Contractions." *The National Bureau of Economic Research (NBER)*, 2018. https://www.nber.org/cycles.html.

While Mahan's ideas were not new, they were especially well-received in the 1890s.[9] Mahan's books and policies received additional support from the arguments of another contemporary academic. Professor Frederick Jackson Turner argued that the American frontier was now closing due to the large-scale westward migration and a growing population. Implicitly, Turner also encouraged foreign policy geared toward commercial expansion abroad and new markets, calling it "vigorous foreign policy."[10]

By the 1890s, such expansionist ideas found credence with leading politicians, including Assistant Secretary of the Navy Theodore Roosevelt. The end of the Spanish-American War in 1898 also set the stage for more aggressive expansionism as the United States annexed and occupied more distant territories in the Pacific, most centrally the Philippines.

Armed with such expansionist logic and political will, American leadership ultimately possessed a battleship navy that allowed the United States to project power far beyond the continent, while claiming the navy only existed as a deterrent or defensive strategy for the formerly isolationist country whenever politically expedient. The task of defending the United States soon became synonymous with imperialist ambitions.

The first test of America's new, imperialist grand strategy was the Spanish-American War of 1898 under President William McKinley. An American victory against a European great power solidified this pathway further by successfully testing America's rising power abroad. As a result of the war, the United States gained control of the Philippines, Cuba, Guam, and Puerto Rico. And there was no stopping there. With this boost of confidence, the United States intensified its expansionist ambitions, annexing Hawaii and Samoa in the following months and other territories in subsequent years.[11]

America's shift from isolationism to imperialism and its new role on the world stage owe much to the presidency of Theodore Roosevelt. Roosevelt believed the United States had a duty to expand its influence internationally.[12] Under Roosevelt, the United States fought in the Banana Wars, and he "gave the Monroe Doctrine its most interventionist interpretation"[13] by adding the Roosevelt Corollary in 1904, which proclaimed the US right to exercise "international police power" in the Western Hemisphere. Through the Roosevelt Corollary, the United States enlarged its armed forces, expanded into the Dutch West Indies, built the Panama Canal, and ultimately cemented its regional hegemony and empire in the Western hemisphere.[14] As illustrated in Figure 2.2, Roosevelt contributed to the exponential rise of US force abroad.

Under both Roosevelt and President William H. Taft, US foreign policy relied heavily on big stick diplomacy and dollar diplomacy, or the use of greater naval capacities to protect American commercial interests in South America and the Caribbean. Yet President Woodrow Wilson's term prompted a stark decline in US military interventions despite serving during America's two longest Banana Wars and World War I.

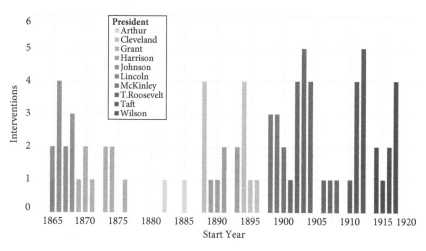

Figure 2.2. US Interventions by President, 1865–1917

The Idealist Moment, 1914–1917

By the early 1910s, the United States had arrived at another juncture of grand strategic importance. While Roosevelt's foreign policy demonstrated the principles of realism, Woodrow Wilson's foreign policy identified with idealism and the embodiment of American exceptionalism. For Wilson, America's mission was to "make the world safe for democracy."[15] Both leaders' approaches were put to the test as World War I broke out among European powers in 1914. While Roosevelt unsuccessfully advocated for US involvement in the war, Wilson initially took a stance for peace and American neutrality. Indeed, his 1916 campaign slogan was, "He kept us out of war!"[16] But gradually, Wilson prepared the country for its new role in international politics. "Roosevelt's approach failed to persuade his countrymen . . . Wilson, on the other hand, tapped his people's emotions with arguments that were . . . morally elevated" and slowly led an isolationist nation to war.[17] In 1917, America was ready to enter World War I and tilt the balance in the Entente's favor.

Figure 2.3 showcases the pinnacle of US power immediately before World War I. As in the previous chapter, we graph US intervention frequencies, applying our National Interests Index that adds up separate measures on

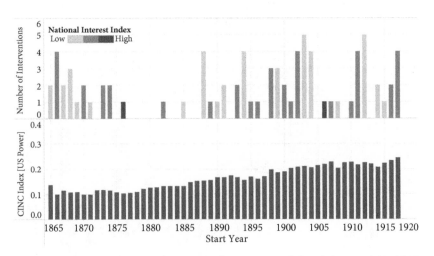

Figure 2.3. US Interventions by National Interests and Capabilities, 1865–1917

Citation: Correlates of War Project. *National Material Capabilities, 1816–2012*. Version 5. http:// www.correlatesofwar.org; J. David Singer, "Reconstructing the Correlates of War Dataset on Material Capabilities of States, 1816–1985," *International Interactions* 14 (1987); 115–132.

contiguity, colonial history, alliances, and natural resources.[18] We also trace how US trends of interventionism relate to national material capabilities, measured by the Composite Index of National Capability (CINC).[19] It seems that US power grew gradually until the 1900s, plateaued, and then grew more right before the US entry into World War I. National interests during interventions increased in the 1900s alongside intervention frequency, mirroring the timing of the key historical events such as the Banana Wars, the Mexican Revolution, and World War I. Therefore, this era sees the United States use its new power capabilities to intervene in pursuit of geopolitical, strategic interests in their immediate neighborhood and region—marking it a regional hegemon.

Nonetheless, under Wilson, American intervention in hotspot countries such as Mexico during the Mexican Revolution was more limited than previous American interventions. Wilsonian foreign policy was more restrained in its usage of force, instead seeking to promote US security and economic interests primarily through the expansion of stable regional democracies, albeit in extremely patronizing ways. This often meant the United States relied relatively more on economic and diplomatic tools of statecraft than militarism. It also held more staunchly to broad principles of good governance and democracy, as showcased in Wilson's refusal to recognize the Huerta regime in Mexico, even though it replaced a more anti-American government. Broadly, these trends also speak to the importance of the executive branch and political elites in driving US foreign policy trends, especially those of rising militarism.

In the next section, we offer a bird's eye view of US military ventures before we detail the implementation of US grand strategies through examples of pivotal historical events.

Empirical Patterns of US Interventions, 1865–1917

Before World War I, having made progress on its manifest destiny, the United States moved away from waging territorial wars within its own continent. Instead, it focused predominantly on securing its economic hegemony and business interests within South America, the Caribbean, and the South Pacific, and negotiating with lingering European powers for control. As Figure 2.4 reveals, during this era, over 63 percent of US interventions occurred within Latin America. The countries of Mexico, Nicaragua, and

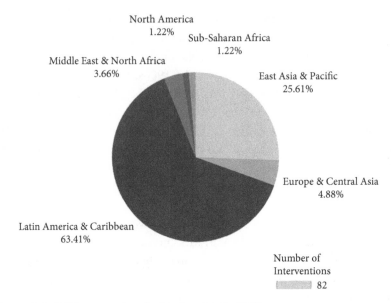

North America
1.22%

Sub-Saharan Africa
1.22%

Middle East & North Africa
3.66%

East Asia & Pacific
25.61%

Europe & Central Asia
4.88%

Latin America & Caribbean
63.41%

Number of
Interventions
82

Figure 2.4. US Interventions by Region, 1865–1917

Colombia suffered the brunt of these interventions, paralleling the Banana Wars, the Spanish-American War, the disputes over the Panama Canal, and the many "small wars" within the Mexican Revolution.

Yet European colonial powers such as Spain and France were not immune to US usage of force in the mid-1800s. Many US interventions in Latin America occurred out of fear of European involvement and economic gains within America's sphere of influence. Unlike patterns from the previous era, the pre–World War I era saw the United States predominantly intervening in noncontiguous regions, especially in the late 1800s. This is, indeed, the hallmark of a growing regional hegemon for the Western hemisphere. Sprinkled throughout these regional interventions were more distant ones in East Asia, making up over a quarter of US interventions in the era. Many of the missions were related to the Spanish-American War, with the eventual US takeover of the Philippines, Samoa, and Guam. Overall, all US interventions increased during this era, from 64 cases to 82 cases—an almost 30 percent bump from the past era. US interventions became dramatically more frequent at the turn of the nineteenth century, as US hegemonic power and naval capabilities became firmly cemented.

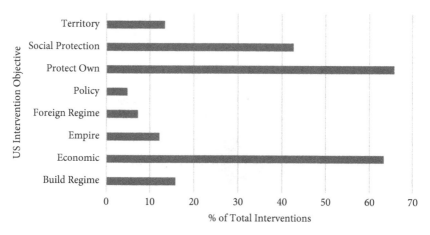

Figure 2.5. US Military Objectives, 1865–1917

In the last era, the United States emerged out of its colonial yoke, but in this new era, the United States embarked on its own mission for colonial conquest and managed to subjugate much of Latin America and parts of South Asia and the Pacific. Over half of US military interventions occurred in regions with an existing or historical colonial relationship to the United States, which parallels the changing grand strategic vision of the era.[20]

Within its growing colonial network in the Western hemisphere, the United States now relied on military interventions not only to carve out new economic markets and opportunities, but to protect existing interests in strategic regions, illustrated in Figure 2.5. In this era of interventionism, the United States seems to have intervened over 60 percent of the time to protect its interests and citizens abroad. This can include protecting US property inside or outside of a target, such as military property, diplomatic property, or diplomats themselves. The second most frequent military objective remained economic objectives, which had defined the previous era of interventionism.[21]

With its growing power, the United States also frequently attained its political objectives via military interventions, as Figure 2.6 reveals. The United States won over half of its military interventions from 1865 to 1917 (and 20 percent of other interventions ended with a yield by the target state), marking a significant increase from the previous era.

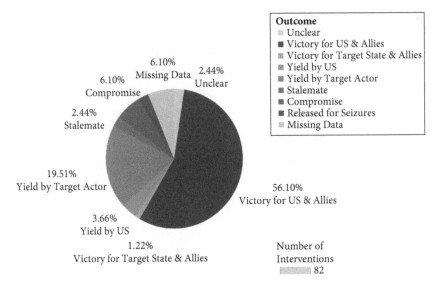

Figure 2.6. Outcomes of US Military Interventions, 1865–1917

Key Cases of America the Western Hegemon, 1865–1917

The period of US history nestled between the end of the American Civil War in 1865 and the beginning of the Spanish-American War in 1898 is often considered unremarkable in terms of foreign policy. The United States avoided involvement in large international conflicts, and while westward expansion into Native American lands continued, the only other significant territorial acquisition occurred in 1867 with the purchase of Alaska from the Russian Empire. However, this "middle, erratic period" marks several crucial developments in US foreign policy, transitioning the nation from a mostly insular, regional power to a globally-minded expansionist empire.[22]

Diplomatic steps toward Western Hegemony, 1865–1898

Prior to the onset of the Civil War in 1861, the United States engaged in limited imperial projects. The Louisiana and Florida Purchases, the Monroe Doctrine, the Mexican-American War, and numerous conflicts with Native American peoples represent the most obvious instances of nascent imperial ambitions. As the United States' borders reached the Pacific Ocean, political leadership faced new questions regarding the extent and character of the American project, specifically whether the United States should continue acquiring territory beyond North America. These questions were complicated by other pressing issues, namely the consolidation of the western territories and the recovery from the material and immaterial wounds of the Civil War.

Secretaries of State William H. Seward and James G. Blaine were instrumental in pushing American foreign policy towards a more expansionist paradigm during this time. Yet Seward and Blaine failed more often than they succeeded. Seward failed in his attempts to annex Haiti, Santo Domingo, and the Dutch West Indies, not to mention less serious efforts to appropriate territories ranging from Greenland to Cuba. Although Seward was able to gain Congressional approval for the purchase of Alaska and the annexation of Midway Island (the first offshore annexation in US history), the interparty dynamics of Congress in the immediate post–Civil War era proved too fractious for Seward to garner the requisite support for his more ambitious expansionist projects.[23] Blaine agreed with Seward's vision of a global United States, though he preferred to rely on his diplomatic skills to assert American power in contrast with Seward's more militaristic vision of expansion.

The State Department prior to Blaine's tenure had a lackadaisical approach to foreign policymaking. William Evarts, Blaine's immediate predecessor, noted, "There are only two rules at the State Department, one, no business is ever done out of business hours; and the other is, that no business is ever done *in* business hours."[24] Blaine adopted a more energetic foreign policy approach, inserting himself and the United States into diplomatic disputes that previous secretaries would likely have avoided. Blaine was particularly active in Latin American disputes, working to settle territorial disputes between Costa Rica and Colombia, and Mexico and Guatemala.[25] Blaine's central innovation was his insistence on engaging with the world, especially Latin America, within the context of a comprehensive vision of American foreign policy. Together, Seward and Blaine helped reorient American foreign policy from an insular and disjointed project into a more active posture toward regional hegemony and active territorial and economic expansion. Seward and Blaine provided the vision, energy, and structure that would transform the United States into a global, imperial power by the conclusion of the nineteenth century.

US engagement with Britain shows some of America's first diplomatic steps in solidifying its regional hegemony and global power. After the War of 1812, the relationship between the United States and United Kingdom further soured during the US Civil War. The burgeoning UK textile manufacturing sector required significant amounts of raw cotton, acquiring 77 percent from the slave economies in the southern United States by the late 1850s.[26] The United Kingdom never recognized the Confederacy during the Civil War, and the British Parliament passed a Declaration of Neutrality in May 1861.[27] However, private British citizens and even government officials sympathized with the Confederacy, and some went so far as to assist the Confederate war effort. Prime Minister Lord Palmerston and his foreign minister, Lord John Russell, were both known for their (private) sympathies for the Confederacy and solidarity with white plantation owners.[28] Future Prime Minister William Gladstone, then the chancellor of the exchequer, gave a speech in October 1862 praising Confederate leader Jefferson Davis.[29] Furthermore, much of the Confederate navy ships were built in Liverpool, England, and the city would remain a hub for Confederate goods.[30]

Some of the British-built Confederate ships sunk Union warships and commercial vessels during the war. The United States sought reparations from the United Kingdom for the losses, called the Alabama Claims, making their first legal claim for reparations in 1869. In 1871, a commission of six British and six American representatives met before an international arbitration tribunal in Geneva, Switzerland to settle the matter and other small disputes along the Canadian border.[31] The tribunal ordered the United Kingdom to pay the United States a $15.5 million indemnity, worth roughly $200 million today.[32]

The Alabama Claims' settlement was critical in two ways. First, it helped pave the way for greater cooperation between the former enemies, both by settling past grievances and establishing a paradigm for the peaceful settlement of disputes. Second, the settlement laid the groundwork for future international arbitrations, most notably the 1895 settlement between Venezuela and the United Kingdom. Venezuela and the United Kingdom had disagreed about the border between eastern Venezuela and western British Guiana for decades, and British forces occupied a Nicaraguan port in April 1895 under the pretenses of protecting British interests under threat.[33] The United States, invoking the Monroe Doctrine's principle against foreign intervention in the Western Hemisphere, stepped in to offer arbitration. The Treaty of Washington, signed in 1897, set the terms of the arbitration and bound the United Kingdom and Venezuela to its outcomes. The arbitration tribunal, composed primarily of British and American officials, awarded

90 percent of the disputed territory to the United Kingdom in 1899.[34] British recognition of US hegemony in the Western Hemisphere and the obvious British-American collusion in the arbitration verdict marked a key pivot in the bilateral relationship, from bitter enemies to military allies engaged in a "special relationship."

Moreover, its diplomatic role demonstrated that the United States was now a world power, willing to exercise its influence unhindered in the Western Hemisphere. Just as the peaceful resolution of the Venezuela crisis in 1895 marked a key pivot in its relationship with Britain, it also marked the culmination of the Monroe Doctrine. The United States had been formally asserting its regional hegemony in the Western Hemisphere since President Monroe outlined the concept in his 1823 State of the Union address. But the young and relatively weak United States could not effectively enforce its prohibition against foreign intervention. European powers, primarily the British, frequently intervened in states from Argentina to Mexico to protect their citizens, investments, and other commercial interests.

The most direct violation of the United States' imperialist sphere of influence via the Monroe Doctrine occurred during the American Civil War. Napoleon III invaded Mexico under the pretense of collecting Mexican government debt to the British, Spanish, and French governments.[35] Napoleon III found allies in the Conservative faction in Mexico's own civil war, who opposed the Liberal faction led by Benito Juárez and supported by the United States.[36] The French-Conservative alliance controlled Mexico City and much of the country by 1863, and Napoleon III invited the Austrian Prince Maximilian to become Emperor Maximilian I of the Second Mexican Empire in 1864.[37] The United States officially remained neutral throughout the conflict while providing Juárez's Liberal faction with crucial support. President Abraham Lincoln's administration continued to recognize Juárez's government-in-exile during the French intervention. Upon the conclusion of the American Civil War, US Generals Grant and Sheridan provided weapons and other support to the Liberal forces, eventually turning the tide of war against the French-Conservative alliance.[38] Napoleon III removed the last French forces in 1867, and Secretary Seward explicitly warned the Austrian Empire against replacing Napoleon's troops with Austrian soldiers.[39]

Yet the expulsion of European forces from Mexico did not immediately end all European violations of the Monroe Doctrine. Besides the UK occupation of a Nicaraguan port in 1895 and the combined British, German, and Italian naval forces blockade of Venezuela in 1902 and 1903, the French were working on connecting the Atlantic and Pacific Oceans via the Panama Canal from 1881 to 1889. The United States also failed to broker peace in the War of the Pacific between Chile and allied Peruvian-Bolivian forces and supported the losing faction in the 1891 Chilean Civil War (while the United Kingdom backed the winners). Thus, the United States did not exercise true hegemony in the Western Hemisphere until the twentieth century, but the foundations were laid in the latter half of the nineteenth century when the United States started to utilize its military and diplomatic tools to enforce the Monroe Doctrine.

The Frontier Wars and Commercial Interests

While the United States was using diplomacy to undergird its future hegemonic order, it was also continuing its militaristic Manifest Destiny against Native American tribes into the nineteenth century. Much of the territory west of the Appalachian Mountains saw some degree of violence between indigenous Native American peoples, European-American settlers, and the United States government. Gold was discovered in Montana in 1852 and again in 1863, and by the early 1860s settlers had begun establishing forts and blazing wagon trails through the territory granted to the tribes in the 1851 Treaty of Fort Laramie.[40] Allied Native American forces raided settler encampments and skirmished with US Army forces until a series of peace agreements were reached in 1865. Red Cloud, the Ute leader of the allied tribes, was at Fort Laramie and ready to negotiate the final agreements when a new US Army force arrived with the intention of building further outposts and forts. The negotiations ended and war broke out.

Red Cloud's War occurred from 1866 to 1888, resulting in a rare strategic victory for the Lakota Sioux and Northern Cheyenne peoples.[41] While the US Army won most of the small-scale engagements, they lacked the manpower to effectively police the expansive territory. A new Treaty of Fort Laramie was signed in 1868, granting specific territorial rights to some of the nations (most notably granting the Black Hills in the Dakota Territory to the Sioux) and demolishing US forts established in contested lands.

This pattern would continue through the rest of the nineteenth century— the United States offered assurances to American Indian nations followed by the discovery of valuable resources and the abrogation of promises. The Great Sioux War in 1876 and 1877 followed directly from the events of Red Cloud's

War. The Black Hills in the Dakota Territory had been granted to the Lakota Sioux, but the land was rich in natural resources and attracted significant numbers of settlers. While timber initially drew prospective settlers, the discovery of gold by Lieutenant Colonel George Custer's US Army expedition in 1874 created a mad frenzy. The accelerated settlement in the region increased tensions, and multiple attempts to avert conflict failed. General Sheridan directed his local subordinates to launch a preemptive attack against the Sioux in February 1876, and the Great Sioux War began.[42] The war is best known for the Battle of Little Big Horn and Custer's "Last Stand," where US Army forces were soundly defeated. However, the Sioux tribes were unable to remain united as the US government attracted defections with benefits distributed to indigenous nations through the Indian Affairs Agency.[43] Critical leaders like Crazy Horse and Sitting Bull were either captured or fled, and the Great Sioux War ended with the Agreement of 1877, which formally annexed all Sioux lands to the United States and relocated the Sioux people to reservations.

The final Native American conflict of note is the 1877 Nez Perce War. The Nez Perce tribe lived in a reservation in the Oregon Territory, following their displacement after the Walla Walla Council of 1855.[44] The discovery of gold in the region facilitated further displacement, as some Nez Perce tribes signed away land rights in 1869. Tensions between the non-reservation tribes and settlers reached their zenith in 1877, and General Oliver Otis Howard ordered the remaining tribes to move onto reservation land within 30 days or face the US Army.[45] Most chose to fight and conducted a "fighting retreat" eastward from June to October 1877. The Nez Perce warriors won several encounters with the US Army, but they finally surrendered on October 5, 1877, and were relocated to reservations in Oklahoma.[46]

American settlers and the US military would continue to fight small engagements with Native American nations until the conclusion of the Apache Wars in 1924, but these nineteenth-century wars proved to be the closing chapter of Native American resistance to Manifest Destiny. The ever-greedier US commercial interests would soon echo throughout the world at large.

The Spanish-American War and American Imperialism

At the end of the nineteenth century, the United States took its most extensive foray into becoming an imperial power on the global stage. Under President

McKinley in 1898, the United States launched the Spanish-American War, which was fought in Cuba as well as the Pacific. The United States was interested in Cuba for decades prior to the Spanish-American War, and on at least five separate occasions the United States offered to buy Cuba from Spain. By the mid-1890s, there was considerable bilateral trade between the two countries ($103 million), though it still represented only a small fraction of US Gross Domestic Product at the time. Most of the trade was in sugar, which represented 59 percent of US cane sugar imports.[47]

In 1895, a rebellion broke out in Cuba, and the Spanish responded with ruthless killings and brutal policies, including re-concentration camps, which led to hundreds of thousands of Cuban deaths. The rebels resorted to scorched earth tactics, burning fields and agricultural land. At the time, US President Grover Cleveland, who tilted pro-Spanish, decided against any kind of intervention. Cleveland's successor in 1897, William McKinley, however, was mildly on the side of the rebels. Throughout 1897, he slowly applied diplomatic pressure on Spain, which led to very modest reforms.

As the situation deteriorated and American property was increasingly put at risk, McKinley deployed the USS *Maine* followed by the USS *Montgomery* to Havana, a standard response to disorder abroad, in January 1898.[48] But in February 1898, the mysterious explosion and sinking of the USS *Maine* in Havana killed 266 Americans, providing the impetus for giving US aid to the Cuban struggle and for diminishing Spain's influence in the Caribbean through both diplomatic and military means.

In response to the explosion, McKinley requested $50 million from Congress for national defense and a naval buildup, which was approved within a day. But McKinley did not blame Spain for the explosion. In late March, the Naval Court of Inquiry issued a report absolving Spain but failing to identify the perpetrator. It also concluded the explosion was externally caused, intensifying suspicion among the public that Spain was, in fact, involved. Still, neither McKinley nor his Navy secretary believed Spain was responsible for the disaster.[49]

A flurry of last-minute diplomatic efforts, including one by Pope Leo XIII and another by six European powers, also failed to prevent war. Spain conceded to a suspension of hostilities, but not an armistice (implying political recognition of the rebels), which McKinley and the rebels demanded. In response, McKinley requested authorization to use military force on April 11, 1898. Congress granted it a week later. McKinley then ordered a naval blockade of Cuban ports and made a call for 125,000 volunteers to join America's army. He formally requested a declaration of war on April 25, with Congress responding that it has already been declared.[50] By way of the Philippines and Cuba, and in alliance with Cuban revolutionaries, the United States defeated Spain by August.

While it was originally initiated to help liberate Cuba, the war concluded with America also in control of the Philippines, Guam, and Puerto Rico.[51] In comparison to other major wars, it was a relatively short and bloodless conflict. Over 327 days, between 300 and 400 US troops and roughly 800 Spaniards were killed in battle, not including the casualties from the USS *Maine* or associated deaths from diseases. Although more than 290,000 US troops were trained and mobilized, only about 54,000 participated in the fighting abroad.[52] But the inherited guerilla war in the Philippines would cost the United States far more lives in the years ahead, killing approximately 4,200 Americans and wounding 2,900.[53]

For the first time, the United States became an overseas imperial power. The McKinley administration also used the war as a pretext to annex Hawaii, which many argued was a vital territory for US economic and militaristic expansion within Asia. Eventually, Cuba gained independence, but it was re-occupied by American forces in 1906. The Philippines was an American territory until 1945, while Guam and Puerto Rico remain American territories today.

As the United States gained control over territories, many locals realized they were simply swapping one imperial overlord for another. Most notably, following the Treaty of Paris that officially ended the Spanish-American War, the Philippine rebels fighting for liberation from Spanish rule since 1896 continued their fight against the Americans. Although it initially seemed like American intervention might grant the Philippines more freedom as US forces partnered with Filipino rebels to wrest control of Manila from Spain, hopes were quickly dashed. Instead, US forces continued to fight, and in some cases, massacre the rebels. Roughly 200,000 Filipino citizens died during the war (mostly from hunger or disease), and 20,000 Filipino insurgents were killed.[54] The war cemented US control of the Philippines and furthered its stake in Pacific affairs, but it also contributed to its image as a ruthless, imperial power, willing to use brutal violence for political and economic domination. For the first half of the twentieth century the US Bureau of Insular Affairs took control, ruling the territory as a de facto colony until it was captured by the Japanese during World War II.[55] US foreign policy therefore echoed the imperialist tendencies of its former masters when the United States amassed enough political and economic power of its own.

A dominant navy became essential to underpin growing US power, and at the same time more colonies provided vital support to the navy. Once the United States grasped the former Spanish colonies, it used them to better control vital shipping lanes and promote American power projection for the first time in America's history.[56] Most important for the long-term goal of many American naval strategists and foreign policymakers was the subsequent building of a canal in Central America to connect the Atlantic and Pacific Oceans. The United States achieved this goal after removing Spain as a potential spoiler in the process. When Colombia backed out of a deal that would have created the canal, the United States championed a rebellion in the breakaway region of Panama. The United States then signed a contract with the new country of Panama to build a canal, granting the United States full sovereignty until 1979 and de facto sovereignty until 1999. The United States ruled over the Panama Canal zone as a colonial power, lording over the territory to maintain naval access.[57] In fact, the United States' involvement in Panama stands as the longest US military intervention of the era, totaling 3,734 cumulative days of occupation.[58]

Overall, the Spanish-American War is notable for commencing American imperialism abroad and providing an opportunity for American power projection for the first time in history.

Hegemony in Full Force: Banana Wars in Latin America

Following the conclusion of the Spanish-American War and with the construction of the Panama Canal underway, the United States fully realized its role as a hegemon in the Western Hemisphere. With power projection capabilities and regional hegemony secured, the United States began acting as the region's policeman through a variety of interventions and foreign military threats that are commonly referred to as the Banana Wars.

Under President Theodore Roosevelt, America undertook the Banana Wars to maintain political and economic interests and promote hegemony. A major fear of American policymakers was that Germany, Britain, and other foreign powers would use the public indebtedness of Caribbean and Latin American states to demand concessions and the placement of naval bases on their territory. This prompted the issuing of the Roosevelt Corollary, which held that the United States would press the claims of European powers in the Western Hemisphere for them. The United States would intervene as needed to stabilize the internal economic conditions of Latin American states that owed European banks, rather than allow European states to press claims themselves.

Throughout this period, multiple American interventions in Cuba, Honduras, Nicaragua, the Dominican Republic, Haiti, and Mexico all followed the logic of attempting to quell internal rebellions and crises while keeping the Europeans out of the way. The goal was to help American investments while not permitting domestic debt to lead to avenues for German or British footholds in the region. Under both Roosevelt and Taft, these interventions were examples of either big stick diplomacy or dollar diplomacy, featuring the use of its growing naval power to protect American commercial interests in the region. In fact, the US Marines Corps doctrine primarily developed during this period to focus on how to win these so-called small banana wars.[59]

Beyond the military strategies of small warfare, the United States under Roosevelt also inaugurated new patterns of regional diplomacy. Roosevelt personally mediated the peace negotiations after the 1904–1905 Russo-Japanese War (for which he won a Nobel Peace Prize) and the Moroccan Crisis of 1911, a proxy conflict between France and Germany.[60] In these instances, the president aimed to promote US influence abroad while at the same time balancing American power against the old European giants.

The United States undertook its two longest Banana Wars under President Wilson in Haiti and the Dominican Republic.[61] Wilson had a slightly different interest in Latin America. While he wanted to protect American commercial interests, he also believed that greater democratic governance in the region was the best way to do so. His paternalistic attitude on how to teach certain Latin American countries to "elect good men" and how to promote enough stability to allow them to be democracies drove much of his policy in the region. After taking control to stabilize the governments, reduce internal rebellions, and decrease the national debt, the United States was the *de facto* government of Haiti from 1915 to 1934 and the Dominican Republic from 1916 to 1924. But instead of allowing democratic governance to emerge, the occupations failed to establish stable democracies in either country.[62]

Changing US Foreign Policy: The Mexican Revolution

The Mexican Revolution began in 1910 and took off in earnest with the over-throw of the Diaz regime and the installation of Francisco Madero as president in 1911. The United States was concerned about unrest on its southern border, threats to American commerce, and British and German interests in Mexico. The conservative Felix Diaz regime was more favorable to American business interests, and the revolution caused US political elites to worry that British and German businesses would gain exclusive access within the new regime.[63]

The first significant American involvement in the Mexican Revolution began during the final months of the Taft administration, which were known as the Ten Tragic Days in Mexico. In a coup, General Victoriano Huerta, a high-ranking military officer under Madero, became president with the support of previous Diaz regime elements and at least tacit assistance from the American ambassador in Mexico, Henry Lane Wilson. Huerta assassinated Madero while he was in custody as President Woodrow Wilson took office. Breaking diplomatic tradition, Wilson refused to recognize Huerta as the legitimate ruler of Mexico and demanded Henry Lane Wilson return to Washington immediately. Even with the United Kingdom and Germany pressuring Wilson to recognize Huerta as the legitimate ruler, he refused, saying he would never allow him to remain president.[64]

Wilson's dislike of Huerta eventually prompted the United States to end its embargo on selling arms to the revolutionaries fighting against his regime, and more significantly led the United States to occupy the city of Veracruz in 1914 to help with his ouster. A mistaken arrest of American marines buying fuel for their ships in Tampico, which was under martial law at the time, precipitated the occupation. Wilson's administration used this as an excuse to plan for the occupation of Tampico, but then switched to Veracruz when it learned a German ship was bringing weapons for Huerta to Veracruz. The United States captured the city quickly, only to discover that its erstwhile allies against Huerta also spoke out against American intervention in the revolution. Instead of marching on Mexico City to oust Huerta as initially planned, Wilson instead decided to work with the Constitutionalist faction led by Carranza. Through mediation by Argentina, Brazil, and Chile, Wilson agreed to leave Veracruz if Huerta stepped down and fled the country, allowing Carranza to become president. After seeing Carranza installed, the United States left Veracruz.[65]

In 1916, the United States intervened again following raids into American territory led by Pancho Villa. Villa felt betrayed when the United States backed Carranza in the battles between the various revolutionary factions. After Villa attacked American territory, US General Pershing led an expeditionary force across the border to capture Villa. However, as the expedition pushed deeper into Mexico, Carranza latched onto growing anti-American sentiment to help push for diplomatic negotiations leading to the withdrawal of US troops. While the United States never captured Villa, he did not lead another raid on American territory during the revolution.[66]

American relations with Carranza were becoming strained and the new Mexican constitution made it easier for him to nationalize and expropriate American commercial interests and territory in Mexico. While Carranza did not act on these powers, the American business community feared the possibility and pressured Wilson for help. During this time, the Zimmerman Telegram came to light after being captured by the British. It revealed a German plot to push Mexico to start a war with the United States, with Germany offering support and promising to give back territory lost to the United States in previous conflicts. The telegram intensified anti-Mexican and anti-German sentiment in the United States, and it almost led Wilson to reinvade Veracruz and other parts of Mexico (which he resisted when Carranza said he would burn the oilfields in Tampico and elsewhere).[67] The Mexican Revolution concluded in 1920 when three generals led a coup against Carranza to prevent him from handpicking a replacement as president, which was seen as a betrayal of the revolution. Carranza was killed trying to flee the country, and the generals consolidated control. Eventually, they secured diplomatic recognition from the United States after negotiating rules on which American commercial interests and property could not be nationalized.

American intervention in the Mexican Revolution appeared more militaristically restrained than previous interventions in Latin America. And Wilson's choice in 1914 to refuse to recognize the Huerta government due to its illegitimacy while continuing to promote US economic interests and American values in Mexico, previews Wilsonian foreign policy in the coming years.

Crisis Event: World War I

In 1914, while the United States was still concerned about European influence in Latin America, Europe erupted into a major war. The United States officially declared itself neutral as World War I began, despite Wilson's dislike of Germany. Wilson attempted to serve as a mediator to end the war and keep the United States out of the European mess. Yet German attacks on American shipping started to increase the likelihood of US intervention. When Germany sank the British-owned *Lusitania* in 1915, killing more than 100 Americans, the US public was outraged, prompting debate on American involvement in the war. Various factions discussed how prepared the United States should be to enter the war and what it would take to stop German aggression. With Wilson campaigning for reelection in 1916 based on the claim that he kept the United States out of the war, however, he was naturally reticent to enter the war.[68]

Yet by 1917, multiple factors changed to prompt a US intervention into the war. First, Germany resumed unrestricted U-boat warfare targeting American shipping, which forced Wilson to place armed units on the ships for self-protection. Second, the revelation in the Zimmerman Telegram about Germany's goal to get Mexico to enter the war raised anti-German sentiment, although Wilson waited a month after the discovery of the telegram to seek a war declaration. Third, the collapse of Russia and its revolution made a German victory more likely. Finally, Wilson seemed to realize that if he did not enter the war, he would not be involved in the war settlement, where he wanted to "make the world safe for democracy." Both public and elite opinion began to support American entry into the war.[69]

On April 2, 1917, the United States officially entered World War I on the side of the Triple Entente powers, providing needed manpower and supplies after the Russian surrender and the *de facto* French collapse on the Western front. The arrival of American troops on the battlefield in 1918 was enough to resist a final German offensive in the spring and allowed the allies to go on the offensive to defeat Germany in November 1918. At the same time, the United States participated in an allied intervention in the Russian Civil War on behalf of the White Russian faction. Some claim this was evidence of the American dislike of communism and Bolshevism, but more likely the intervention was an attempt to help the faction still committed to the war effort against Germany gain power.[70]

In the end, Wilson was eager for the opportunity offered by the Paris Peace Treaty. It gave him a chance to promote his vision for collective security and a new global order, outlined famously in his Fourteen Points speech to the US Congress. This included his proposal for the creation of a League of Nations and the redrawing of national borders for self-determination. Wilson also sought to create a peace treaty that would eliminate future wars, open the world to free trade, and not be overly harsh on Germany and other losers of the war. However, once the peace treaty negotiations took off in earnest, Wilson fell ill, and the French and other allied negotiators were able to concoct a harsher peace settlement on Germany and Austria-Hungary that would echo for decades to come. Most notably, the League of Nations concept and the transformation of borders and the colonial system did make it through the peace negotiations, but this transformation did not include freedom for everyone. Wilson consented to the mandate system under League of Nations auspices for administering territories previously controlled by the Triple Alliance, and he also refused to meet with anticolonial activists, like a young Vietnamese nationalist, Ho Chi Minh, who requested American aid to fuel decolonization.[71]

Unfortunately, US domestic politics prevented the United States from joining the League of Nations, and the treaty signing never occurred. With greater global status and involvement, US domestic political elites and the public faced growing dilemmas on how to balance US sovereignty with rising international obligations and interventionism. Moreover, the impulse to avoid costly European conflicts across the sea remained a strong factor that tempered US global hegemonic aspirations. Despite these ideological defeats, Wilson relentlessly pursued his efforts to make the world safe for democracy, albeit with a staunch Western and racial bias that continues to impact debates on democratization to this day.[72]

Conclusion and Parallels to the Present

After the Civil War, the United States began to accumulate significant economic strength, expanded its military footprint in the Western hemisphere, and started its ascent to great power status. It built a strong navy to defend its commercial interests overseas, and intervened in the affairs of other nations, mainly in Latin America, to safeguard its economic investments, prop up foreign regimes favorable to US interests, and prevent allies from accruing debt to US adversaries. President Roosevelt was the first leader to expressly link world affairs to US national interests and stress to the American people the importance of US global interests. Wilson also introduced democracy promotion as a key objective of US foreign policy, which would last well into the late twentieth century and beyond.

Toward the end of this era of US foreign policy, American imperialism forged ahead unabated, as the United States expanded westward, sparking increased conflicts with indigenous nations, and as politicians debated the annexation of international territories like the Philippines, Guam, and Puerto Rico. The period ended with the outbreak of World War I, which the United States reluctantly joined in 1917.

The relevance of democracy promotion and economic interests in deciding where and when to intervene can be seen in more recent trends in US interventionism. The second Gulf War, beginning in 2003, is the most notorious contemporary example of this alleged use of military force for economic gain. As historian Steven Hurst wrote, "American policy towards Iraq since 1979 has been driven, ultimately, by the need to maintain a dominant position in the international oil system."[73] Further, before the war, American leadership "came to see regime change in Iraq as the potential catalyst for the spread of market-democracy throughout the wider Middle East."[74] More recently, President Trump chose to keep US troops in Syria "because I kept the oil,"[75] and State Department employees confirmed that a US presence is justified by the need to protect Syrian oil reserves.[76] These conflations of economic and security interests echo the gunboat diplomacy and Banana Wars of the prior century. The rhetoric of democratization as part of these recent regime change wars also echo the Wilsonian legacy of making the world safer for democracy by meddling in the domestic politics of Latin American countries.

Like the European challenges to America's spheres of influence in Latin America, the United States now faces challenges to its hegemony in a number of regions. America's historically generous international aid dramatically increased its influence worldwide, however its adversaries are now adopting similar tactics. The United States competes with China's Belt and Road Initiative in Africa, Central Asia, and the Middle East, with many countries choosing China's less restrictive and cheaper economic assistance and development aid over US assistance. As in the previous century, the United States is again using its military and economic might to ward off foreign interference in its spheres of influence, although today America's sphere of influence includes the world at large.

Historical parallels may also be drawn directly to contemporary US military interventions that span the entire globe, with the United States controlling over 750 military bases abroad as of 2020.[77] While the United States is no longer annexing territory overseas or battling Native American nations in pursuit of Manifest Destiny in the West, its legacy of gunboat diplomacy, imperialistic protection of spheres of influence, military interventions in the domestic politics of other countries, and regime change policies have increased despite lower levels of existential and regional threats.

Perhaps most importantly, contemporary US militarism has grown at the expense of US diplomacy and economic statecraft. While in the past the United States often relied on diplomacy, economic tools, and threats or displays of force, its modern-day self has resorted to more direct militaristic tactics, rather than reserving force as the policy of last resort. Such a militaristic foreign policy today is further magnified by the United States' transformed role from a regional power to an unmatched global superpower. In other words, while imperial overstretch[78] may not have been a concern for the United States in the 1800s and 1900s despite its clear expansionism, it is very much an urgent concern today.

Notes

1. Second Inaugural Address of Woodrow Wilson. The Avalon Project: Yale Law School. https://avalon.law.yale.edu/20th_century/wilson2.asp.
2. Cavanna, "U.S. Grand Strategy."
3. Fareed Zakaria, *From Wealth to Power: The Unusual Origins of America's World Role* (Princeton, NJ: Princeton University Press, 1998), 5.
4. Thomas D. Shoonover, *Dollars over Dominion* (Baton Rouge: Louisiana State University Press, 1978), 249–250.
5. Zakaria, *From Wealth to Power: The Unusual Origins of America's World Role,* 11.
6. Kissinger, *Diplomacy,* 35.
7. Kevin Narizny, *The Political Economy of Grand Strategy* (Ithaca, NY: Cornell University Press, 2007), 126.
8. Zakaria, *From Wealth to Power: The Unusual Origins of America's World Role,* 130.
9. Secretary of State William Seward had attempted to expand US commercial markets to Asia by purchasing Alaska in 1867, and by crafting a reciprocity treaty that would connect Hawaii's economy to that of the United States. He had also attempted to procure Caribbean naval bases, amongst other expansionist actions in Latin America.

But in the aftermath of the Civil War, Congress had rejected all of Seward's ideas and plans.

10. "Mahan's The Influence of Sea Power upon History: Securing International Markets in the 1890s," Office of the Historian: U.S. Department of State, https://history.state.gov/milestones/1866-1898/mahan; Frederick Jackson, Turner. 1893. "The Significance of the Frontier in American History," https://quod.lib.umich.edu/m/moa/ABL0 350.0001.001?rgn=main;view=fulltext.

11. Zakaria, *From Wealth to Power: The Unusual Origins of America's World,* 11.

12. Kissinger, *Diplomacy,* 38.

13. Kissinger, *Diplomacy,* 39.

14. Zakaria, *From Wealth to Power: The Unusual Origins of America's World Role,* 165.

15. Address of President Wilson to Joint Session of Congress, April 2, 1917, Woodrow Wilson Papers, Manuscript Division, Library of Congress, Electronic source available here: https://www.loc.gov/exhibitions/world-war-i-american-experiences/about-this-exhibition/arguing-over-war/for-or-against-war/wilson-before-congress.

16. "Wilson for 'America First,'" *The Chicago Daily Tribune* (October 12, 1915), https://chicagotribune.newspapers.com/.

17. Kissinger, *Diplomacy,* 44.

18. Full codebook is available upon request.

19. The CINC measure reflects an average of a state's share of the system total of each of the six elements of capabilities in each year, weighting each component equally. The six components are: military expenditures; military personnel; iron and steel production; primary energy consumption; total population; and urban population. The CINC will always range between 0 and 1. "0.0" would indicate that a state had 0% of the total capabilities present in the system in that year, while "1.0" would indicate that the state had 100% of the capabilities in a given year. Correlates of War Project. (d). *National Material Capabilities, 1816–2012.* Version 5. http://www.correlatesof war.org; J. David Singer, "Reconstructing the Correlates of War Dataset on Material Capabilities of States, 1816–1985," *International Interactions* 14 (1987): 115–132.

20. We measure whether the United States and State B share a colonial border during the year in question. The original data and coding arise from: Correlates of War Project, *Colonial/Dependency Contiguity, 1816–2016,* Version 3.1, http://correlatesofwar.org.

21. For the original MIPS coding that we heavily rely on, see Sullivan, Patricia and Michael Koch, MIPS Codebook, 2008, https://plsullivan.web.unc.edu/wp-content/uploads/sites/1570/2011/09/MIPS_codebook_Sullivan.pdf.

22. Jeannette P. Nichols, "The United States Congress and Imperialism, 1861–1897," *The Journal of Economic History* 21, no. 4 (December 1961): doi:10.1017/s0022050700109039.

23. Nichols, "The United States Congress and Imperialism, 1861–1897."

24. Allan Peskin, "Blaine, Garfield and Latin America: A New Look," *The Americas* 36, no. 1 (1979): doi:10.2307/981139.

25. Peskin, "Blaine, Garfield and Latin America: A New Look."

26. Sven Beckert, "Emancipation and Empire: Reconstructing the Worldwide Web of Cotton Production in the Age of the American Civil War," *The American Historical Review* 109, no. 5 (December 2004): doi:10.1086/ahr/109.5.1405.

27. Stève Sainlaude et al., *France and the American Civil War: A Diplomatic History* (Chapel Hill: University of North Carolina Press, 2019).

28. "British Support During the U.S. Civil War," *Liverpool's Abercromby Square and the Confederacy During the U.S. Civil War*, Lowcountry Digital History Initiative (LDHI), https://ldhi.library.cofc.edu/exhibits/show/liverpools-abercromby-square/brit ain-and-us-civil-war.

29. Tom Bingham, "The Alabama Claims Arbitration," *International and Comparative Law Quarterly* 54, no. 1 (2005): 1–25, doi:10.1093/iclq/54.1.1.

30. Matthew Shaw, "Anglo-American Relations during the Civil War," *The British Library*, The British Library, September 9, 2013, www.bl.uk/onlinegallery/onlineex/uscivil war/britain/britainamericancivilwar.html.

31. Bingham, "The Alabama Claims Arbitration."

32. Bingham, "The Alabama Claims Arbitration."

33. James Breck Perkins and Lindley Miller Keasbey, "The Nicaragua Canal and the Monroe Doctrine," *Political Science Quarterly* 12, no. 2 (1897): doi:10.2307/2140128.

34. Clifton J. Child, "The Venezuela-British Guiana Boundary Arbitration of 1899," *The American Journal of International Law* 44, no. 4 (October 1950): doi:10.2307/2194986.

35. "French Intervention in Mexico and the American Civil War, 1862–1867," *Milestones: 1861–1865*, U.S. Department of State: Office of the Historian, http://hist ory.state.gov/milestones/1861-1865/french-intervention.

36. "French Intervention in Mexico and the American Civil War, 1862–1867," *Milestones: 1861–1865*.

37. "French Intervention in Mexico and the American Civil War, 1862–1867," *Milestones: 1861–1865*.

38. "French Intervention in Mexico and the American Civil War, 1862–1867," *Milestones: 1861–1865*.

39. "French Intervention in Mexico and the American Civil War, 1862–1867," *Milestones: 1861–1865*.

40. "Famous Historical Indians: Red Cloud." *Central States Archaeological Journal* 17, no. 2 (April 1970).

41. "Famous Historical Indians: Red Cloud." *Central States Archaeological Journal*.

42. Robert M. Utley, "Origins of the Great Sioux War: The Brown-Anderson Controversy Revisited," *Montana: The Magazine of Western History* 42, no. 4 (1992).

43. Utley, "Origins of the Great Sioux War."

44. John A. Carpenter, "General Howard and the Nez Perce War of 1877," *The Pacific Northwest Quarterly* 49, no. 4 (October 1958).

45. Carpenter, "General Howard and the Nez Perce War of 1877."

46. Carpenter, "General Howard and the Nez Perce War of 1877."

47. Louis Pérez, *The War of 1898: The United States and Cuba in History and Historiography* (Chapel Hill: University of North Carolina, 1998).

48. Lewis L. Gould, *The Spanish-American War and President McKinley* (Lawrence: University Press of Kansas, 1982); Mark Hayes, "Spanish-American War; War Plans and Impact on U.S. Naval Operations in the Spanish-American War," Naval History and Heritage Command, The Navy Department Library, March 23, 1998, https://www.history.navy.mil/research/library/online-reading-room/title-list-alphabetically/s/spanish-american-war-war-plans-and-impact-on-u-s-navy.html.

49. Kenneth E. Hendrickson, *The Spanish-American War* (Westport, CT: Greenwood Press, 2003); John L. Offner, *An Unwanted War: The Diplomacy of the United States and Spain Over Cuba, 1895-1898* (Chapel Hill: University of North Carolina Press, 1992).

50. Offner, *An Unwanted War.*

51. George C. Herring, *From Colony to Superpower: U.S. Foreign Relations Since 1776* (Oxford: Oxford University Press, 2008), chs. 8–9; Philip S. Foner, *The Spanish-Cuban-American War and the Birth of American Imperialism Vol. 2: 1898–1902* (New York: NYU Press, 1972); Lester D. Langley, *The Banana Wars: United States Intervention in the Caribbean, 1898–1934* (Lanham, MD: Rowman & Littlefield Books, 1983), chs. 1–2; Zakaria, *From Wealth to Power: The Unusual Origins of America's World Role,* ch. 4.

52. Patrick McSherry, "Casualties During the Spanish American War," *The Spanish American War Centennial Website*, accessed January 23, 2021, https://www.spanam war.com/casualties.htm.

53. Trevor K. Plante, "Researching Service in the U.S. Army During the Philippine Insurrection," *Prologue Magazine* 32, no. 2 (2000): https://www.archives.gov/publi cations/prologue/2000/summer/philippine-insurrection.html.

54. "The Philippines," *Digital History,* accessed April 2, 2022, https://www.digitalhistory. uh.edu/disp_textbook.cfm?smtid=2&psid=3161.

55. Daniel Immerwahr, *How to Hide an Empire: A Short History of the Greater United States* (New York: Random House, 2019), chs. 4–6; Julian Go and Anne L. Foster, eds., *The American Colonial State in the Philippines: Global Perspectives* (Durham: Duke University Press, 2003).

56. Alfred Thayer Mahan, *The Influence of Sea Power Upon History, 1660–1783* (Boston: Little, Brown, and Company, 1890); George C. Herring, *From Colony to Superpower: U.S. Foreign Relations Since 1776* (Oxford: Oxford University Press, 2008), ch. 9.

57. David McCullough, *The Path Between the Seas: The Creation of the Panama Canal, 1870–1914* (New York: Simon & Schuster, 1977); Noel Maurer and Carlos Yu, *The Big Ditch: How America Took, Built, Ran, and Ultimately Gave Away the Panama Canal* (Princeton, NJ: Princeton University Press, 2010); John Major, *Prize Possession: The United States Government and the Panama Canal 1903–1979* (Cambridge: Cambridge University Press, 1993), chs. 2 & 6.

58. See Table A2.1 in the appendix for a complete list of interventions and their duration.

59. Keith B. Bickel, *Mars Learning: The Marine Corps' Development of Small Wars Doctrine, 1915–1940* (New York: Westview Press, 2001), chs. 3–4; Noel Maurer, *The Empire Trap: The Rise and Fall of U.S. Intervention to Protect American Property Overseas,*

1893–2013 (Princeton: Princeton University Press, 2013), chs. 3–4; Michel Gobat, *Confronting the American dream: Nicaragua under U.S. Imperial Rule* (Durham: Duke University Press, 2005); Dana G. Munro, "Dollar Diplomacy in Nicaragua, 1909–1913," *The Hispanic American Historical Review* 38, no. 2 (1958): 209–234.

60. Cavanna, "U.S. Grand Strategy."

61. See Table A2.1 in the Appendix for a complete list of US interventions and their duration.

62. Lester D. Langley, *The Banana Wars: United States Intervention in the Caribbean, 1898–1934* (Lanham, MD: Rowman & Littlefield Books, 1983), chs. 10–12; Bruce J. Calder, *The Impact of Intervention: The Dominican Republic During the U.S. Occupation of 1916–1924* (Austin: University of Texas Press, 1984); Ellen D. Tillman, *Dollar Diplomacy by Force: Nation-Building and Resistance in the Dominican Republic* (Chapel Hill, NC: UNC Press Books, 2016); Hans Schmidt, *The United States Occupation of Haiti, 1915–1934* (New Brunswick, NJ: Rutgers University Press, 1971).

63. Friedrich Katz, *The Secret War in Mexico: Europe, The United States and the Mexican Revolution* (Chicago: University of Chicago Press, 1981).

64. Katz, *The Secret War in Mexico: Europe, The United States and the Mexican Revolution*; Cole Blasier, "The United States and Madero," *Journal of Latin American Studies* 4, no. 2 (1972): 207–231; Stanley R. Ross, *Francisco I. Madero: Apostle of Mexican Democracy* (New York: Columbia University Press, 1955), 276–329.

65. Langley, *The Banana Wars: United States Intervention in the Caribbean, 1898–1934*; Jack Sweetman, *The Landing at Veracruz: 1914* (Annapolis, MD: U.S. Naval Institute, 1968); Robert E. Quirk, *An Affair of Honor: Woodrow Wilson and the Occupation of Veracruz* (New York: W.W. Norton & Company, 1962).

66. John S. D. Eisenhower, *Intervention!: The United States and the Mexican Revolution, 1913–1917* (New York: WW Norton & Company, 1993), chs. 16–24; Friedrich Katz, "Pancho Villa and the Attack on Columbus, New Mexico," *The American Historical Review* 83, no. 1 (1978): 101–130; James A. Sandos, "Pancho Villa and American Security: Woodrow Wilson's Mexican Diplomacy Reconsidered," *Journal of Latin American Studies* 13, no. 2 (1981): 293–311.

67. Katz, *The Secret War in Mexico: Europe, The United States and the Mexican Revolution*, 344–383, 493–503; Thomas Boghardt, *The Zimmermann Telegram: Intelligence, Diplomacy, and America's Entry into World War I* (Naval Institute Press, 2012); Douglas W. Richmond, *Venustiano Carranza's Nationalist Struggle, 1893–1920* (Lincoln: University of Nebraska Press, 1983) 189–218.

68. Kendrick A. Clements, "Woodrow Wilson and World War I," *Presidential Studies Quarterly* 34, no. 1(2004): 62–82; Arthur S. Link, *Wilson: The Struggle for Neutrality 1914-1915, Volume III* (Princeton, NJ: Princeton University Press, 1960).

69. Arthur S. Link, *Wilson: Campaigns for Progressivism and Peace 1916-1917, Volume V* (Princeton, NJ: Princeton University Press, 1965), chs. 5–9; Barbara Wertheim Tuchman, *The Zimmermann Telegram* (New York: Macmillan, 1985).

70. David Woodward, *The American Army and the First World War* (Cambridge: Cambridge University Press, 2014); Edward M. Coffman, *The War to End All Wars: The American Military Experience in World War I* (Lexington: University

Press of Kentucky, 1998); John W. Long, "American Intervention in Russia: The North Russian Expedition, 1918–19," *Diplomatic History* 6, no. 1 (1982): 45–68.

71. Tony Smith, *Why Wilson Matters: The Origin of American Liberal Internationalism and Its Crisis Today* (Princeton, NJ: Princeton University Press, 2017), ch. 3; Tony Smith, *America's Mission: The United States and the Worldwide Struggle for Democracy* (Princeton, NJ: Princeton University Press, 1994), ch. 4.

72. Errol Henderson, "Hidden in Plain Sight: Racism in International Relations Theory," *Cambridge Review of International Affairs* 26, no. 1 (2013): 71–92; Lloyd E. Ambrosius, *Woodrow Wilson and the American Diplomatic Tradition: The Treaty Fight in Perspective* (Cambridge: Cambridge University Press, 1990), chs. 7 and 8.

73. Steven Hurst, *The United States and Iraq Since 1979* (Edinburgh: Edinburgh University Press, 2009), 12, https://www.jstor.org/stable/10.3366/j.ctt1r27xm.

74. Hurst, *The United States and Iraq Since* 1979, 226.

75. David Brennan, "Trump Says U.S. Troops Stayed in Syria 'Because I Kept the Oil,'" *Newsweek*, January 15, 2020, https://www.newsweek.com/onald-trump-us-troops-syria-oil-bashar-al-assad-kurds-wisconsin-rally-1482250.

76. Jack Detsch, "U.S. Troops Really Are in Syria to Protect the Oil—for the Kurds," *Foreign Policy*, August 5, 2020, http://foreignpolicy.com/2020/08/05/kurds-oil-syria-us-troops-trump/.

77. Data on U.S. military bases abroad from David Vine, *The United States of War: A Global History of America's Endless Conflicts, from Columbus to the Islamic State* (Berkeley: University of California Press, 2020). https://www.basenation.us/maps.html.

78. Jack Snyder, *Myths of Empire: Domestic Politics and International Ambition* (Ithaca, NY: Cornell University Press, 1991).

Chapter 2 Appendix

Table A2.1 List of US Military Interventions with Duration and Fatalities, 1865–1917

Start Year	Name	Duration (Days)	US Battle Deaths	State B Battle Deaths	Total Battle Deaths	US Total Deaths	State B Total Deaths
1865	"Glorious Revolution" of the 9 (Panama)	1	0	0	0	0	4
1865	French Intervention in Mexico	153	0	0	0	0	0
1866	US Consul Protection in China	17	0	0	0	0	0
1866	Occupation of Matamoros	3	0	0	0	0	
1866	Blockade Dispute with Brazil	1	0	0	0	0	0
1866	Bombardment of Valparaiso	31	0	0	9	0	0
1867	Formosa Expedition	1	1	0	1	1	0
1867	Show of Force in Nicaragua	1	0	0	0	0	0
1868	Boshin War	234	0	0	0	0	1
1868	Chiriquí Intervention	22	0	0	0	0	0
1868	Montevideo Uprising	9	0	0	0	0	0
1869	Dominican Republic Interference	30	0	0	0	0	0
1870	Tianjin Massacre	73	0	0	0	0	0
1870	Battle of Boca Teacapan	2	7	0	7	4	0
1871	Korea Shipwreck Incident	3	2	250	252	2	250
1873	Isthmus Revolutions	33	0	0	0	0	0
1873	Mexico Border Crossings by US Troops	3333	100	10	110	100	100
1874	Honolulu Courthouse Intervention	9	0	0	0	0	1

(continued)

Table A2.1 Continued

Start Year	Name	Duration (Days)	US Battle Deaths	State B Battle Deaths	Total Battle Deaths	US Total Deaths	State B Total Deaths
1874	The USS *Saranac* in Mexico	161	0	0	0	1	1
1876	Evacuation of Matamoros	7	0	0	0	0	0
1882	Alexandria intervention	5	0	0	0	0	0
1885	Rebel Takeover of Colón & Panama City	127	0	18	18	0	18
1888	Baby Riots in Korea	12	0	0	0	0	0
1888	Protective mission in Samoa	126	0	0	0	0	0
1888	Samoan Crisis	14	56	118	174	56	118
1888	Haitian Revolution	398	0	0	0	0	0
1889	Coup attempt in Hawaii	2	0	0	0	0	0
1890	Buenos Aires protective mission	57	0	0	0	0	0
1891	Chilean Civil War & the Baltimore Affair	362	2	0	2	2	0
1891	Attempt to Lease Mole St. Nicolas	87	0	0	0	0	0
1893	Hawaiian Coup Troop Landing	45	0	0	0	0	0
1893	Havana Ranch Incident	12	0	0	0	0	0
1894	Sino-Japanese War	188	0	0	0	0	0
1894	Korea Crisis in Sino-Japanese War	621	0	0	0	0	0
1894	Rio de Janeiro Affair	1	0	0	0	0	0
1894	Protective mission in Nicaragua	32	0	0	0	0	0
1895	Bocas del Toro Landing	3	0	0	0	0	0
1896	Protective mission	3	0	0	0	0	0

Year	Event						
1898	Marine stationing in Beijing and Tientsin	8	0	0	0	0	0
1898	Spanish-American War	327	330	800	1130	3550	Unclear
1898	Protective mission in Nicaragua	2	0	0	0	0	0
1899	The Philippine–American War	2589	4200	17500	21700	4200	217500
1899	War of Succession in Samoa	90	10	200	210	10	200
1899	Protective mission in Nicaragua	11	0	0	0	0	0
1900	Boxer Rebellion	123	21	10000	10983	21	75000
1900	Anticipated Protective Mission in DR	5	0	0	0	0	0
1901	Retaking Colón	15	0	0	0	0	0
1902	Return to Bocas del Toro	32	0	0	0	0	0
1902	Continued Isthmus Unrest	65	0	0	0	1	0
1902	Venezuelan Crisis	24	0	0	0	0	0
1902	Alaska Boundary Dispute	511	0	0	0	0	0
1903	Landing During 1903 Revolution	23	0	0	0	0	0
1903	Conservative Rebellion of 1903	17	0	0	0	0	0
1903	US Recognition of Independent Panama	3734	0	0	0	0	0
1903	Beirut intervention	31	0	0	0	0	0
1903	Skinner Mission to Ethiopia	60	0	0	0	0	0
1904	Korea Crisis in Russo-Japanese War	677	0	0	0	0	0
1904	Huerta's Resignation	8	0	0	0	0	0
1904	Seven Red Flags Battle	146	1	100	101	1	100
1904	Tangiers Hostages	29	0	0	0	0	0
1906	Occupation of Cuba	848	0	0	0	0	0
1907	Honduran Rebellion	83	0	0	0	0	0

(continued)

Table A2.1 Continued

Start Year	Name	Duration (Days)	US Battle Deaths	State B Battle Deaths	Total Battle Deaths	US Total Deaths	State B Total Deaths
1908	1908 Panamanian Election	36	0	0	0	0	0
1910	Nicaraguan civil war	195	0	0	0	0	0
1911	Chinese Revolution	686	0	0	0	0	0
1911	General Bonilla's Counter-Rebellion	60	0	0	0	1	0
1911	Rebellion Against Antoine Simon	19	0	0	0	0	0
1911	The Mexican Revolution	3106	131	554	685	265	878
1912	Constantinople Interv/1st Balkan War	16	0	0	0	0	0
1912	Cuban rebels	74	0	0	0	0	0
1912	Attempted Seizure at Puerto Cortez	8	0	0	0	0	0
1912	Liberal Uprising in Nicaragua	91	7	Unclear	0	7	Unclear
1912	1912 Panama Election	619	0	0	0	0	0
1914	Instability in the Dominican Republic	162	0	Unclear	0	0	500
1914	Landings During Instability in Haiti	335	0	0	0	0	0
1915	US Occupation of Haiti	1755	14	2750	2764	14	2774
1916	Nanjing Incident (Nanking)	1	0	0	0	0	0
1916	Occupation of Dominican Republic	3122	16			195	
1917	Chungking Incident	3	0	0	0	0	0
1917	Seizure of German ships	1	0	0	0	0	0
1917	World War I	584	53402	3409442	3462844	116516	7415000
1917	US Force Deployment in Cuba	883	0	0	0	0	0

3

America the Hesitant Helper

Let us no longer blind ourselves to the undeniable fact that the evil forces which have crushed and undermined and corrupted so many others are already within our own gates . . . We must be the great arsenal of democracy.[1]

Franklin D. Roosevelt, December 29, 1940

Judging by the previous era's momentum, stretching from the American Civil War to the end of World War I, the United States could have been expected to ramp up its international involvement into the next era, expanding its imperialist ambitions beyond Latin America and pushing its objectives more stridently around the world. That did not happen. Instead, there was a stark reversal in US foreign policy during the interwar era with isolationist voices dominating foreign policy decisions. The United States moved away from its previously imperialist ambitions toward relatively isolationist tendencies, before finally becoming a hesitant, last-minute helper of its European allies during World War II. Dire domestic economic conditions in the 1930s spread like wildfire across the Atlantic, and America's political and economic isolationism fanned the flames of rising global fascist movements, which ultimately awoke the reluctant United States from its hibernation.

This chapter traces momentous events in US foreign policy during the interwar era, from 1918 to 1945. We first contextualize the main themes and patterns using data from the Military Intervention Project before delving deeper into representative events. The era concludes with the United States using its tools of war, trade, and diplomacy far beyond its neighborhood to come to the rescue of Europe and end another world conflagration. The era propelled the United States from an emergency ally to an often-benign great

Dying by the Sword. Monica Duffy Toft and Sidita Kushi, Oxford University Press. © Oxford University Press 2023. DOI: 10.1093/oso/9780197581438.003.0004

power, ready to act on the world stage and shape the post–World War II order for decades to come.

After first synthesizing the grand strategies of the era, the next section of the chapter summarizes the main historical moments of US foreign policy during the so-called twenty years' crisis.[2] We then introduce data-driven patterns and graphics of US military interventionism to contextualize the historical narratives of the most critical crisis moments of the era, concluding with the US entry into World War II. The chapter's concluding section places this interwar US foreign policy within a broader theoretical and policy perspective.

Grand Strategy during the Twenty Years' Crisis

President Woodrow Wilson led the United States into World War I, where America's military intervention ultimately decided the conflict in favor of the Entente alliance. Wilson's grand strategy of liberal interventionism, however, did not take root in American politics after the war, and the country soon returned to its relative isolationism. For the postwar period, Wilson proclaimed his idealistic Fourteen Points and advocated for the establishment of the League of Nations, the first global institution of collective security. Nevertheless, Wilson could not ensure the acceptance of his principles of collective security, international free trade, and open diplomacy either at the Paris peace talks, where French leadership successfully pushed for brutally punitive terms with Germany and Austria-Hungary, or in the US Congress, where the Republican opposition rejected US membership in the League.

Henry Cabot Lodge—Senate majority leader and chairman of the Foreign Relations Committee—spearheaded resistance against US membership in the League. Echoing the spirit of selective isolationism that defined the era, Lodge and his supporters were concerned that the League would commit the United States to an expensive organization that would reduce the country's ability to defend its interests.[3] Moreover, Lodge and others still adhered to a vision of a United States that only engaged within the Western Hemisphere and avoided commitments outside of its sphere of influence. Ultimately, Lodge feared the consequences of involvement in European politics, especially in the aftermath of the less-than-ideal World War I peace settlement.

Despite Wilson's lasting influence on US foreign policy, the grand strategy of the United States was based on isolationism in the 1920s and 1930s. In fact, even after World War I, many Americans still did not believe events outside of the Western hemisphere could impact their security or America's national interests. The United States feared that deeper engagement would lead it down the path of more entanglements into distant, unimportant conflicts—which ultimately came to define its political reality in time. Still, the United States saw the need to maintain its military and economic influence within the Western hemisphere to support American commercial growth and maintain overseas private investments.

America looked upon the settlement of World War I with much disappointment: "the framers of the Versailles settlement achieved the precise opposite of what they had set out to do. They had tried to weaken Germany physically, but instead strengthened it geopolitically."[4] Even the most ardent American liberal internationalist did not see any worthwhile reasons to enforce the post–World War I settlement as it had evolved.[5] Moreover, in the aftermath of World War I, a report by Senator Gerald P. Nye, a Republican from North Dakota, fanned the flames of isolationism by declaring that it was American bankers and arms manufacturers that pushed the United States to join the war for their profit. This narrative continued to appear in popular media and books, such as the 1934 *Merchants of Death* by H. C. Engelbrecht and F. C. Hanighen, further cementing public opinion toward US neutrality in international affairs.[6]

Disillusionment with the treaties, lack of international leadership, and the great costs of war brought about historian E.H. Carr's aptly named "twenty years' crisis." Germany, Italy, and Japan turned to authoritarianism, militarism, and aggressive territorial revanchism, while Britain and France chose appeasement. According to Carr, "the characteristic feature of the crisis of the twenty years between 1919 and 1939 was the abrupt descent from the visionary hopes of the first decade to the grim despair of the second, from a utopia which took little account of the reality to a reality from which every element of utopia was rigorously excluded."[7] Grappling with enormous internal problems due to the Great Depression of 1929 to 1933, America's interventionist impulses from previous eras were effectively muted, even as the world moved toward another war. In this moment, continued relative American isolationism was a strong contender for the long-term vision of the country. In other words, US military expansion was not inevitable, but arose from a wide set of foreign policy choices across each era.

Another shift towards isolation occurred even before the economic collapse of 1929, when the United States turned away from the Mahan-era naval build-ups and decided to sign the Washington Naval Treaty (or Five-Power Treaty) at the Washington Naval Conference in 1922. The treaty limited the American, British, and Japanese navies' tonnage of ships. This prevented naval arms races from taking off and limited the amount of power projection the US Navy could pursue. The treaty kept the ratio of battleships and newly developed aircraft carriers at five for the United States, five for the United Kingdom, and three for Japan. The terms of the disarmament were further negotiated in 1927 and 1935, with much less success as the Japanese delegation eventually walked out of the last conference. Japan ultimately broke the disarmament treaty in 1936 as it began the march toward war against the United States.[8]

The final agreement made at the Washington Naval Conference was the Nine-Power Treaty, which formally internationalized the United States' open door policy in China. Within the treaty, the United States, United Kingdom, Japan, France, Italy, Belgium, Netherlands, Portugal, and China promised to respect China's territorial integrity and affirmed the importance of equal opportunity for international commercial interests in China. China promised not to discriminate against any country seeking business opportunities.[9]

Together, the treaties arising from the Naval Conference maintained the status quo in the Pacific and attempted to stem the threat of Japanese expansion in the area. This meant America's ongoing open-door policy in China and US interests in the Philippines were reinforced for a time. Thus, by the 1930s, the United States had spearheaded efforts to disarm itself and its competitors, resolved some of the ongoing economic competition for new markets in the East, continued to maintain its regional hegemony in Latin America, and was seemingly well positioned to enforce a relatively inward political orientation to the rest of the world.

President Franklin Delano Roosevelt's leadership finally mobilized Americans to want to get involved in World War II. His approach transformed US grand strategy from one of isolationism to one of deep engagement and international leadership as a great power. As political scientist Jeffrey Taliaferro shows, Roosevelt's shrewdness in political maneuvering built popular support for US intervention in Europe against Germany and in Asia against Japan.[10] Moreover, Roosevelt's grand strategic adjustment did not stop at intervention in World War II, as he also had broader designs for US grand strategy after the war. "He saw to it that, this time, America's involvement would mark the first step toward permanent international engagement. During the war, his leadership held the alliance together and shaped the multilateral institutions which continue to serve the international community to this day."[11] With Roosevelt at the helm, the United States prepared for the postwar era and its new international leadership role, laying the foundations for institutions like the United Nations and the Bretton Woods organizations (the World Bank, International Monetary Fund, and ultimately the World Trade Organization) and the postwar American-led liberal international order with its many military operations to come.

Empirical Patterns of US Interventions, 1918–1945

US interventions dropped significantly during the interwar period, particularly in Latin America with the Good Neighbor Policy. By the mid-1930s, US interventions in Latin America became almost nonexistent as the economic depression spurred further isolationist impulses in American political circles. The severity of the economic collapse demanded an inward orientation for any political elite attempting to maintain their seat of power. Moreover, the Great Depression shook one of the pillars of American power projection, economic growth, as well as the ideal of American exceptionalism via rugged individualism and free markets.

A wide range of international military incidents occurred during the early 1930s, including the Japanese seizure of northeast China in 1931 (and then the invasion of China in 1937), the Italian invasion of Ethiopia in 1935, and the German expansion in Central and Eastern Europe. Yet the United States did not engage in any meaningful way with these repeated developments. Instead, the United States limited its reactions to statements of disapproval to maintain its neutrality.[12] But by the late 1930s, our data reveal America's hesitant and slow involvement in World War II efforts through US interventions in East Asia and the Pacific (predominantly Japan) and in the Mediterranean front in Europe.

During this era, the United States intervened mainly in three regions of the world—Latin America, East Asia, and Europe/the Mediterranean—as seen in Figure 3.1. As its interventions in Latin America declined, US military interventions in Europe and Central Asia grew, although the total number of interventions was lower than previous and future eras. Still, it is important to note the regional shift in US interventionism gradually beyond the Western hemisphere, even during an era often marked as staunchly isolationist.

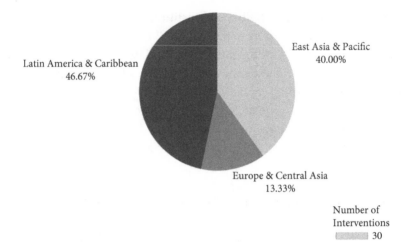

Figure 3.1. US Interventions by Region, 1918–1945

Figure 3.1 highlights the overall decline in the numbers and scope of US interventionism, relative to the previous era of US imperialism. Despite the advent of World War II, US interventions decreased from 82 in the previous era to 30—a steep decline of over 60 percent. The vast majority of these interventions occurred in the western and southern hemispheres, reflecting the United States' role as a regional hegemon and imperial power in Latin America before the mid-1930s.

Trends of US interventionism by presidential administration also mirror the general foreign policy of isolationism during the time. As seen in Figure 3.2, the presidential administrations prior to the Great Depression were much more interventionist than the ones that followed. Even then, Wilson's and Coolidge's hawkishness appears dovish when comparing it to presidential administration trends of the previous eras.

During this era of relative isolationism, the United States undertook most of its interventions in pursuit of social protective and economic objectives, as Figure 3.3 shows.[13]

The United States also continued to achieve most of its political objectives via its interventions, as Figure 3.4 confirms.

The Great Depression is also associated with decreased US intervention frequencies. The economic depression drove the United States to become more isolationist across all tools of statecraft (war, trade, and diplomacy). Three examples of the increasingly isolationist foreign policy tendency

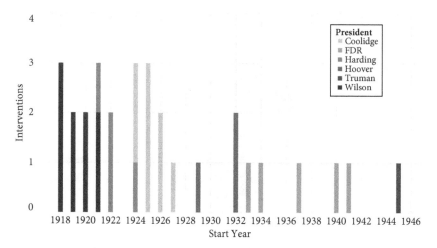

Figure 3.2. US Interventions by President, 1918–1945

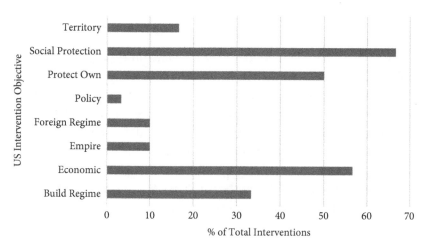

Figure 3.3. US Military Objectives, 1918–1945

and its effects include the (1) cancellation of German reparations credits after the stock market collapsed in 1929;[14] (2) the adoption of the Smoot-Hawley tariffs to protect American industries;[15] and (3) the Good Neighbor Policy, which was a commitment to not intervene in Latin America that will be discussed in more detail in later sections.[16] Moreover, the collapse of the US economic system nullified the option of expansionary economic-based

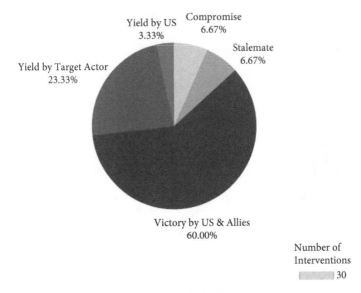

Figure 3.4. Intervention Outcomes, 1918–1945

foreign policy for much of the decade, which also perpetuated deeper isolationism.

This period reveals a series of self-imposed restrictions across all US tools of statecraft, including military noninterventionism, trade limitations, and diplomatic isolation. Instead of recalibrating the balance of its foreign policy arsenal and tools of engagement with the world, the United States simply abandoned its effort to engage beyond its own neighborhood. But as the United States pulled away from the world, the world pulled away from US ideals and ideologies, turning to dangerous alternatives.

Historical Narratives of America the Helper, 1918–1945

Though the United States was relatively isolationist towards the rest of the world during the interwar era, Central America was a notable exception. The United States continued to follow the ethos of the Monroe Doctrine, which asserted its sphere of influence over South and Central America. Under President Calvin Coolidge, Secretary of State Charles Evans Hughes sought to repair relations with America's southern neighbors and promised to negotiate border disputes and to intervene militarily in the region only as a last resort.[17] Despite this promise, however, the United States continued to play an active role in Central America.

While many American elites and citizens could not yet envision how distant global engagements could affect US national interests, they could easily justify US interventions in Latin America for economic interests, the protection of domestic industries, and the defense of foreign regimes conducive to US goals. The continued interventionism in the Western hemisphere foreshadowed more global interventionist trends to come, typically justified under the same protectionist rhetoric.

Persistent US Military Occupations in Latin America

The United States wielded frequent and persistent military tools to protect its economic interests and promote favorable foreign regimes. Indeed, it intervened frequently at the request of its preferred national governments during civil wars, including in Haiti, Panama, Nicaragua, and Mexico.

Decades of US Military Occupation in Haiti

In the Caribbean, the United States occupied Haiti for over two decades from 1915 to 1934, justifying its military presence to establish peace and defend the lives and interests of US citizens after the assassination of Haiti's president, Jean Vilbrun Guillaume Sam. But the United States had been monitoring Haiti's domestic politics for many years prior to his death. Eyeing Haiti as a potentially vital naval base, US political elites feared growing foreign influence within Haiti, especially given the increasing German business and trade at the beginning of the twentieth century.[18] The US military intervention of 1915 therefore served to protect American assets in the region and deter possible German invasion or economic gains following a series of presidential assassinations and instability in Haiti.

Haiti and the United States signed a treaty the following year that effectively sanctioned this US occupation and pledged cooperation over national security and government affairs. This agreement led to the creation of a military force made up of US citizens and Haitians, yet controlled by US Marines. In addition to military control, the United States also obtained complete control over the country's finances and domestic politics. In 1915, the Wilson administration coerced Haiti into electing a new pro-American president, Philippe Sudré Dartiguenave, which exacerbated civil unrest.[19]

Two years later, the United States attempted to bully the Haitian legislature into adopting a new constitution that would legalize foreign land ownership and thus intensify foreign influence within Haiti. The legislature rejected the new constitution and began drafting an anti-American constitution instead, but the Haitian president dissolved the legislature following pressure from the United States.

America's blatantly racist and discriminatory rule, defined by racial segregation, press censorship, and forced labor, fomented additional civil unrest and local calls for revolution in Haiti. By December 1929, twenty US Marines quelled a Haitian student revolt, killing twenty-five people and injuring seventy-five more.[20] The continuing protests in 1930 drew negative international attention to the American occupation of Haiti, compelling President Hoover to try to end the arrangement diplomatically. The United States ultimately withdrew its troops from Haiti in August 1934 after nearly twenty years of relatively unhindered military occupation.

Sanctioned US Military Interventions in Panama

Around the same time as the occupation of Haiti, the American military was present in Panama, outstaying its welcome well after the completion of the Panama Canal in 1914. With the assistance of the United States, Panama had separated from Colombia in 1903, and in the same year signed the Hay-Buneau-Varilla Treaty with the United States. The treaty effectively gave the US authority over a 10-mile strip of land along the canal, including the right to fortify the so-called canal zone, and the right to intervene militarily in Panama to support its independence.

In the first quarter of the twentieth century, the United States was deeply involved in Panama's domestic political affairs. From 1903 onward, the United States permanently stationed 10,000 troops in the canal zone to guard the strategically significant waterway.[21] When Panama's president disbanded the Panamanian military in 1904, the United States assumed full control of the country's national security affairs. Article 135 in Panama's 1904 Constitution went even further, allowing US troops to "intervene in any part of the Republic of Panama to reestablish public peace." The United States used its increased authority to supervise nearly every national election between 1906 and 1918, which were largely fraudulent.[22] Panama City and Colon, two of Panama's largest cities, were technically excluded from the canal zone even though they were situated within its geographical limits, but the United States nevertheless succeeded in disarming the police in these two cities and incorporating US troops into their police forces by 1916.[23]

At the time, the Panamanian government was content to have such an all-encompassing security guarantee from the United States, but resentments grew among Panamanian citizens.[24] Still, the United States' military involvement in Panama expanded. Following the death of President Ramón Valdés in June 1918, Ciro Urriola took over as provisional president with elections set for later that month. However, Urriola issued a decree delaying the election by six months as he needed more time to build his coalition, inciting widespread protests across the country. In response, US Secretary of State Robert Lansing demanded that Urriola hold the election on time, and when Urriola refused, US troops moved to occupy Panama City and Colon in 1918. Although Urriola quickly backed down, civil unrest sparked by the election turned into a rebellion in Panama's northern province of Chiriquí. Asserting US privilege under the 1904 Constitution, Lansing ordered an unknown number of US soldiers to Chiriquí to crush the uprising. The fact that the United Fruit Company had significant holdings in Chiriquí undoubtedly influenced Lansing's order. But the US troop presence went further than ensuring the elections or protecting commercial interests, as the garrison commander in charge also sought to eliminate prostitution—still legal in Panama—and close the saloons suspected of corrupting US soldiers.[25] US troops and this ethos of American puritanism remained as an occupying force in Chiriquí until August 1920.[26]

US troops were again activated in October 1925 when the Panamanian government directly requested US assistance to quell a massive but largely peaceful renters' strike. A group of unionists and left-wing organizers started a riot in Santa Ana Plaza in Panama City, protesting a recent tax levied on income gained from rentals, which owners then passed on to poor tenants.[27] The riot ended up killing one person and wounding eleven others, and Panamanian police fired on the rioters. The next day, the minister of foreign affairs requested the support of 300 American soldiers to restore order alongside the local police.[28] Six hundred American soldiers entered Panama City that same afternoon from the nearby canal zone.[29] Order was quickly restored, and a commission of tenants and landlords was organized to lodge the complaints of Panamanian citizens.[30]

Ultimately, the US military involvement strengthened the elites in Panama against the urban poor. Similar to its legacy in Haiti, the American intervention fomented domestic unrest that eventually required additional US military engagements in order to stabilize the country.

The United States Takes Sides in Mexico

Since taking power in 1920, Mexican President Álvaro Obregón lobbied for diplomatic recognition from the United States without success. Oil was main reason for the diplomatic standstill. At the time, Mexico produced a quarter of the world's oil supply, and many of the fields were owned by US companies. But Article 27 of Mexico's 1917 Constitution nationalized its natural resources.[31] While Obregón insisted he would not apply this principle to US oil companies, he still refused to sign an official agreement given the anti-American sentiment in Mexico. But with an upcoming presidential election in September 1923, Obregón finally relented and signed the Bucareli Agreements, protecting US oil fields in Mexico. In return, President Coolidge normalized diplomatic relations.[32] This was a clear diplomatic win for the United States at the time, requiring no direct military might to resolve.

The normalization came just in time for Obregón. In December 1923, Obregón's former secretary of the treasury, General Adolfo de la Huerta, launched a rebellion from the port city of Vera Cruz. De la Huerta enjoyed substantial support from many Mexican military leaders, and Obregón desperately needed US assistance to stay in power. At Obregón's request, the United States placed an arms embargo on de la Huerta and provided significant military support to Obregón, including airplanes. And when the rebels threatened to blockade and mine the oil port of Tampico in January 1924, the United States became directly involved in the conflict. On January 15, the USS *Tacoma* was dispatched to Vera Cruz, near Tampico. The USS *Richmond* soon followed, before the USS *Omaha* arrived escorted by six destroyers. The rebels reversed their decision to blockade Tampico by January 25, but the United States continued to play a significant role for the duration of the rebellion.[33]

As a clear threat and display of force, the United States stationed warships off the coast of Mexican cities under de la Huerta's control. The United States was ready to use its military might if the rebels acted against its interests. In total, twenty US warships and one repair ship were stationed in Mexican waters during the rebellion.[34] The United States also provided direct support to the Mexican air force, and a small number of US service members traveled to Mexico to train their allies on new aircrafts. In time, these American troops became directly involved in flying bombing missions, and US pilots may have even participated in the bombing of civilians at Morelia in February 1924.[35]

By March 1924, de la Huerta fled to the United States. But Mexico's civil strife and leadership struggles continued for years on end, with the United States paying close attention to changing presidents, rebellion factions, and Mexico's treatment of its natural resources.[36]

US Military in Nicaragua

The American military was extensively involved in Nicaragua, where it deployed forces from Panama following the breakout of civil war in 1926. In fact, this military occupation was the longest lasting of the era, with the United States remaining militarily active for over 3,000 days.[37] The United States first sent troops to Nicaragua in 1912 to protect its mining interests amid a civil war between Liberals and Conservatives, before leaving 100 soldiers in the country to maintain peace. Less than one month after finishing their mandate in 1925, civil war broke out once more.

To protect its regional economic interests by blocking a possible Liberal victory as well as to protect American citizens, the United States sent warships in 1926 to Bluefields, a community captured by Liberal rebel forces. The United States maintained two warships in the region and exercised an element of gunboat diplomacy prior to direct intervention. Among other tactics, the United States imposed an arms embargo and requested the presence of all parties at a peace conference on board one of the ships in October 1926. Eventually, under intense US pressure, Nicaraguan President Emiliano Chamorro resigned, and the crisis abated. In the aftermath, Adolfo Diaz, a favored US candidate, ascended to the presidency.

Political instability, however, remained a persistent issue in Nicaragua. By 1927, additional US ships and marines entered the country to help Diaz maintain order and to protect foreign lives and property. Undersecretary of State Robert Olds wrote in January 1927, "Nicaragua has become a test case. It is difficult to see how we can afford to be defeated." Nicaragua was then a test case of the United States' resolve to maintain a stable region, favorable to its interests, despite any domestic considerations for the foreign citizens on the ground. More than 2,000 Marines were deployed in the first few months of 1927, and the former secretary of state and war, Henry Stimson, was sent as a personal envoy to end the civil war—though the peace he negotiated did not hold.[38] The Liberal commander Augusto Cesar Sandino refused to accept the terms of the deal, and American troops quickly became involved in

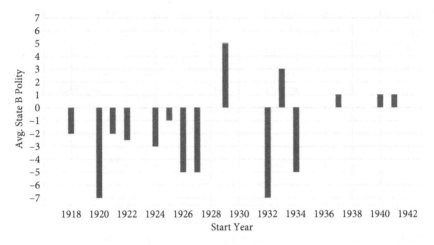

Figure 3.5. State B Democratization, 1918–1945

Citation: Monty Marshall and Ted Robert Gurr, "POLITY IV Project: Political Regime Characteristics and Transitions, 1800–2017," *Center for Systemic Peace,* http://www.systemicpeace.org/polityproject.html.

a guerrilla war against the Sandinistas that lasted for the next five years. US troops finally withdrew from the country in 1933, and with their departure Nicaragua's fragile democracy quickly devolved into dictatorship.[39]

With its many interventions in Latin America, often to prop up certain political factions over others, it is not surprising that the US record of democratization in the region was unimpressive. In Latin America, US foreign policy prioritized stability and geopolitical interests over democratic ideals in practice. Figure 3.5 traces the regime type of US Target States using the Polity Index, a trusted measure of democratization ranging from −10 (full autocracy) to +10 (full democracy).[40]

As illustrated, during this era, the United States intervened mainly in states with autocratic regimes (scores below 0 mark nondemocracies), while it maintained a perfect 10 score itself.[41] Honduras and Cuba are the only US intervention targets that had relatively democratic regimes during the era.

The US Military to the Rescue?

In these cases and others, the United States served as the third-party intervener altering the balance of power toward incumbent regimes during times of civil unrest. The United States often came to the rescue of favorable regimes in strategic regions possessing valuable resources, helping them to maintain power and stability.

But in the dispute between Honduras and El Salvador, the US military was asked to prevent a war between two states. Honduras and El Salvador had various political and geographical disputes dating back to the nineteenth century, and by 1921 these disputes escalated with Honduras fearing El Salvador was on the brink of invading its territory. The Honduran government issued an urgent request to the United States to deploy its forces to prevent war. In May 1921, the United States sent a warship to Honduras, signaling that El Salvador needed to demobilize. El Salvador yielded to this display of force and backed down from the dispute.[42]

The United States was also able to alter domestic politics in Cuba without deploying troops in the country. Cuba held an inconclusive election in 1920, with both sides claiming victory. The tense situation threatened to erupt into civil war. In an attempt to resolve the stalemate, Wilson sent a special representative to Cuba in January 1921.[43] Meanwhile, the State Department deployed a military warship to Havana, claiming that it was merely providing transportation for the special representative. In practice, however, the warship constituted a threat of open military intervention. In this climate, local parties in Cuba quickly reached an agreement and the United States helped preserve the stability.[44] It did so by making use of threats and displays of force before embarking upon direct military interventions in the target country—a trend that would erode in the decades to come. Its ability to deter El Salvador and influence Cuban politics with a show of force illustrated America's hegemonic position, "policeman" status, and rule-making influence in the Western hemisphere.

Until the 1930s, the United States intervened numerous times in Latin America to protect its commercial interests, natural resources, and favored regimes during an era otherwise marked by US isolation. It left behind fractured countries, either rife with unrest or led by authoritarian regimes. But these decades of direct US economic and militaristic interference within the domestic politics of Latin American countries came to a halt by 1934 with the Good Neighbor Policy. Under the policy, the United States renounced its right to unilaterally intervene in Latin American affairs.[45] Roosevelt began to emphasize trade relations and cooperation in Latin America rather than the use of American military force, declaring, "The definite policy of the United States from now on is one opposed to armed intervention."[46]

Neighborly restraint was not fully altruistic or simply due to Wilsonian principles. It came in the aftermath of the Great Depression, which solidified the United States' isolationist stance for the next decade.

Interventions in the East

As the engagements within Latin America reveal, isolationism did not stop the United States from choosing to deploy troops when its interests were directly threatened, which occasionally overlapped with the international community's goals of limiting land grabs by aggressive states or stopping perpetual civil wars. In addition to Latin America, US troops were fairly active in the "Far East" during the interwar period, most notably in the Soviet Union, China, and in the Manchurian Crisis.

When Wilson involved the United States in conflicts within Russia and the Far East, US policy circles and the public initially pushed back against the distant engagements and demanded less interventionism. But as the United States started to end its contiguous neighborhood interventions to focus on economic recovery and domestic politics, the United States began a consistent pattern of noncontiguous interventions. Such patterns begin to hint at the changing nature of US national interests, or at least how political elites at the time began to understand the United States' interactions toward the rest of the world.

Interventions in the "Near East"

After the Russian Revolution in March 1917, the United States supported the newly formed provisional government. Under intense pressure from the allies, Wilson agreed to intervene in Siberia after a legion of abandoned Czechs clashed with German and Austrian ex-prisoners of war. In August 1917, 5,000 American soldiers were sent to Murmansk and another 10,000 joined the Japanese at Vladivostok.[47] Historian George Herring writes that Wilson's motives for approving this military operation "remain elusive,"[48] but it seems he was worried about Japanese expansionism, sought to limit Japanese ability to maneuver in the Russian Far East, and wanted to protect German shipping interests in Vladivostok. But the American public was not convinced by these justifications. Oswald Garrison Villard wrote in *The Nation*, "The President has assured us that it is only to be a little intervention, and we are to forgive it or approve it on the grounds of its littleness."[49] The intervention was widely seen as a failure and greatly hurt Wilson's progressive credibility, lending credence to the isolationists among US policy circles.

Despite the pushback, the United States' interventionist patterns in the east continued for a while longer. In 1918, the Allied Powers intervened in the Russian Civil War to support the White Movement, a confederation of anticommunist forces. There were limited amounts of US military forces across Russia, particularly in Russia's Far East, where the US maintained a consulate, trade routes, and businesses.[50] In June 1918, as Bolshevik and Czech troops (backing the White Movement) continued to clash, the United States deployed a contingent of thirty-one Marines to guard the US Consulate. During this time, the Allied Powers established an occupation force in Vladivostok in hopes of transitioning control to the White Movement.[51] As the White Movement in Siberia collapsed and Soviet-communist forces took power, the United States and Allied Powers withdrew from the city, accepting defeat and seeing no further strategic potential for a military footprint in the region.[52]

While military interventions in the Soviet Union came to a stop, diplomatic missions continued. In March 1919, an attaché to the US delegation to the Paris Peace Conference, William Christian Bullitt, entered Soviet Russia on a secret mission. He was only authorized to report on the political and economic conditions he saw, but unbeknownst to Wilson, Bullitt's true objective was to broker an agreement between the allies and Russia's new Bolshevik government that would end the civil war, lift the allied blockade, and allow the allies to withdraw troops dispatched to Russia in 1918. Bullitt ultimately received a viable proposal from the Bolshevik government that would have attained all these goals, but allied leaders at the Paris Conference were unwilling to accept the offer, because they simply refused to negotiate with Vladimir Lenin's Bolshevik government, and they received news that anti-Bolshevik forces would soon recapture Moscow.[53]

Unfortunately, the Bullitt mission was a missed opportunity. Bullitt believed the greatest danger facing the United States was the rise of more radical political factions in the aftermath of continued allied interventions in Soviet Russia. He wrote that Lenin was willing to compromise with the United States and "[no] Government save a Socialist Government can be set up in Russia today except by bayonets." Lenin's faction of the Bolshevik Party was "as moderate as any Socialist Government which can control Russia."[54] Had the Bullitt mission succeeded, the United States might have recognized the Soviet Union sixteen years sooner, perhaps helping to stem Japanese aggression within Asia. It might have also decreased the US demonization of Bolshevism in Russia that fanned the flames of the Cold War after World War II.

Interventions in "the Far East"

Further east, as Chinese nationalism and discontent with the imperial system grew, civil war broke out in China in 1916. Between April 1922 and November 1923, Marines landed ashore five times to protect Americans during antiimperial turmoil.[55] In 1926, forces loyal to Sun Yat-sen's Kuomintang party launched a northern expedition and occupied the city of Nanjing, where there were increased attacks on foreign individuals and properties. US and British gunboats responded and suppressed the violence, but six foreigners, including one American, were killed in the violence.[56]

The biggest challenge to US isolationism outside of the Western Hemisphere during this period was the war in Manchuria, where China and Japan were fighting over control of the resource-rich territory from 1931 to 1933. The US government was distracted by both the Great Depression at home and a split between those supporting the Japanese or Chinese governments, with different factions believing each was a better partner for the United States. Yet when Japanese aggression became a clear threat, the United States realized it needed to take sides. Thus, it tried to work with the League of Nations for the first time to limit any further Japanese action. But these multilateral diplomatic efforts were ultimately futile, and Japan withdrew from the League altogether. The United States then sent troops to Shanghai in 1932 to protect American interests in a dispute between Japan and China, and again in 1934 in Fuzhou to protect the American Consulate.[57] Despite a pattern of aggressive expansionism and Japan's breach of the disarmament treaties with the United States, the US government failed to intervene definitively to prevent the Japanese from occupying Manchuria. Part of its reluctance was due to the legacy of the Great Depression, as will be explained below.

World War II

The global economic depression and the turn to isolationism in the United States produced a variety of international effects. The economic crisis

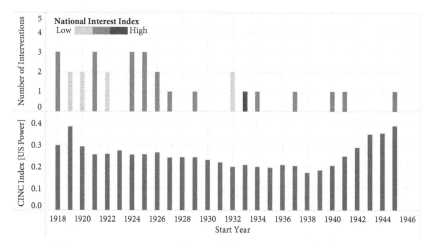

Figure 3.6. US Interventions by National Interests and Capabilities, 1918–1945

Citation: Correlates of War Project. *National Material Capabilities, 1816–2012.* Version 5. http://www.correlatesofwar.org; J. David Singer, "Reconstructing the Correlates of War Dataset on Material Capabilities of States, 1816–1985," *International Interactions,* 14 (1987); 115–132.

originating in the United States, followed by the doubling down on US isolationism, eventually discredited US-style democracy[58] and inadvertently aided the rise of fascism, and to a lesser extent, communism, as alternatives. First in Italy, and later in Germany and Japan, the rejection of American democracy, driven by the perception that it was not accurately responding to the challenges posed by the Great Depression, encouraged the rise of fascist political systems. The relative success of Germany and Italy especially led to further institutional emulation by other states. Even in the United States, doubts about the efficacy of American democracy emerged.

The Great Depression destroyed US national power capabilities into the 1930s, but the mid-1940s saw the rise of the most powerful United States of America yet. Figure 3.6 illustrates these swings. Paradoxically, the interwar era marked the United States' lowest and highest levels of power yet for the country.

The rise of expansionary fascism and militarism set the stage for World War II, where US isolationist tendencies eventually had to contend with growing elite and public impulses to pursue global US interests, which culminated in a wide-range of attacks on US territory. Despite many efforts not to involve itself abroad, by the end of the interwar era, the United States had no choice but to flip its grand strategy and usher in an era marked by

US imperial power and involvement in distant conflicts within East Asia and Europe.

As efforts to disarm the great powers failed one by one and as the peace movement of the era appeared more futile, the road to World War II became increasingly apparent. Nazi Germany expanded following the Austrian Anschluss and the Munich Conference, which permitted the annexation of the nominally German areas of Czechoslovakia, the Sudetenland. While World War II started in earnest in Europe after the German invasion of Poland in 1939, the United States did not enter the war immediately. Continuing with its more isolationist tendencies characterized by the passing of increasingly lax Neutrality Acts in the 1930s, the United States also resisted joining the war during the Battle of Britain and the fall of France.

In East Asia, World War II began with the Second Sino-Japanese War in 1937. The United States did not see any vital interests in getting involved militarily or aiding China before 1937, especially given uncertainties over US success amid rivalries between Chinese Nationalists and Communists. But after July 1937, as the United States watched Japanese forces sweep into the capital of Nanjing, US popular opinion swung in favor of the Chinese. Tensions with Japan rose once again when the Japanese Army bombed the USS *Panay* as it evacuated American citizens from Nanjing, killing three. The US government, however, continued to placate the Japanese by merely accepting an apology and indemnity at the time.

It was the Japanese expansion into Indochina in 1940 that finally triggered a strong response from the United States, partially due to the need to preserve an ally in the region and partially due to the growing internal Communist challenge. The United States formalized aid to China via increased Lend-Lease credits and initiated oil and military material embargoes on Japan. Ultimately, following the Japanese Neutrality Pact of 1941 with the Soviet Union and the agreement with Vichy France allowing Japanese forces to move into Indochina and advance south, the United States instituted a full export embargo against Japan, froze Japanese assets in US banks, and halted negotiations with Japanese diplomats. Overall, while the United States was still formally neutral, its economic penalties limited Japan's much-needed access to oil.[59]

Around the same time, Roosevelt secretly began aiding allies against German and Japanese aggression. Most notably, he relied on US diplomatic channels and attended a meeting with British Prime Minister Winston Churchill off the coast of Halifax to work out the Atlantic Charter. While not a binding treaty, the charter helped enhance US war efforts. Furthermore, it pushed the United Kingdom to commit to tangible war aims that were consistent with American goals, showcased solidarity between the two powers, and crafted a vision of the Wilsonian post-war order based on the principles of international free trade, collective security, self-determination, among others. Still, Churchill hoped that the Atlantic Conference would bring America into the war, which it failed to do.

But the United States sent additional support through the Lend-Lease program, which allowed the United States to lend or lease war supplies while technically staying neutral, ultimately expanding the program to more than thirty countries throughout the war. While remaining formally neutral, American leadership was forced to deal once again with unrestricted U-Boat warfare from Germany trying to sink American ships. But it was the December 1941 Japanese attack on Pearl Harbor, which was primarily an attempt to knock America out of the war before it joined and to free up oil assets, that propelled the United States into the war in both Europe and Asia. The next day, Congress declared war against Japan, and three days later the House of Representatives approved declarations of war against the Axis Powers of Germany and Italy. The war declarations led to the military campaigns in Europe (notably the Mediterranean theater first) and naval battles and island-hopping campaigns in East Asia.[60]

Initially, Japan had the upper hand in the Pacific theater, pushing the United States out of the Philippines, but American naval power eventually helped turn the tide and revoke Japanese territorial gains. The United States was able to recapture the Philippines and worked with allies in other parts of East Asia to push the Japanese back to the home islands. In the Mediterranean, the United States initially joined the war in the fight against Germany and Vichy France in North Africa, setting the stage to invade the European homeland through Italy at first and then through France. While the United States was focused on the Mediterranean and East Asia, its new ally the Soviet Union was dealing with the full thrust of Nazi forces invading its homeland, which compelled the United States and United Kingdom to open a second front in France.

After knocking Italy out of the war in 1943 and landing in France to liberate it in 1944, the American victory over Germany came in April 1945. While the Soviet Union had faced an even larger struggle on the Eastern Front, both allies met in Germany and began planning how to keep German militarism from propelling future wars. But brewing Soviet resentment at American and British delays in opening a second front in France coupled with American fears of Stalin's ambitions made the celebratory meeting in Germany quite tense.[61]

The end of World War II marked the time when the United States became a world superpower. The United States emerged as the rescuer of Europe, which also effectively pulled the United States out of its economic depression for good as the US war production revved the economy to unprecedented levels. The end of World War II also prompted historic cooperation between the British, Americans, Soviets, and Chinese. In fact, during the Moscow Conference of the Foreign Ministers in 1943, these four allies signed a four-power declaration that spearheaded the creation of the United Nations, a "general international organization" designed to promote "international peace and security" that eventually evolved to include discussions of "four policemen" to monitor and respond to threats to international peace and security.[62] By 1944, the US-led postwar international economic order was coming into being through the creation of the International Monetary Fund and World Bank at the Bretton Woods Conference. By October 1945, the United Nations had come into existence with the ratification of twenty-nine states, this time including the United States.

The end of World War II, however, also left a terrifying legacy in many parts of the world, including America's use of the first atomic bomb against Japanese civilian cities twice, prompting Japan's surrender in 1945. These weapons killed 150,000 people in just a couple of days. Fears over the destructive power of new nuclear weapons prompted international discussions on the creation of a world government that would regulate atomic technology to save humanity. During this time, the United States was unaware that the Soviet Union had well-placed sources to steal its nuclear secrets, paving the way for the Soviet's atomic arsenal to challenge America's.[63]

Thus, tensions still abounded, especially between the ambivalent World War II allies, the United States and the Soviet Union. Concerns over how to manage occupied Germany, the new distribution of economic and military power, ideological divisions over communism and liberal capitalism, and the postwar period led to disagreements and distrust that became the Cold War.

Conclusion

After World War I, US policymakers and the public alike were disillusioned with the consequences of internationalism and the steep human and financial cost of global war. Many believed the United States would be better served with an isolationist foreign policy that safeguarded US domestic security and economic interests, only maintaining US primacy in the Western hemisphere. Congress chose not to join the League of Nations, thus kneecapping the nascent organization and limiting the rise of multilateralism. The Great Depression only exacerbated this antiinternationalist sentiment, both by distracting the US government from dealing with international issues and by limiting the funds and thus the foreign policy tools available to do so. The rise of fascism continued unabated in Europe and growing tensions with revisionist powers such as Japan caused division within the American foreign policy apparatus. As historian Benjamin Rhodes writes, "If there is one thing that all commentators can agree on about United States foreign policy during the interwar period, it is that it was a time when a great many well-intentioned policies went awry . . . it is difficult to imagine a portrayal of American diplomacy from 1918 to 1941 as a bright, shining example of what should be done in the future."[64]

However, the United States' interwar dynamics appear to repeat themselves decades later. After the lengthy struggle in Vietnam through the 1960s and 1970s, and then the so-called endless wars in Iraq and Afghanistan in the 2000s, the American public was leery of further military engagements abroad and the legacy of America's strategy of primacy. Amid the 2008 Great Recession, then-presidential candidate Barack Obama vowed to pull US troops from Iraq and Afghanistan—a promise he knew would be well-received in a cash-strapped and war-weary electorate. Almost a decade later, his Republican successor capitalized heavily on this isolationist bent, as President Trump's election-winning "America First" policy promised to halt wasteful spending abroad and focus on American strength and prosperity. Like in the interwar period, the Trump administration rejected multilateralism—pulling out of the Paris Climate Accords and the Iranian nuclear deal, disparaging North Atlantic Treaty Organization (NATO) allies, and refusing to fund the World Health Organization (WHO).

Even with the end of the Trump administration, the forces of fascism, populism, and ethnonationalism continue to gain traction across the world, with the United States often looking the other way as autocratic tendencies take hold in regions of interest, such as Eastern Europe, the Balkans, India, and East Asia. Today's geopolitical arena is also crowded with revisionist powers similar to those that dominated the interwar era. Both China and Russia—like imperial Japan—are occasional partners of the United States, but their landgrabs and rising military power pose serious challenges to US security and the international order. The foreign policy establishment remains divided over how to best manage these power relationships, and a good number fear that great power conflict or even war is inevitable.[65]

If the interwar period taught US policy circles anything, it may be that isolationism is not the answer to fears of hypermilitarism. Though the United States was not quite the established global leader it is today, a world absent of a strong US presence devolved into a war on an unprecedented scale. Had a global economic downturn not stifled international trade, had the League of Nations not been so ineffective, and had the United States extended its diplomatic and economic tools outward, perhaps the aggressive revisionist and fascist powers of the interwar era may have been deterred enough to avoid war.

The United States can thus learn from the mistakes of its past. This means renouncing its military-forward policies in the past decades and supporting the multilateral institutions it recently turned against. The United States should not tolerate the aggression and territorial seizures of China and Russia, eerily similar to those of Japan and Germany before them, but this doesn't mean relying on direct military interventions either. America can instead rely on international organizations and allies to make aggressive actions costly to other states. The US government in the interwar period believed that World War I was an aberration; policymakers today should guard against such naiveté as well. In the current polarized geopolitical climate, diplomatic initiatives, economic sanctions, and other types of tools (including threats of force) should be adopted before the direct use of force to deescalate tensions and engage with the world. There are middle grounds available within US foreign policy that do not rely on either complete isolationism or global imperialism and/or primacy.

Notes

1. Fireside Chat: Radio Address Delivered by President Roosevelt From Washington, December 29, 1940. The American Presidency Project. https://www.presidency. ucsb.edu/documents/fireside-chat-9; see also Josh Zeitz, "The Speech That Set Off the Debate About America's Role in the World," *Politico*, December 29, 2015, https:// www.politico.com/magazine/story/2015/12/roosevelt-arsenal-of-democracy-speech-213483/.

2. E. H. Carr, *The Twenty Years' Crisis, 1919–1939: An Introduction to the Study of International Relations* (New York: Palgrave, 1939, 2001).

3. Henry Cabot Lodge, *"Constitution of the League of Nations," The Senate: Classic Speeches, 1830–1993* (Washington, DC: Government Printing Office, 1919). https://www.senate.gov/artandhistory/history/resources/pdf/LodgeLeagueofNations.pdf.

4. Kissinger, *Diplomacy*, 245.

5. Kissinger, *Diplomacy*, 372.

6. "Milestones in the History of U.S. Foreign Relations: American Isolationism in the 1930s," Office of the Historian, United States Department of State. https://history.state.gov/milestones/1937-1945/american-isolationism.

7. Carr, *The Twenty Years' Crisis, 1919–1939*, 207.

8. Charles L. Glaser, "When Are Arms Races Dangerous? Rational Versus Suboptimal Arming," *International Security* 28, no. 4 (2004): 44–84; John H. Maurer, "Arms Control and the Washington Conference," *Diplomacy and Statecraft* 4, no. 3 (1993): 267–293.

9. Maurer, "Arms Control and the Washington Conference."

10. Jeffrey W. Taliaferro, "Strategy of Innocence or Provocation? The Roosevelt Administration's Road to World War II," in *The Challenge of Grand Strategy: The Great Powers and the Broken Balance between the World Wars*, eds. Jeffrey W. Taliaferro, Norrin M. Ripsman, and Steven E. Lobell (Cambridge: Cambridge University Press, 2012), 193–223.

11. Kissinger, *Diplomacy*, 370.

12. "Milestones in the History of U.S. Foreign Relations: The Great Depression and U.S. Foreign Policy," Office of the Historian, United States Department of State, https://history.state.gov/milestones/1921-1936/great-depression.

13. Social protective objectives are coded using the standards adapted mainly from the Military Interventions by Powerful States (MIPS). It occurs when the United States "uses or threatens military force to protect civilians from violence and/or other human rights abuses; restores social order in a situation of unrest (e.g., violent protests, rioting, looting); or suppresses violence between armed groups within another state." As per MIPS, "Peacekeeping operations that are intended to prop up an incumbent regime or maintain empire are not coded as social protection and order operations. Similarly, 'humanitarian' operations in which military force is used to coerce the incumbent government into changing the way it is treating a minority group within its borders should be coded as policy change operations. A Social Protective Intervention occurs to protect a socio-ethnic faction(s) or minority of the target country." For the original MIPS coding that we heavily rely on, see Sullivan, Patricia and Michael Koch, MIPS Codebook, 2008, https://plsullivan.web.unc.edu/wp-content/uploads/sites/1570/2011/09/MIPS_codebook_Sullivan.pdf.

14. Adam Tooze, *The Deluge: The Great War, America and the Remaking of the Global Order, 1916–1931* (New York: Penguin Books, 2014), chs. 24 and 26; Albrecht Ritschl, "Reparations, deficits and debt default: The great depression in Germany," In *The Great Depression of the 1930s: Lessons for today*, eds. Nicholas Crafts and Peter Fearon (Oxford: Oxford University Press, 2013), 110–139.

15. "Protectionism in the Interwar Period," Office of the Historian, United States Department of State, https://history.state.gov/milestones/1921-1936/protectionism.

16. Douglas A. Irwin, *Peddling Protectionism: Smoot-Hawley and the Great Depression* (Princeton, NJ: Princeton University Press, 2017); George C. Herring, *From Colony to Superpower: US Foreign Relations Since 1776* (Oxford: Oxford University Press, 2008), ch. 12.

17. Herring, *From Colony to Superpower: U.S. Foreign Relations since 1776*, 472.

18. "Milestones in the History of U.S. Foreign Relations: U.S. Invasion and Occupation of Haiti," Office of the Historian, United States Department of State, https://history.state.gov/milestones/1914-1920/haiti.

19. "Milestones in the History of U.S. Foreign Relations: U.S. Invasion and Occupation of Haiti," Office of the Historian, United States Department of State.

20. Chantalle F. Verna, *Haiti and the Uses of America: Post-U.S. Occupation Promises* (New Brunswick, NJ: Rutgers University Press, 2017), 62.

21. George W. Baker, "The Wilson Administration and Panama, 1913-1921," *Journal of Inter-American Studies* 8, no. 2 (April 1966): 279–923, https://www.jstor.org/stable/165110.

22. "Panama Protests Our Policing Zone Cities: United States Troops Will Stay There and in Colon Till after Elections." *Los Angeles Times (1886–1922),* Jun 30, 1918, https://www.proquest.com/historical-newspapers/panama-protests-our-policing-zone-cit ies/docview/160542585/se-2?accountid=14434.

23. Thomas Lee Pearcy, "The Military and Politics in Modern Panama," Order No. 9401828, University of Miami, 1993, https://www.proquest.com/dissertations-the ses/military-politics-modern-panama/docview/304071340/se-2?accountid=14434.

24. "Hay–Bunau-Varilla Treaty," Encyclopædia Britannica, August 10, 2016, accessed January 6, 2019, https://www.britannica.com/event/Hay-Bunau-Varilla-Treaty.

25. John Lindsay-Poland, *Emperors in the Jungle: The Hidden History of the US in Panama*, American Encounters/Global Interactions (Durham, NC: Duke University Press, 2003), 41.

26. Special to The New York Times, "America Assumes Control in Panama: General Blatchford Will Take Over Police in Cities of Panama and Colon. Political Situation Acute Serious Disorders Feared Through Postponement of Election of a New President," *New York Times (1857–1922),* Jun 29, 1918, https://www.proquest.com/historical-newspapers/america-assumes-control-panama/docview/100022853/se-2?accountid=14434.

27. J. A. Zumoff, "The 1925 Tenants' Strike in Panama: West Indians, the Left, and the Labor Movement," *The Americas: A Quarterly Review of Latin American History* 74, no. 04 (October 22, 2017): 513–546, accessed January 6, 2019, doi:10.1017/tam.2017.88.

28. *Papers Relating to the Foreign Relations of the United States, 1925, Volume II*, edited by Joseph Fuller, US Department of State, (Washington, DC: United States Government Printing Office, 1940), 664.

29. *Papers Relating to the Foreign Relations of the United States, 1925, Volume II*, edited by Joseph Fuller.

30. *Papers Relating to the Foreign Relations of the United States, 1925, Volume II*, Edited by Joseph Fuller.

31. John Womack, "The Mexican Revolution, 1910–1920," in *Mexico since Independence*, ed. Leslie Bethell (Cambridge: Cambridge University Press, 1991), 125–200, https://www.cambridge.org/core/books/mexico-since-independence/mexican-revolution-19101920/67622C42BB61F0158C48F9F01C1FD253.

32. *Papers Relating to the Foreign Relations of the United States, 1923, Volume II, Mexico*, eds. Joseph Fuller and Tyler Dennet (Washington: Government Printing Office, 1938), documents 471–502, https://history.state.gov/historicaldocuments/frus1923v02/comp12.

33. Gregory Alan Andrews, "The Decisive Role of the United States in Suppressing the De La Huerta Rebellion In Mexico, 1923–1924," Order No. 1313372, Northeast Missouri State University, https://www.proquest.com/docview/303020403?accountid=14434; David Allen Brush, "The De La Huerta Rebellion in Mexico, 1923–1924," Order No. 7607574, Syracuse University, https://www.proquest.com/docview/302783280?accountid=14434.

34. "Fleet Sent to Mexico: Uprising Near Acapulco One Thousand Rebels Give Up Arms; Villa Planning Complete Surrender Obregon Assures League of Complete Peace in Twenty Days," *Los Angeles Times (1923-1995)*, Mar 08, 1924, 1, https://www.proquest.com/docview/161587293?accountid=14434; "Order Eight U.S. Warships to Mexican Rebels' Base: Omaha and Six Destroyers Instructed to Hurry To Vera Cruz to Join Admiral Magruder and His Flagship, the Richmond Ports Held by Insurgents Mined," *Boston Daily Globe (1923-1927)*, Jan 20, 1924, 1. https://www.proquest.com/docview/497642721?accountid=14434; Special to The New York Times, "Another Warship Sent to Mexico: Gunboat Tulsa Is Dispatched to Tuxpam on Request of Hughes to Guard Americans. Federals to Attack Port Revolutionary Headquarters Predicts a Combined Assault by Rebels on Mexico City." *New York Times (1923-Current File)*, Feb 22, 1924, 4, https://www.proquest.com/docview/103413756?accountid=14434.

35. Andrews, "The Decisive Role of the United States," 1970.

36. Andrews, "The Decisive Role of the United States," 1979, https://www.proquest.com/docview/303020403?accountid=14434.

37. See Table A3.1 in the appendix for a complete list of US military interventions with durations and fatalities.

38. Max Boot, *The Savage Wars of Peace: Small Wars and the Rise of American Power*, Revised paperback edition (New York: Basic Books, 2014), 235.

39. Boot, *The Savage Wars of Peace*, 251.

40. Monty Marshall and Ted Robert Gurr, "POLITY IV Project: Political Regime Characteristics and Transitions, 1800–2017," *Center for Systemic Peace*, http://www.systemicpeace.org/polityproject.html.

41. Polity's perfect 10 score of US democracy during this time ignores the country's ongoing racial and gender oppression. The US maintains a perfect 10 score of democracy according to these measures despite Jim Crow laws and related discriminatory policies of the era. We suggest that readers assess these measures of US democracy with strong skepticism.

42. Thomas Karnes, *The Failure of Union: Central America, 1824–1960* (Chapel Hill: University of North Carolina Press, 1961).

43. Dana Munro, *Intervention and Dollar Diplomacy in the Caribbean, 1900–1921* (Princeton: Princeton University Press, 1964).

44. Leslie Bethell, *Cambridge History of Latin America* (Cambridge: Cambridge University Press, 1984).

45. *Britannica Academic*, s.v. "Good Neighbor Policy," accessed June 3, 2020, https://www.britannica.com/event/Good-Neighbor-Policy-of-the-United-States.

46. "Milestones in the History of U.S. Foreign Relations: Interwar Diplomacy," Office of the Historian, United States Department of State, https://history.state.gov/milesto nes/1921-1936.

47. Thomas J. Knock, *To End All Wars, New Edition: Woodrow Wilson and the Quest for a New World Order* (Princeton, NJ: Princeton University Press, 2019), 156, https://doi. org/10.1515/9780691191928.

48. George C. Herring, *From Colony to Superpower: U.S. Foreign Relations since 1776*, The Oxford History of the United States (New York: Oxford University Press, 2008), 414.

49. Michael Wreszin, *Oswald Garrison Villard, Pacifist at War* (Bloomington: Indiana University Press, 1965), 96.

50. Leo J. Daugherty, "'In Snows of Far Off Northern Lands': The U.S. Marines and Revolutionary Russia, 1917–1922," *The Journal of Slavic Military Studies* 18, no. 2 (2005): 227–303.

51. Harry A. Ellsworth, "One Hundred Eighty Landings of United States Marines 1800-1934," History and Museums Division Headquarters, US Marine Corps, (1974), 142.

52. Daugherty, "'In Snows of Far Off Northern Lands,'" 255.

53. "Milestones in the History of U.S. Foreign Relations: The Bullitt Mission to Soviet Russia," Office of the Historian, United States Department of State, https://history. state.gov/milestones/1914-1920/bullitt-mission.

54. "Milestones in the History of U.S. Foreign Relations: The Bullitt Mission to Soviet Russia," Office of the Historian, United States Department of State.

55. Barbara Salazar Torreon and Sofia Plagakis, "Instances of Use of United States Armed Forces Abroad, 1798-2020," Congressional Research Service, January 13, 2020, https://fas.org/sgp/crs/natsec/R42738.pdf.

56. Herring, *From Colony to Superpower*, 469.

57. Torreon and Plagakis, "Instances of Use of United States Armed Forces Abroad."

58. Seva Gunitsky, *Aftershocks: Great Powers and Domestic Reforms in the Twentieth Century*, (Princeton: Princeton University Press, 2017), Chapter 4.

59. Herring, *From Colony to Superpower: US Foreign Relations Since 1776*, 503-537; Michael A. Barnhart, *Japan Prepares for Total War: The Search for Economic Security, 1919-1941*, (Ithaca: Cornell University Press, 1987).

60. Nicholas J. Cull, "Selling peace: The origins, promotion and fate of the Anglo-American new order during the second world war," *Diplomacy and Statecraft* 7, no. 1 (1996): 1–28; John M. Schuessler, "The deception dividend: FDR's undeclared war," *International Security* 34, no. 4 (2010): 133–165; George C. Herring, "Lend-lease to

Russia and the origins of the Cold War, 1944-1945," *The Journal of American History* 56, no. 1 (1969): 93–114.

61. Herring, *From Colony to Superpower: US Foreign Relations Since 1776*, Chapter 13.

62. "The Tehran Conference," Office of the Historian, United States Department of State, https://history.state.gov/milestones/1937-1945/tehran-conf.

63. Herbert Feis, *The Atomic Bomb and the end of World War II*, (Princeton: Princeton University Press, 1966); Louis Morton, "The Decision to Use the Atomic Bomb," Foreign Affairs, 35, No. 2 (January 1957), 334–353.

64. Benjamin D. Rhodes, *United States Foreign Policy in the Interwar Period, 1918-1941: The Golden Age of American Diplomatic and Military Complacency*, Praeger Studies of Foreign Policies of the Great Powers (Westport, Conn: Praeger, 2001).

65. cf. Allison and Mearsheimer.

Chapter 3 Appendix

Table A3.1 List of US Military Interventions with Duration and Fatalities, 1918–1945

Start Year	Name	Duration (Days)	US Battle Deaths	State B Battle Deaths	Avg. Total Battle Deaths	US Total Deaths	State B Total Deaths
1918	Vladivostok deployment	1050	0	0	0	0	0
1918	Adriatic Question in Croatia	698	0	0	0	0	0
1918	Election & Chiriquí Rebellion	766	Unclear	Unclear	Unclear	Unclear	Unclear
1919	Allied Occupy Ottoman lands	50	0	0	0	0	0
1919	Tegucigalpa Uprising	4	0	Unclear	Unclear	0	100
1920	Kiukiang Incident	1	0	0	0	0	0
1920	The Unionista Revolution	33	0	800	800	1	800
1921	Election dispute in Cuba	1	0	0	0	0	0
1921	Border dispute in Panama	183	0	0	0	0	100
1921	Deterring War with Honduras	31	0	0	0	0	0
1922	Landings in China	27	0	0	0	0	0
1922	Evacuation Greek-Turkish War	80	1	Unclear	Unclear	1	Unclear
1924	Shanghai Landing	45	0	0	0	0	0
1924	De la Huerta Rebellion	154	0	100	100	0	100
1924	Honduran Civil War of 1924	201	0	Unclear	Unclear	1	Unclear
1925	Protection of Shanghai	196	0	Unclear	Unclear	0	Unclear

1925	Uprising of 1925 in Honduras	2	0	Unclear	Unclear	0	Unclear
1925	Panama Rent Riots	11	0	1	1	0	1
1926	Hankow deployment	69	0	0	0	0	0
1926	Remove Nicaraguan President	3119	0	0	0	0	0
1927	Nanjing Incident	6	0	40	40	0	40
1929	Las Limas Bombing	1	0	Unclear	Unclear	0	Unclear
1932	Shanghai Incident	97	0	0	0	0	0
1932	Communist Uprising El Salvador	15	0	0	0	0	35000
1933	Cuban Revolution of 1933	165	0	0	0	0	0
1934	Foochow Protective Mission	2	0	0	0	0	0
1937	Panay Incident	1	2	0	2	3	0
1940	Deterrence Against Japan	585	0	0	0	0	0
1941	World War II	1681	291557	5025766	5317323	405399	7651441
1945	Operation Beleaguer	1324	34	—	—	34	

4

America the Leader of the Free World

In the councils of government, we must guard against the acquisition of unwarranted influence, whether sought or unsought, by the military-industrial complex. The potential for the disastrous rise of misplaced power exists, and will persist.[1]

President Dwight D. Eisenhower, farewell
address, January 17, 1961

From secrecy and deception in high places; come home, America. From military spending so wasteful that it weakens our nation; come home, America.[2]

Senator George McGovern (D, SD), speech accepting the
Democratic nomination for president, July 14, 1972

The United States emerged from World War II as a hero to its European allies and as a world superpower, largely unaffected by the devastation of the war. Indeed, World War II emboldened US industrial production, military technological advancements, and the promotion of American values and institutions worldwide. The Soviet Union (USSR), however, emerged as a devastated country, with 40 million citizens killed in the fight against Nazi Germany. Although the United States and USSR emerged from World War II as allies, their power trajectories as well as early disputes over how to handle postwar Germany encouraged suspicion, fear, and rising militarism between them. By then, the United States had already created, tested, and used the atomic bomb, threatening Soviet power. At the same time, the European balance of power shifted, and European states struggled to maintain their empires in the context of the decolonization movement. Thus, the United States and the Soviet Union remained as the two great powers of the era—one was staunchly capitalist while the other was communist.

Dying by the Sword. Monica Duffy Toft and Sidita Kushi, Oxford University Press. © Oxford University Press 2023.
DOI: 10.1093/oso/9780197581438.003.0005

As this chapter will reveal, the United States was one of two superpowers in a new bipolar world order, driven by ideological, economic, and political rivalries during the atomic age. During the Cold War era from 1946 to 1989, the United States' greatest objective was to deter Soviet Union expansion, whether it be territorial, militaristic, economic, or ideological. Foreign policy specialists and leaders came to a shaky consensus on how to deal with the Soviet threat: the policy of containment, which demanded high diplomatic engagement alongside selective military involvement, to limit Soviet influence and power globally. As political elites broadened interpretations of the strategy of containment, another policy alternative lingered in the background: the doctrine of rollback. The persistent proponents of rollback pushed for greater, sustained US militaristic commitment to completely "roll back" new Soviet territorial gains in Europe and its political influence around the world. While muted for part of the Cold War, the rollback camp never fully disappeared. Instead, they came to push the policy of containment toward more belligerent ways and shape US foreign policy decisions in the future.

During the Cold War, America established the signature institutions, including the Central Intelligence Agency (CIA) and the Department of Defense, which are at the forefront of US foreign policy and military formulations today. Most US military interventions during this era, both overt traditional operations and covert CIA operations, sought to maintain or change a foreign regime to contain communism and deter Soviet influence.

Despite its aggressive rivalry with the Soviet Union, the United States was still perceived as a strategic, often restrained, actor on the world stage, and one that stood for the sought-after principles of democracy, human rights, and capitalistic freedom. The Cold War spanned over four decades replete with political intrigue and frequent crises and contests. Instead of delving into the minutiae of the historical details, this chapter will outline the key foreign policy trends during the era, especially those that continue to relate to modern-day US foreign policy priorities and strategies. As with previous chapters, this chapter first synthesizes the grand strategy of the era, followed by a data snapshot of the dominant interventionist trends of the period. The chapter then offers a range of historical narratives that characterized US foreign policy. It concludes with a theoretical outline of the Cold War's implications for the future of US foreign policymaking.

Cold War Grand Strategy

Containment was not one specific grand strategy. Instead, it was an over-arching framework that subsequent US administrations during the Cold War interpreted in different ways according to their changing situations, ideologies, and policy preferences. As political scientist Nina Silove argues, containment "did not mandate a specific set of means to be mobilized for particular ends."[3] John Lewis Gaddis, the leading chronicler of US grand strategy during the Cold War, emphasizes that there were "strategies of containment" during this period,[4] but containment as an organizing principle held these together and led them to success: "The United States and its allies sustained a strategy that was far more consistent, effective, and morally justifiable than anything their adversaries were able to manage."[5]

The containment strategy was the result of a string of events and the work of several people, but George Kennan stands out as its chief architect.[6] "George Kennan came as close to authoring the diplomatic doctrine of his era as any diplomat in our history," writes Henry Kissinger.[7] Kennan, a junior diplomat at the time, was serving as the Chargé d'Affaires of the American embassy in Moscow, when he authored the *Long Telegram* in February 1946, which came to be the foundational document for the new strategy. "Despite its verbosity, the cable's central theme was relatively succinct: 'At the bottom of the Kremlin's neurotic view of world affairs is [a] traditional and instinctive Russian sense of insecurity,'" writes historian James Chace.[8] He continued, "Kennan stressed a program based not on military adventurism but on rehabilitating the 'health and vigor of our own society,' so that the Russians would be met at all contested points by the only thing they understood—strength."[9] *The Long Telegram* gave a new direction to US Soviet policy and propelled Kennan's career forward. "The Long Telegram undoubtedly had an impact on the thinking of senior policymakers in Washington . . . Kennan's message helped construct the intellectual supports for the already developing disposition of firmness towards the Soviet Union."[10]

In May 1947, incoming Secretary of State George Marshall appointed Kennan to be the first director of the new Policy Planning Staff, charged with formulating America's new foreign policy and grand strategy.[11] *Foreign Affairs* magazine published Kennan's article, "The Sources of Soviet Conduct," under the pseudonym X because of Kennan's official government position in July 1947. Although the article's anonymity was supposed to prevent it from being seen as a reflection of official thinking within the administration,

Kennan's name was soon leaked, and the article came to be considered the blueprint for the new US strategy vis-à-vis the Soviet Union. In the article, Kennan argued that "it must invariably be assumed in Moscow that the aims of the capitalist world are antagonistic to the Soviet regime," and that "the main element of any United States policy toward the Soviet Union must be that of a long-term, patient but firm and vigilant containment of Russian expansive tendencies."[12]

Drafted somewhat hastily, Kennan's article was quickly misunderstood to advocate for US opposition to Soviet communism wherever it reared its head. While this was not Kennan's intention, it became the essence of the *Truman Doctrine*, delivered by President Harry S. Truman to Congress in March 1947. The Truman Doctrine arose during the Greek civil war between communists and a right-wing pro-Western government. When the British pulled out of the war due to financial issues, the United States feared the imminent victory of communist factions. This is when Truman delivered his speech to Congress to sway public opinion. Truman proclaimed that "it must be the policy of the United States to support free peoples who are resisting attempted subjugation by armed minorities or by outside pressures." The tension between Kennan's advocated strategy of mostly psychological warfare, shows of strength, and strong-point defense, and the Truman Doctrine's "open-ended commitment to resist Soviet expansionism"[13] defined the contested nature of US strategy making throughout the Cold War.

The first departures from Kennan's containment concept occurred when the Truman and later Eisenhower administration adopted a rollback strategy. Truman codified the rollback in document NSC-68 and then applied it during the US intervention in the Korean War. NSC-68 "provided the blueprint for the militarization of the Cold War from 1950 to the collapse of the Soviet Union at the beginning of the 1990s."[14] As Hal Brands argues, "what NSC-68 represented . . . was an effort to fill the holes that were opening up in the nation's strategic posture as commitments expanded and Soviet military power grew."[15]

The Eisenhower administration continued zigzagging between containment and rollback. Initially, it adopted a rollback position when John Foster Dulles first became secretary of state, but in 1953 Eisenhower adopted NSC-162/2, which essentially returned to containment. Eisenhower's new strategy, whose foundations were seen in the 1955 defense budget, was the "New Look," which emphasized the need to better balance ends and means. The new strategy also aimed to rely on strategic nuclear weapons with Dulles saying, "local defenses must be reinforced by the further deterrent of massive retaliatory power."[16] In line with this strategy, Eisenhower involved the United States in conventional limited wars and enforced unprecedented executive authority in deploying US forces abroad without congressional authorization. Indeed, his administration's policies increased the influence of the executive branch in foreign policymaking and expanded America's international responsibilities.

President John F. Kennedy broke with Eisenhower's "New Look" and massive retaliation policies, offering "Flexible Response" in its place. "Kennedy was appalled by the cataclysmic consequences of the still-dominant military doctrine of massive retaliation . . . He strove to develop a strategy that created military options other than Armageddon and capitulation."[17]

But the arrival of President Richard M. Nixon and National Security Advisor Henry A. Kissinger in 1969 brought about a major reformulation of US grand strategy once again. As Kissinger explains, "America's nuclear superiority was eroding, and its economic supremacy was being challenged." Despite these claims, however, this era of hyperinterventionism occurred amid economic growth, as Figure 4.1 illustrates. US GDP grew since World War II, with the vast majority of years showcasing economic gains from the previous year.

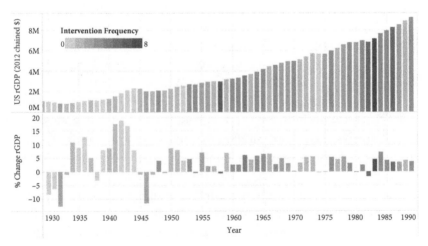

Figure 4.1. US GDP Trends and Interventions, 1930–1989

Citation: Bureau of Economic Analysis (BEA). Gross Domestic Product. *U.S. Department of Commerce, 2019.* https://www.bea.gov/data/gdp/gross-domestic-product; Louis Johnston and Samuel H. Williamson. "What Was the U.S. GDP Then?" *Measuring Worth,* 2018. https://www.measuringworth.com/datasets/usgdp/.

Especially in the 1960s, the United States saw large, persistent increases in GDP per capita despite several oil crises. By the 1980s, these economic gains appear correlated to higher intervention frequencies per year, as illustrated in Figure 4.2. As shown below, by the 1980s, US intervention frequency increased from prior decades and the level of national interests remained constant at "medium," whereas in decades prior, many interventions had exhibited "high" levels of national interest, yet the US less frequently.

To address the perceived decrease in US superiority at the time, as also evidenced in the decreasing National Material Capabilities index (CINC) in the figure above, the Nixon administration sought to create a new balance of power. This was a "strategy of transforming the two-power world into a strategic triangle" and was successful as it "managed to create a major incentive for Soviet moderation by achieving a dramatic opening to China."[18] Nixon and Kissinger's interpretation of the opportunities afforded to the United States within the international system of the time were instrumental in "ushering in the most sweeping changes in United States foreign policy since the idea of containment had first emerged two decades earlier."[19] The result was détente, an era of easing tensions with the Soviet Union and an alliance with China. The new strategy left its mark on US diplomacy for the rest of the Cold War. "It was Nixon's focus on a new balance of power in Asia

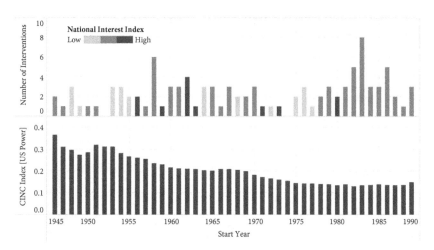

Figure 4.2. US Interventions by National Interests and CINC Capabilities, 1946–1989

Citation: Correlates of War Project. *National Material Capabilities, 1816–2012*. Version 5. http://www.correlatesofwar.org; J. David Singer, "Reconstructing the Correlates of War Dataset on Material Capabilities of States, 1816–1985," *International Interactions* 14 (1987); 115–132.

to which Jimmy Carter would later turn in the face of Soviet expansion [in Afghanistan] . . . and that Ronald Reagan would refine and resource to push the Soviets out of the Pacific."[20]

Unlike previous eras of US foreign policy and despite such different interpretations of containment among policymakers, American presidents did not seem to alter the trajectory of interventionism during the Cold War until Reagan. This may have occurred because there was still long-term consistency in the perceived existential threats facing the country. Moreover, the United States held to relatively steady objectives and grand strategy throughout these decades, as long as the policy of containment remained in some form. We see in Figure 4.3, however, that President Ronald Reagan was an outlier as he spearheaded the rollback policy.

Reagan's administration was responsible for a large spike in US military interventions, moving the maximum number of interventions per year from six (before Reagan) to eight—an increase of over 30 percent.

Whatever the continuities, Reagan denounced the Nixon-Kissinger strategy of détente, offering his vision in its place. Hal Brands argues that indeed "there was a Reagan grand strategy . . . It was premised on the idea that the Soviet Union was far weaker than it had looked in the late 1970s, and that the United States could take advantage of that weakness by exerting pressure in the military, economic, political, and ideological realms . . . Reagan's grand strategy . . . was meant to capitalize on America's competitive advantages vis-à-vis Moscow, to reverse the tide of the Cold War, and then to begin the

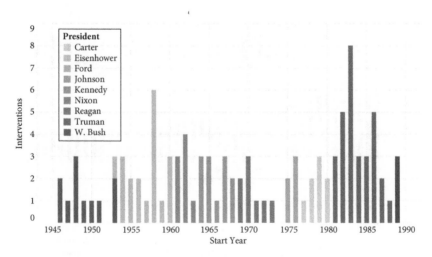

Figure 4.3. US Interventions by President, 1946–1989

process of forging a more stable superpower relationship."[21] While Reagan's statecraft strengthened America's geopolitical position, "the president could not initially translate these gains into productive diplomacy with Moscow," so he had to "execute a key tactical shift by toning down his incendiary rhetoric . . . and seeking to build trust with the . . . Kremlin leadership" in 1983 and 1984.[22] Thus, Reagan also saw a need to temper militarism and growing tensions with diplomacy and softer forms of engagement. His administration increased spending on radio programming such as the Voice of America and Radio Free Europe. It also spearheaded and completed a program of nuclear non-proliferation in the landmark Strategic Arms Reduction Treaty (START).

When Mikhail Gorbachev attained leadership of the Soviet Communist Party in 1985, initiating the new policies of *glasnost* (openness) and *perestroika* (restructuring), his "revised approach left the [US] administration well-placed to respond" to the changes in Moscow.[23] As a result, US-Soviet relations significantly improved, America's position was enhanced, and eventually the Cold War ended when the Soviet Union collapsed in 1989.

Even though Reagan is known for his victories during the Cold War rivalry, his administration promoted initiatives that heightened tensions and increased the risk of confrontations with the Soviet Union and its allies. He also oversaw significant increases in US defense spending that left a long shadow in the decades to come even in the absence of an archnemesis superpower, as shown in Figure 4.4 using Stockholm International Peace Research Institute (SIPRI) military expenditure data.

Reagan's administration sought to build a larger navy, deploy intermediate-range nuclear missiles in Europe, and militarize outer space via the Strategic Defense Initiative, which would prevent intercontinental nuclear missile warheads from reaching targets, amongst other projects.

Empirical Patterns of US Interventions, 1946-1989

The United States undeniably emerged as a global hegemon after World War II, as seen in its many anticommunist interventions across the world. The United States wielded military force across all continents in about equal measure, except for sub-Saharan Africa as it rarely posed communist threats. The frequency of interventions increased dramatically after the 1970s. The United States intervened in proxy conflicts against the Soviet Union

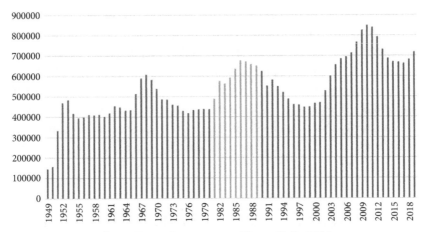

Figure 4.4. US Military Expenditures across Years, 1949–2019

Citation: Stockholm International Peace Research Institution (SIPRI). Extended Military Expenditure Database. Beta. https://www.sipri.org/databases/milex.

Note: Reagan's term in office marked in lighter shade.

consistently in Europe and East Asia, and by the late 1980s it heavily involved itself in the Middle East under the Carter Doctrine, with sprinklings of antileftist conflicts in Latin America.

The United States increased its interventions from thirty in the interwar era to 104 during the Cold War, a 245 percent increase. The vast majority of target states leaned heavily autocratic, with a few exceptions in European targets and then Guatemala in the 1960s and Panama and the Philippines in the late 1980s. The United States often overthrew leftist governments in support of conservative, pro-US dictatorships. Figure 4.5 shows that almost 30 percent of US interventions concluded in a stalemate, while 23 percent of them ended in a US victory.

Only a tiny fraction culminated with US surrender or victory for its opponent (State B). Comparatively, the United States was also more hostile to its target states than the target states were to it, as Figure 4.6 shows. The hostility gap increased dramatically from the mid-1960s onward as the policy of containment grew to include even more interventions against perceived communist threats worldwide.

Figure 4.7 indicates that building or maintaining foreign regimes was the second most frequent objective, after protecting US citizens, diplomats, embassies, and properties abroad. The third most common objectives were linked to territorial gains and social protection.[24]

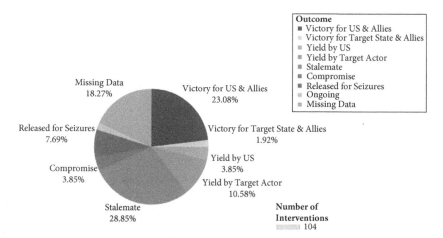

Figure 4.5. Outcomes of US Interventions, 1946–1989

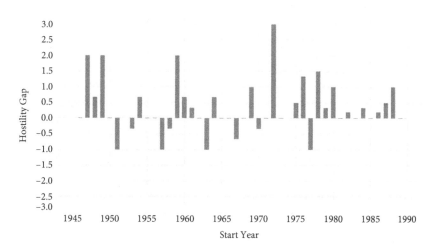

Figure 4.6. Comparative Hostility Levels, 1946–1989

Historical Narratives of America the Leader, 1946–1989

During the Cold War, the United States saw the Soviet Union as an existential threat—an ideological monolith bent on world domination and the spread of its communist system. The United States' greatest objective was to deter Soviet expansion using all available foreign policy tools. It is unsurprising then that the Cold War era stands as America's most military interventionist one, eclipsing all eras before it. In other words, this hypermilitarism reflected

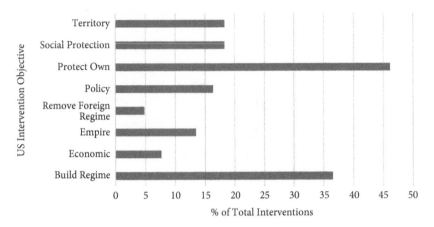

Figure 4.7. US Intervention Objectives, 1946–1989

the need to protect vital security interests against an archnemesis in a time of existential crisis for the country. American militarism also frequently occurred in response to another country's hostilities. The United States and the Soviet Union did, however, manage to prevent a full-blown "hot" war between themselves by relying on diplomacy, threats of force, atomic deterrence via mutually assured destruction, and proxy wars across the globe.

Early Cold War: Occupation of Europe and Marshall Plan

By the end of World War II, the United States and its allies occupied Germany, Austria, Italy, and many other parts of Europe. In Germany and Austria, the United States, United Kingdom, France, and the Soviet Union split the country and the capital of each country into four zones to co-occupy the territories. Eventually, these four zones merged into two—one overseen by the three western powers and the other by the Soviet Union. The Soviets initially believed the postwar occupation period would focus on reparations and deindustrializing Germany to prevent future wars. When the United States decided to implement a different strategy of reconstruction to avoid future conflict, it marked the beginning of the breakdown of bilateral relations.[25]

In the backdrop of the newly established Bretton Woods agreement in 1944 and the creation of the CIA in 1947, the United States' rising dominance continued to antagonize the Soviet Union. By 1948, the United States was spearheading the Marshall Plan to guard domestic European markets against protectionist backlashes and Soviet influence. The Marshall Plan aided European economic recovery and post-war rebuilding and drew states closer to US economic, political, and cultural influences, but none of the Eastern European countries where the Soviet Union enjoyed influence or imposed new governments joined the US-led program. A clear line was being drawn, which was fully solidified in 1949 when the Soviet Union shut down American access to Berlin to coerce concessions and force the United States to withdraw. Instead, the Soviets backed down once the United States was able to organize an airlift of food and economic goods to resupply the city.

Beyond this, the Soviet Union and the United States began competing for political control in Western Europe. The Soviet Union retained influence with communist parties in France and Italy, where both were trying to win elections. In response, the United States used covert aid to help other parties win elections. At this time, Kennan sent the infamous *Long Telegram* outlining what he saw as Soviet efforts to establish more power and arguing for the United States to take active measures to contain Soviet influence.[26]

The creation of NATO in 1949 further formalized the Truman Doctrine, solidifying US military commitments to Western Europe. As the United States consolidated the NATO bloc in the West, the Soviet Union used its control in the East to set up the Warsaw Pact, cementing the lines between western and eastern Europe. A challenge to this order emerged in 1956 with the Budapest uprising in Hungary. But once the United States decided not to intervene in favor of those protesting Soviet influence and Soviet tanks flowed into the country, it became clear that overt intervention was a line that both sides wouldn't cross in the newly emerging Cold War order. The two evenly matched nuclear powers started to understand how delicate the power balancing must be to avoid mutually assured destruction. Finally, in 1961, as the Soviets erected the Berlin Wall to stop defections from East Germany, they solidified the East-West lines in stone.[27]

In Asia: Occupation of Japan, Chinese Civil War, and Korean War

While the United States and the Soviet Union drew the Iron Curtain across the European continent, the Cold War was fought as much in Asia and as it was in Europe. Following the defeat of Japan in World War II, the United States occupied the country, reorganizing its politics while also keeping the emperor as a figurehead. During this period, General Douglas MacArthur was the de facto emperor of Japan, ruling via edict while the United States reconstructed the country in its liberal image. As the Soviet threat grew, Japan became a more reliable American ally. At the same time, the United States retook control of the Philippines, neglecting to follow through on its promise to grant the country independence, and took over the international mandates Japan held for various pacific island territories after World War I, administering them as UN trust territories.[28]

Civil war continued in China between the Soviet-supported communist force (CCP) under Mao Zedong and the American-backed Republic of China (ROC) forces under Chiang Kai-shek. As Japanese troops were surrendering, American forces in East Asia attempted to keep the Japanese military in place in Manchuria to allow time for ROC forces to arrive. But Soviet forces pressured the Japanese to surrender and send all captured weapons to the CCP. Eventually, Mao and the communist forces won the battle for mainland China in 1949, and ROC forces retreated to Taiwan. The United States did not recognize the Communist Chinese government as legitimate for many years, instead maintaining that the ROC was the rightful government of China, which prompted recurring conflict in the region.[29]

China's Communist revolution permanently altered the balance of power in the region, with the United States now left to rely on Japan as its main anticommunist ally in East Asia. In Washington's eyes, it became more important than ever to safeguard some of the other key regional players, such as Korea and Vietnam, from the communist menace.

The United States and Soviet Union split another former Japanese territory, Korea, into a northern and southern occupation zone. Both took total control over their newly occupied territories, building new government institutions, and both sides wanted to reunify the country into one. In South Korea, a communist insurgency began with support from the north, and clashes along the border started in 1950. As this happened, US Secretary of State Dean Acheson did not include South Korea as part of his outlined strategic Asian defense perimeter, which some argue was a key indicator allowing the Soviet Union to permit North Korea's military action aimed at taking back control of the South. While the United States was surprised by the invasion from the North, they were able to receive support from the UN (largely because of a Soviet boycott) to intervene in the war.

The Korean War clearly reflected the expansion of the containment doctrine from diplomatic threats to alliances to direct military interventions. Korea also marked the beginning of US military interventions within the so-called third world, culminating in the Vietnam War from 1965 to 1973. Given its staunch anticommunist ideology, the United States interpreted the Korean War as a coordinated plan of communist domination by Moscow, rather than just an internal civil war between two local factions. Truman saw America's intervention as an exercise of his new containment doctrine, where communist expansion needed to be resisted all around the world.[30]

Eventually, American-led forces arrived to help South Korea push North Korea back across the 38th parallel and even further towards the Chinese border. Irregular Chinese intervention then managed to prevent an American and South Korean victory. With fighting mainly coming to a standstill, a ceasefire with borders along the 38th parallel was reached once again. At various points throughout the war, the United States threatened to use atomic weapons, especially if China intervened. This was one reason why China used irregular forces to intervene instead of its traditional military. But fears of Soviet nuclear retaliation also made it hard for Truman and others to authorize nuclear attacks, indicating for the first time that nuclear parity might be at work. While the war was never officially ended and American troops remain in South Korea, there has not been a resumption of full-scale hostilities since 1953.[31]

The Cold War was not limited to competition in Europe and East Asia near the Soviet Union's borders—it was truly global, extending to decolonial struggles and featuring competition in the Western Hemisphere. The United States saw any leftist government as a potential vector for the Soviet Union to challenge American power. By 1953, partially due to the Defense Production Act of 1950, US military production ballooned to seven times the amount in 1950 and the army had grown by 50 percent.[32]

In 1953, the United States tacitly aided the overthrow of Iran's newly elected leftist government to reinstall the conservative and US-friendly Shah. CIA operatives identified local proxies who were willing to act in accordance with US interests in exchange for large sums of cash. While the coup successfully removed the leftist Prime Minister Mohammed Mossadegh who sought to nationalize oil resources, replacing him with General Fazlollah Zahedi who became a reliable American ally, it also stoked anti-American sentiments, ultimately helping to foment the Iranian revolution of 1979 and the rise of a virulently anti-American Islamist regime.[33]

After the Korean War, the United States also sent military aid to French forces fighting communist-led anticolonial factions in Indochina. While the United States did not directly intervene to help French forces at Dien Bien Phu in 1954, it did provide material support before it began directly aiding the South Vietnamese noncommunist government. In February 1955, the United States sent 327 military advisors to assist South Vietnamese forces, contributing not only tactical and strategic advice and training, but also direct logistical support, such as flying helicopters. The number of advisors continued to rise in the years ahead, culminating in the Vietnam War.[34]

In Latin America: CIA Operations in Guatemala, Cuba, and the Dominican Republic

The United States was even more attuned to potential leftist uprisings in Latin America, making its foreign policy especially militant and corrosive. The driving fear behind its interventions was that the United States could lose the Cold War by failing to perpetuate its political ideology in its own backyard as the Soviet Union did in Eastern Europe.[35] Leftist parties in Latin America, with real or perceived ties to the Soviet bloc, were often banned, repressed, or toppled by military coups backed by the United States.[36] In Latin America in particular, leftist transformations were seen as a manifestation of anti-Americanism and a challenge to the US-led socioeconomic order, causing the United States to respond with force. Competition for political hegemony therefore drove US interventions in Latin America.

Most notably in the early Cold War, the United States sponsored the overthrow of Jacobo Árbenz Guzman and the installation of a right-wing government in Guatemala in 1954. The intervention showed how the competitive and fearful mindset in Washington ushered in an exaggerated idea of communist proliferation in the region and promoted military interventions to protect corporate interests.[37] A 1944 revolution in Guatemala resulted in successive democratically elected leftist governments, culminating in the 1950 election of Jacobo Árbenz. In 1952, the Truman administration authorized an unsuccessful Central Intelligence Agency (CIA) collaboration with the Nicaraguan dictator Anastacio Somoza to put Guatemalan general Carlos Castillo Armas in power. For the rest of Truman's presidency, the administration remained hesitant to directly aid Guatemalans on the ground trying to overthrow Arbenz.[38]

By 1954, Árbenz wanted to shift the country toward a more autonomous economy that relied on its natural resources, increased employment rates, and encouraged the development of a diverse, technologically oriented economy.[39] In building this new economic structure, Árbenz announced an agrarian reform bill that would expropriate and redistribute idle land from landowners to produce more staple foods, rather than goods for export.[40] At this time, Guatemala's United Fruit Company leveraged the saliency of anticommunist fervor in the United States and launched a publicity campaign against the agrarian reform bill based on the communist conspiracy (rather than economic grievance) to gain support from an already sympathetic US audience.[41] Thus, the agrarian bill quickly became fodder for Washington's predispositions to view Guatemala's reforms as a marker of communist influence. Stoked by the United Fruit Company campaign, fear of communism ultimately led the United States to intervene in Guatemala.

The United States organized a CIA task force to arrange for a new Guatemalan leader and run a campaign to influence public opinion. Subsequently, the United States passed a resolution stating that communist control of any country would justify "appropriate action in accordance with existing treaties."[42] When the Árbenz administration imported a shipment of Soviet-sourced arms in anticipation of a potential US invasion, Washington became furious and supported the troops of its preferred leader, Castillo Armas. A CIA psychological warfare campaign, PBSUCCESS, helped persuade people that a major invasion was imminent, resulting in the defection of the Guatemalan military. Árbenz quickly resigned in fear.[43] Washington was now practiced in both creating and supporting coups.

The United States then turned its anticommunist attentions to Cuba, where it wanted to dislodge Fidel Castro's regime and place a right-wing government back in control. By 1959, the Eisenhower administration came up with the idea to leverage its existing CIA task force infrastructure in its dealings with the Castro regime in Cuba. The overly confident administration thought a similar operation to the one that succeeded in Guatemala would function just as smoothly, assuming Castro would capitulate to US pressure as quickly and painlessly as Árbenz did. This eventually culminated in the disastrous Bay of Pigs operations where American support for Cuban exiles was supposed to lead to an invasion and domestic uprising. But the utter failure of the operation reinforced Castro's position in Cuba. While the United States continued to seek ways to overthrow his regime, it never succeeded.[44]

Ironically enough, the Cuban government anticipated a US intervention after its actions in Guatemala. This may have even influenced Cuba to adopt more militant policies as a means of better protecting the country from American intervention. These preemptive defensive security responses, such as nuclear proliferation programs, have become commonplace across Middle Eastern and South Asian countries in the post-9/11 era.[45]

Partially due to the United States' regime change aspirations and hostility, Cuba and Soviet ties grew, which led to the Soviet Union's decision to place missiles in Cuba. This kicked off the Cuban Missile Crisis, raising real concerns that the Soviet Union and the United States were about to start a global nuclear exchange. But despite bouts of miscommunication and coercion, the crisis was resolved through cautious diplomacy, with the Soviet Union removing its missiles in Cuba and the United States removing some missiles from bases in Turkey.

The Dominican Republic was another regular target of aggressive US behavior as the United States did not want the country to become "a second Cuba."[46] From 1960 to 1965, the United States engaged in its largest intervention in Latin America since the inauguration of the Good Neighbor Policy. Attempts to sway domestic politics in the Dominican Republic began years before the US military intervention. Economic sanctions against Rafael Trujillo began with Eisenhower's attempt to isolate the Dominican Republic from Cuba, and Kennedy expanded those sanctions to coax a more liberal political system.[47] In early 1961, the United States was also operating a covert anti-Trujillo campaign involving the transfer of small arms and "sabotage equipment" to dissidents with links to political assassins.[48] The failure at the Bay of Pigs paused its actions in the Dominican Republic, but the United States remained prepared to invade if there was any sign of a new communist takeover.[49] Kennedy wanted credit for the eventual removal of Trujillo but needed to avoid being accused of assassinating a foreign leader.

In May 1961, a group of US-supported dissidents assassinated Trujillo. In November 1961, when two of Trujillo's brothers returned to regain control of the country, Secretary Rusk warned that the United States would not "remain idle." By the next day, US military attaches were encouraging key Dominican Air Force officers to oppose the Trujillos, and US Navy jets were seen flying over Santo Domingo.[50] The next day, both the *New York Times* and the *Wall Street Journal* reported that the US government was prepared to land US Marines, if necessary. On November 20, the Trujillo brothers and a planeload of relatives and close associates left the Dominican Republic. Fearful of a left revolution among anti-government protests and unrest, the United States actively pressured and achieved the regime's departure with the threat of military intervention and constant military presence near the country's shores.

In May 1965, President Lyndon B. Johnson, despite the disapproval of his civilian advisors, used Eisenhower's original Guatemala playbook once more to intervene in the Dominican Republic after the overthrow of the Trujillo regime spiraled into a civil war. The goal was to prevent the installation of a leftist government and another Cuban revolution. In a televised address, Johnson acknowledged that the military intervention in the Dominican Republic was motivated by anticommunist objectives, stating, "What began as a popular democratic revolution that was committed to democracy and social justice moved into the hands of a band of communist conspirators."[51] The Organization of American States (OAS) authorized an inter-American force to restore order on May 6. US forces reached their zenith of 24,000 troops a few weeks later and cleared the rebels from Santo Domingo by May 20th. A ceasefire was established the next day, and within a week the Inter-American Peace Force assumed command and US Marines began returning home.[52]

Many consider the relative success in the Dominican Republic to be the basis for future American interventions in Haiti, Grenada, and Panama. However, the unilateral American intervention and subsequent approval from the OAS seriously damaged both the prestige of the United States in Latin America and the regional perception of the OAS as an independent body. And despite all its interventions in the region, the United States' main target, the communist Castro regime, remained in place. Cuba continued to support leftist movements throughout the rest of the Cold War, which the United States tried to overthrow or defeat using a range of tools, including covert operations in places like Guatemala and Nicaragua.[53]

Crisis Event: The Vietnam War and Beyond

The Vietnam War formalized America's more militant version of containment and altered international expectations and perceptions of US foreign policy. After France withdrew its forces, Vietnam was temporarily partitioned on the 17th parallel between North Vietnam and South Vietnam and the two sides were to hold a national election to determine how to unify again. Instead, 1956 brought about a partition into two separate states, with the communists under Ho Chi Minh ruling the North and the US-backed Ngo Dinh Diem regime governing the South. The United States provided military and financial support, fearing "contagion"—if Vietnam fully fell to communist forces, it could create a domino effect across the entire region. But the United States struggled to get its local allies to pursue its preferred policies. The United States used various tools to support Diem, including psychological operations trying to make the communists in the North look more nefarious, and consulting on how best to rig national elections. Most importantly, however, the United States advised the Diem regime in its fight against communist rebels as the Viet Cong continued its insurgency in South Vietnam.[54]

By 1957, tensions between North and South Vietnam intensified. In July, North Vietnamese forces bombed a military base and killed several US officers. In May 1960, the United States responded to increased aggression in Vietnam by doubling the number of military advisors in the country from the original 327 to 685.[55]

As the Cold War intensified in the early 1960s, Southeast Asia became an important battleground with multiple proxy conflicts where the two rival superpowers took alternate sides. Vietnam was rapidly becoming the most important proxy battle. After President Kennedy's election, American military efforts in Vietnam escalated with an increased desire to show resolve and prevent communism from spreading in Southeast Asia. By the end of 1961, Kennedy increased the number of military advisors embedded within South Vietnamese military units to over 3,400 and increased the amount of financial assistance to the South Vietnamese army to $144 million a year. By 1964, the US military presence in Vietnam expanded to 23,000 troops.[56]

Yet with the US-backed regime failing to make a dent in the insurgency and struggling to gain control of rural areas, support grew for overthrowing Diem as the leader of South Vietnam. Unfortunately, an internal coup in 1963 only fractured the government of South Vietnam further, benefitting Northern factions.[57] By 1965, the United States was left with two choices—get out and let the local government deal with the communist forces or become more involved in the conflict by directing the war in the countryside against the Viet Cong.

After Kennedy's assassination, President Lyndon B. Johnson escalated the war in Vietnam. The United States reinstituted the draft to begin an American ground war effort in South Vietnam and initiated a strategic bombing campaign in North Vietnam, to compel the North to stop aiding the insurgency in the South. The strategic bombing operation, Rolling Thunder, dropped over a million tons of ordnance, including attacks in neighboring Laos to prevent North Vietnamese forces from using the Ho Chi Minh trail in the country. The strategic bombing and ground campaign failed, however, and the failure eventually prompted Johnson not to seek reelection.[58]

With the election of Richard Nixon, the new focus was to build up the domestic South Vietnamese forces and reduce the number of American troops in the country. Nixon also tried to use strategic bombing to help push the North Vietnamese to the negotiating table and encourage a ceasefire agreement. He also controversially widened the scope of the intervention to target sites in Cambodia as well as Laos.[59] Eventually, the United States and North Vietnam reached a ceasefire agreement that allowed Nixon to achieve his promise of removing American troops. However, after the withdrawal of US forces in 1973, the South Vietnamese military was not strong enough to resist renewed Northern aggression, and Saigon fell in 1975.[60]

The Vietnam War was the longest and most unpopular American war of the twentieth century. US operations were extensive, costly, and destructive.[61] Approximately 2,594,000 American troops served in Vietnam, and the entire intervention cost $732 million.[62] Around 2 million civilians on both sides were killed throughout the conflict,[63] and perhaps most shockingly, 6.7 percent of the overall civilian population in North and South Vietnam perished.[64]

Détente and Nixon Goes to China

Beyond ending America's most unpopular and destructive war, the Nixon administration also reduced hostile relations with the two largest communist powers, the Soviet Union and China. First, Nixon made a concerted effort to deescalate tensions with the Soviet Union and find ways to reduce the likelihood of nuclear escalation following the crises of the 1960s. The two powers engaged in arms control talks to decrease nuclear stockpiles and discussed normalizing relations. This eventually led to the Anti-Ballistic Missile (ABM) Treaty and the Strategic Arms Limitation Talks (SALT) I agreement in 1972, which reduced the number of deployed nuclear warheads, as well as the Helsinki Accords of 1975, which normalized relations between the NATO and Warsaw Pact blocs and accepted the principles of free elections and fixed borders.[65]

While the efforts did not fully normalize US-Soviet relations, they did prompt some improvements through joint space missions and increased agricultural trade. The Soviet Union was also involved in helping the United States end the war in Vietnam. Some leaders in the United States, however, were concerned about normalizing relations too much without concessions on human rights issues, particularly the Soviet Union's refusal to let the Soviet Jewish population and others emigrate from the country. As such, the Jackson-Vanik Amendment was passed, tying US trade deals with the Soviet Union to allowing emigration. There were also remaining concerns about communist expansion, so proxy wars in Latin America, South Asia, and elsewhere continued. The era of détente ended with the Soviet invasion of Afghanistan and Reagan's election.[66]

The Nixon administration was also interested in normalizing relations with communist China, especially following the break between the Soviet Union and China. It made perfect sense with its power-balancing strategy to foster closer ties with China. Before the 1970s, Chinese intervention in the Vietnam War and the development of Chinese nuclear weapons made US-China relations perpetually hostile. But in 1972, Nixon traveled to the country and was the first American president to recognize the legitimacy of the communist Chinese regime. The meeting in China allowed the United States and China to take the first step towards a settlement on the Taiwan issue and led to normalized relations in 1979. After 1979, the United States did not have formal diplomatic contacts with Taiwan but did continue its arms sales. US-China relations mostly progressed in this positive matter throughout the rest of the Cold War until the Tiananmen Square protests in 1989.[67]

Late Cold War: The Middle East's Oil Crisis and the Carter Doctrine

During the late Cold War, the United States increased its involvement and intervention in the Middle East, which cast a long shadow in US foreign policy. The 1973 Yom Kippur War began when Egypt crossed the Suez, and not only raised tensions between Israel and the Arab world but also between the Soviet Union and the United States. The UN brokered a ceasefire ending the 1973 war, and Egypt and Israel signed the Camp David Accords in 1978, giving captured territory back and reducing tensions permanently between the states. One of the most significant legacies of the 1973 war was the oil crisis it produced. Arab oil producers imposed an embargo on the United States and its allies for supporting Israel in the war, massively raising global oil prices even after the embargo ended. While the embargo did not force Israel back to its 1949 borders, it did permanently increase the effectiveness of the Organization of Petroleum Exporting Countries (OPEC) in the international economy and showed how these tools could be used to pressure American foreign policy.[68]

During the Carter administration, several different crises set up the future of US policy in the Middle East. First, following the Soviet invasion of Afghanistan and the fear of increased Soviet assertiveness in the Middle East, articulated the so-called Carter Doctrine to ensure the Persian Gulf remained free of outside influence. Initially, the strategy was premised on keeping the Soviet Union out of the region and led to the formation of US Central Command (CENTCOM). Eventually, however, Reagan morphed the doctrine into ensuring the stability of Saudi Arabia and deterring threats from other regional powers. Most importantly, the doctrine laid the groundwork for a permanent US presence in the Middle East and provided justification for various interventions to stabilize the region and oil prices.

The Iranian Revolution and subsequent Iran-Iraq War, however, triggered another global oil shock and large economic effects.[69] In 1979, the Carter administration responded to growing instability in Iran, where the pro-US Shah was overthrown and the American embassy was stormed, with American diplomatic staff taken hostage for more than 400 days. Carter tried to negotiate an end to the hostage crisis and launched a military rescue mission, but both efforts failed. Iran only released the hostages after the election of Reagan. While Iran was once seen as one of the twin pillars of stability in the region, from 1979 onwards it became a chief threat to American interests.

In 1980, Iraq invaded Iran, launching the Iran-Iraq War, with both sides attempting to become the dominant power in the region. The United States nominally supported Iraq, providing some nonmilitary aid, but primarily sought to prevent an Iranian victory. For most of the 1980s, the United States retained a heightened military presence in the Strait of Hormuz (which Iran had threatened to close off) with naval and air power, partly to maintain certain protected international zones for commercial shipping. Finally, the 1983 Marine barracks bombing in Lebanon cemented the dislike of the new Islamic Republic among American policymakers. At the time, US Marines were participating in a multinational force enforcing a ceasefire following the

1982 crisis between Israel, the Palestine Liberation Organization, and various Lebanese factions when terrorists linked to Iran bombed their barracks. While Reagan eventually removed American forces from Lebanon and sold arms to Iran as part of the Iran-Contra affair, the legacy of distrust and dislike continue to loom over relations.[70]

Late Cold War: From Afghanistan to the Berlin Wall

Détente ended after the Soviet invasion of Afghanistan. Coupled with Reagan's election, the Cold War heated up again as both sides pursued more assertive foreign policies. The Afghanistan war was meant to be a quick military mission to prop up the government after an internal conflict but turned into a decade-long quagmire for the Soviet Union. The United States, however, supported the Afghan mujahideen militarily against the Soviets and the Soviet-imposed regime, primarily by providing covert military aid through the CIA and collaborating with Pakistan to help fund the rebels.

The so-called Reagan Doctrine emerged, with the United States supporting every anticommunist movement in the world in an attempt to turn back the tide of communist expansion. Finally, the supporters of rollback got their wish. Rather than containment, in places like Afghanistan, Angola, Cambodia, and Nicaragua there was a concentrated effort to roll back communism and support all rebels fighting against communism anywhere in the world. This mostly included supplying arms, but it led to many covert US interventions to provide funding and weapons during civil conflicts. The covert funding was most controversial in Nicaragua where the United States sent weapons to the Contras, a US-backed insurgency, made up of former regime elements, carrying out more terrorist acts than the local anticommunist insurgency. Eventually, Congress forbade sending aid to the Contras, which the Reagan administration tried to overcome by illegally selling arms to Iran to gain resources to send to the Contras.[71]

As part of its rollback strategy, the Reagan administration also made a concerted effort to turn back on nuclear cuts and engage in a new form of technological arms racing. The expectation was that greater arms racing, coupled with lower oil prices, would significantly strain the already dysfunctional Soviet economy. This included new attempts at grand strategic advances such as the Strategic Defense Initiative, colloquially known as "Star Wars." These efforts led to a few nuclear scares as military exercises and broken sensors indicated possible first strikes of a major war. However, after Gorbachev came to power in the Soviet Union, there was a desire to reduce tensions that could lead to an accidental nuclear war. Relations thawed between Gorbachev and Reagan, which allowed for nuclear arms control talks to take place, including the signing of the Intermediate-Range Nuclear Forces (INF) Treaty that reduced the number of intermediate nuclear forces deployed in Europe.[72]

In 1989, during George H. W. Bush's presidency, the Cold War finally came to an end as the Berlin Wall came down. Protest movements and revolutions against the communist system broke out, and the United States watched the Warsaw Pact and Soviet sphere of influence break down. As communist regimes fell, the United States was involved in two crucial decisions about the future of European politics: the reunification of Germany and NATO expansion. Indeed, these two issues remain connected. Some argue that the United States promised not to expand NATO further toward the Soviet Union after it consented to German reunification. In 1991, however, when the Soviet Union fully collapsed and fifteen separate republics emerged in the aftermath, the United States remained the sole great power in the international system, giving it the opportunity to rethink American power and American military strategy.[73]

Conclusion

The United States and the Soviet Union emerged from the ashes of World War II as political allies only to transform into existential rivals. A cycle of fear and paranoia grew as the Sovietization of East-Central Europe intensified with the Soviet Union eliminating noncommunist forces across the region and coercing countries into the Soviet economic system. The United States now saw the Soviet Union as an illiberal rival and threat. At the same time, the Soviets saw the United States as a threat as well, endangering its economic and security interests in its own backyard.

Whether founded in reality or not, the Cold War was perceived by both rivals as an existential crisis of identity—where a rival's successes and influences could wipe out the other, both politically and ideologically. Throughout this era, US leadership believed that many leftist movements, causes, or factions were directly inspired or organized by Moscow and other communist elements. The United States believed the Soviet Union sought to expand its power and communist system globally and eventually even invade the United States. In this cycle of mutual paranoia and fear, both the United States and Soviet Union built up massive militaries and invested in new, highly destructive weapons systems while sending their troops to all areas of the world to balance out the other rival in proxy conflicts.

Realist theory tends to see the Cold War through the lens of power and security interests. It interprets the era as one of stability brought about by the bipolar distribution of power and by the balancing of the two superpowers against each other. In this view, the Cold War is known as the long peace, brought about by successful deterrence and power balancing.

However, we cannot ignore the reality that both the United States and the Soviet Union eventually caved to ideological motivations. The United States involved itself in regions of little to no security interests just to prevent the rise of communism, such as the war in Vietnam. The Soviets did the same thing in Afghanistan. In this perspective, the United States didn't fear Soviet power expansion alone in the traditional sense as it also feared the spread of Soviet ideologies across the world. Thus, the Cold War was, in part, a clash of two globally expansionist ideologies, which had its origins in America's virulent anti-communism since the early 1900s. If these ideological motivations and perceptions were not fanned by policymakers, then perhaps the level of militarism might have been lower, saving many lives in the process.

The ideological perspective supplements the leaner security-based perspective on the Cold War. Since the United States believed that all socialist leaders and movements in other countries were controlled by Moscow, they were also seen as direct threats to US economic and security interests. No distinction was made between Soviet-dominated communist regimes and socialist movements globally. Without such a dogmatic perception, the United States would not have assumed many of the civil wars and leadership changes in developing countries directly affected US security interests, reducing the incentives to intervene.

But US interventions during this time also served the interests of America's capitalist and industrial classes. Instead of balancing its power against a rival or fighting back against communism, this economic perspective sees the Cold War as a sort of economic imperialism, where the United States needed to protect emerging markets and safeguard private property rights abroad. If the Soviet economic system were to replace the US capitalist system in many parts of the world, including in the new states arising from decolonial movements, it would cut off potential markets for US industries and international capital. And it wasn't just the Soviet Union that was a threat in this game. All global revolutionary movements, whether linked to the Soviets or not, threatened capitalism too if they wanted to nationalize industries or limit capitalism.

Ultimately, no matter which perspective of the era one prefers, the Cold War ended with a political, economic, and ideological victory for the United States. The United States emerged as the world's uncontested hegemon in the 1990s. With unrivaled military power, the United States could determine when, where, and whether to intervene while arguably facing fewer existential threats to its homeland.

Notes

1. "Ike's Warning Of Military Expansion, 50 Years Later," *NPR,* January 17, 2011, https://www.npr.org/2011/01/17/132942244/ikes-warning-of-military-expans ion-50-years-later.
2. James Lindsay, History of the Cold War in 40 Quotes, *Council on Foreign Relations,* November 7, 2014, https://www.cfr.org/blog/history-cold-war-40-quotes.
3. Nina Silove, "Beyond the Buzzword: The Three Meanings of Grand Strategy," *Security Studies* 27, no. 1 (2018): 27–57, 40.
4. John Lewis Gaddis, *Strategies of Containment: A Critical Appraisal of American National Security Policy during the Cold War* (Oxford: Oxford University Press, 1982, 2005), 381.
5. Gaddis, *Strategies of Containment,* 381.
6. Zoltan Feher, "Obituary: George F. Kennan—A realist diplomat shaping American foreign policy," *Kül-Világ Foreign Policy Magazine* 2–3 (2005), 83–92, 83, https:// www.researchgate.net/publication/341298385_Obituary_George_F_Kennan_A_re alist_diplomat_shaping_American_foreign_policy.
7. Henry Kissinger, *White House Years* (Boston: Little, Brown, 1979), 135.
8. James Chace and Caleb Carr, *America Invulnerable: The Quest for Absolute Security from 1812 to Star Wars* (New York: Summit Books, 1988), 234.
9. Chace and Carr, *America Invulnerable,* 234.
10. Wilson D. Miscamble, *George F. Kennan and the Making of American Foreign Policy, 1947–1950* (Princeton, NJ: Princeton University Press, 1992), 26–27.
11. Zoltan Feher, "Obituary: George F. Kennan—A realist diplomat shaping American foreign policy," *Kül-Világ Foreign Policy Magazine* 2–3, (2005), 83–92, 86-87, https:// www.researchgate.net/publication/341298385_Obituary_George_F_Kennan_A_re alist_diplomat_shaping_American_foreign_policy.
12. George Kennan ("X"), "The Sources of Soviet Conduct," *Foreign Affairs,* 25, no. 4 (July 1947), 566–582.
13. Gaddis, *Strategies of Containment,* 23.
14. Ernest May, *American Cold War Strategy: Interpreting NSC-68,* (New York: St. Martin's, 1993).

15. Hal Brands, *What Good is Grand Strategy: Power and Purpose in American Statecraft from Harry S. Truman to George W. Bush* (Ithaca, NY: Cornell University Press, 2014), 46.

16. Quoted in Bernard Brodie, *Strategy in the Missile Age*, (Princeton, NJ: Princeton University Press, 1959), 248.

17. Kissinger, *Diplomacy*, 612.

18. Kissinger, 703–732.

19. Gaddis, *Strategies of Containment*, 272–273.

20. Michael Green, *By More Than Providence: Grand Strategy and American Power in the Asia Pacific Since 1783* (New York: Columbia University Press, 2017), 323.

21. Hal Brands, *What Good Is Grand Strategy: Power and Purpose in American Statecraft from Harry S. Truman to George W. Bush* (Ithaca, NY: Cornell University Press, 2014), 103.

22. Brands, *What Good Is Grand Strategy,* 104.

23. Brands, *What Good Is Grand Strategy,* 104.

24. For the original MIPS coding that we heavily rely on, see Sullivan, Patricia, and Michael Koch, MIPS Codebook, 2008, https://plsullivan.web.unc.edu/wp-content/uploads/sites/1570/2011/09/MIPS_codebook_Sullivan.pdf. Adapted from MIPS, Maintaining/Building Foreign Regime Authority is coded when US military force is employed to preserve the governing authority of an incumbent regime or the existing political institutions in another state. Refer to the Appendix for comprehensive coding and definitions of the types of intervention objectives. Social protective objectives, for instance, can be further disaggregated into Socially protective interventions and humanitarian interventions.

25. Carolyn Woods Eisenberg, *Drawing the line: The American decision to divide Germany, 1944–1949* (Cambridge: Cambridge University Press, 1996); James Jay Carafano, *Waltzing into the Cold War: The Struggle for Occupied Austria* (College Station: Texas A&M University Press, 2002); James Edward Miller, *The United States and Italy, 1940–1950: The Politics and Diplomacy of Stabilization* (Chapel Hill: University of North Carolina Press, 1986), chs. 6–9.

26. Benn Steil, *The Marshall Plan: Dawn of the Cold War* (Oxford: Oxford University Press, 2018); Lindsey A. O'Rourke, *Covert Regime Change: America's Secret Cold War* (Ithaca, NY: Cornell University Press, 2018), 107–110; George F. Kennan, "The Sources of Soviet Conduct," *Foreign Affairs* 25, no. 4(1947): 566–583; Carolyn Woods Eisenberg, *Drawing the line: The American decision to divide Germany, 1944–1949* (Cambridge: Cambridge University Press, 1996), ch. 10.

27. Anne Applebaum, *Iron Curtain: The Crushing of Eastern Europe 1944–1956* (New York: Doubleday, 2012), 455–461; Frederick Kempe, *Berlin 1961: Kennedy, Khrushchev, and the Most Dangerous Place on Earth* (New York: Penguin, 2011); A. James. McAdams, *Germany Divided: From the Wall to Reunification* (Princeton, NJ: Princeton University Press, 1994), ch. 1.

28. John W. Dower, *Embracing Defeat: Japan in the Wake of World War II* (New York: WW Norton & Company, 2000); Michael Schaller, *The American Occupation of Japan: The Origins of the Cold War in Asia* (Oxford: Oxford University Press, 1985).

29. Odd Arne Westad, *Decisive Encounters: The Chinese Civil War, 1946–1950* (Palo Alto: Stanford University Press, 2003); Steven I. Levine, "A New Look at American Mediation in the Chinese Civil War: The Marshall Mission and Manchuria," *Diplomatic History* 3, no. 4 (1979): 349–376; Chen Jian, "The Myth of America's "Lost Chance" in China: A Chinese Perspective in Light of New Evidence," *Diplomatic History* 21, no. 1 (1997): 77–86.

30. George M. McCune, "Post-War Government and Politics of Korea," *Journal of Politics* 9, no. 4 (1947): 605–623; George M. McCune, "Korea: The First Year of Liberation," *Pacific Affairs* 20, no. 1 (1917): 3–17.; Gregg A. Brazinsky, *Nation Building in South Korea: Koreans, Americans, and the Making of a Democracy* (Chapel Hill, NC: University of North Carolina Press, 2007); James I. Matray, "Hodge Podge: American Occupation Policy in Korea, 1945–1948," *Korean Studies* 19, no. 1 (1995): 17–38; Herring, *From Colony to Superpower*, 639–645; David S. McLellan, "Dean Acheson and the Korean War," *Political Science Quarterly* 83, no. 1 (1968): 16–39.

31. Bruce Cumins, *The Korean War: A History* (New York: Modern Library, 2010); William Stueck, *The Korean War: An International History* (Princeton, NJ: Princeton University Press, 1995).

32. Michael Cox and Doug Stokes, *US Foreign Policy*, 3rd edition, (New York: Oxford University Press, 2018), ch. 6.

33. Stephen Kinzer, *All the Shah's Men: An American Coup and the Roots of Middle East Terror* (Hoboken, NJ: John Wiley & Sons, 2003).

34. George S. Eckardt, *Vietnam Studies: Command and Control, 1950–1969* (Washington, DC: Department of the Army, 1974).

35. Paul Musgrave and Daniel H. Nexon, "Defending Hierarchy from the Moon to the Indian Ocean: Symbolic Capital and Political Dominance in Early Modern China and the Cold War," *International Organization* 72, no. 3 (2018): 610.

36. Steven Levitsky and Kenneth M. Roberts, eds., *The Resurgence of the Latin American Left* (Baltimore: JHU Press, 2011), 8.

37. Richard H. Immerman, "Guatemala as Cold War History," *Political Science Quarterly* 95, no. 4 (1980): 653.

38. Kate Doyle and Peter Kornbluh, "CIA and Assassinations: The Guatemala 1954 Documents," CIA and Assassinations: The Guatemala 1954 Documents, accessed December 7, 2018, https://nsarchive2.gwu.edu/NSAEBB/NSAEBB4/.

39. Immerman, "Guatemala as Cold War History," 633.

40. Immerman, "Guatemala as Cold War History," 634.

41. Immerman, "Guatemala as Cold War History," 638.

42. Immerman, "Guatemala as Cold War History," 645.

43. Immerman, "Guatemala as Cold War History," 645.

44. Lindsey A. O'Rourke, *Covert Regime Change: America's Secret Cold War* (Ithaca, NY: Cornell University Press, 2018), 53–57, 118–120, 194–224.

45. Immerman, "Guatemala as Cold War History," 652.

46. Stephen G. Rabe, "The Johnson Doctrine," *Presidential Studies Quarterly* 36, no. 1 (March 2006): 45–58.

47. Michael R. Hall, *Sugar and Power in the Dominican Republic: Eisenhower, Kennedy, and the Trujillos*, No. 13 (Westport: Greenwood Publishing Group, 2000).

48. Stephen G. Rabe, *The Most Dangerous Area in the World: John F. Kennedy Confronts Communist Revolution in Latin America* (Chapel Hill: University of North Carolina Press Books, 2014), 37.

49. Rabe, *The Most Dangerous Area in the World*, 39.

50. Abraham F. Lowenthal, "The United States and the Dominican Republic to 1965: Background to Intervention," *Caribbean Studies* 10, no. 2 (1970): 30–55, https://www.jstor.org/stable/25612211; Adam B. Siegal, *The Use of Naval Forces in the Post-War Era: U.S. Navy and U.S. Marine Corps Crisis Response Activity, 1946–1990*, Center for Naval Analysis, accessed April 3, 2022, https://www.history.navy.mil/research/library/online-reading-room/title-list-alphabetically/u/use-naval-forces-post-war-era.html.

51. "LBJ Regretted Ordering U.S. Troops into Dominican Republic in 1965, White House Tapes Confirm; Yet He Insisted," National Security Archive, April 28, 2015, https://nsarchive2.gwu.edu/NSAEBB/NSAEBB513.

52. Major Lawrence M. Greenberg, "United States Army Unilateral and Coalition Operations in the 1965 Dominican Republic Intervention," *U.S. Army Center of Military History*, 1987, https://history.army.mil/html/books/093/93-5-1/CMH_Pub _93-5.pdf.

53. Graham T. Allison, "Conceptual models and the Cuban missile crisis," *American Political Science Review* 63, no. 3 (1969): 689–718; Ernest R. May and Philip Zelikow, eds., *The Kennedy Tapes: Inside the White House During the Cuban Missile Crisis* (New York: WW Norton & Company, 2002); Susan Peterson and Christopher Wenk, "Domestic Institutional Change and Foreign Policy: A Comparative Study of U.S. Intervention in Guatemala and Nicaragua," *Security Studies* 11, no. 1 (2001): 53–76.

54. Edward Miller, *Misalliance: Misalliance: Ngo Dinh Diem, The United States, And The Fate Of South Vietnam* (Cambridge, MA: Harvard University Press, 2013); Elizabeth N. Saunders, *Leaders at War: How Presidents Shape Military Interventions* (Ithaca, NY: Cornell University Press, 2011), ch. 3.

55. Eckhardt, *Vietnam Studies*.

56. Eckhardt, *Vietnam Studies*; Campbell Craig and Fredrik Logevall, *America's Cold War* (Cambridge, MA: Harvard University Press, 2009).

57. Saunders, *Leaders at War: How Presidents Shape Military Interventions*, ch. 4.

58. Fredrik Logevall, *Choosing War: The Lost Chance for Peace and the Escalation of War in Vietnam* (Berkeley: University of California Press, 1999); Herring, *From Colony to Superpower: U.S. Foreign Relations Since 1776*, ch. 16; Saunders, *Leaders at War: How Presidents Shape Military Interventions*, ch. 5.

59. The US involvement in Laos would become the longest lasting intervention of the era, with a cumulative duration of 4,063 days. See Table 1 in the appendix for details on all other military interventions.

60. Robert A. Pape, *Bombing to Win: Air Power and Coercion in War* (Ithaca, NY: Cornell University Press, 1996), ch. 6; Leslie H. Gelb, *The Irony of Vietnam: The System*

Worked, (Washington, DC: Brookings Institution Press, 1979); Herring, *From Colony to Superpower: U.S. Foreign Relations Since 1776*, ch. 17.

61. "U.S. Spent $141-Billion In Vietnam in 14 years." *The New York Times,* January 19, 1975, https://www.nytimes.com/1975/05/01/archives/us-spent-141billion-in-viet nam-in-14-years.html.

62. "U.S. Spent $141-Billion In Vietnam in 14 years."

63. "Vietnam War U.S. Military Fatal Casualty Statistics," *U.S. National Archives*, accessed May 20, 2020, https://www.archives.gov/research/military/vietnam-war/casualty-sta tistics.

64. As calculated by MIP's case study analysis on Vietnam, included as supplemental documentation.

65. Herring, *From Colony to Superpower*, 770–797; Robert S. Litwak, *Détente and the Nixon Doctrine: American foreign policy and the pursuit of stability, 1969–1976* (Cambridge: Cambridge University Press, 1986); John Lewis Gaddis, *The Cold War: A New History* (New York: Penguin, 2005), 179–194.

66. Herring, *From Colony to Superpower*, 803–805.

67. Evelyn Goh, *Constructing the U.S. Rapprochement with China, 1961–1974: From "Red Menace" to "Tacit Ally"* (Cambridge: Cambridge University Press, 2005); Margaret MacMillan, *Nixon and Mao: The Week that Changed the World* (New York: Random House, 2007); Herring, *From Colony to Superpower*, ch. 17; Steven M. Goldstein and Randall Schriver, "An uncertain relationship: the United States, Taiwan and the Taiwan relations act," *The China Quarterly* 165 (2001): 147–172.

68. Herring, *From Colony to Superpower*, 804–811; Roy Licklider, "The Power of Oil: The Arab Oil Weapon and the Netherlands, the United Kingdom, Canada, Japan, and the United States," *International Studies Quarterly* 32, no. 2 (1988): 205–226.

69. Herring, *From Colony to Superpower,* 854–855; Bruce R. Kuniholm, "The Carter Doctrine, the Reagan Corollary, and Prospects for United States Policy in Southwest Asia," *International Journal* 41, no. 2 (1986): 342–361; Hermann F. Eilts, "Security Considerations in the Persian Gulf," *International Security* 5, no. 2 (1980): 79–113.

70. Herring, *From Colony to Superpower,* 847–851, 872–875, 878–880; David Patrick Houghton, *U.S. Foreign Policy and the Iran Hostage Crisis* (Cambridge: Cambridge University Press, 2001); Charles Kurzman, *The Unthinkable Revolution in Iran*, (Cambridge, MA: Harvard University Press, 2004); Gary Sick, "Trial by Error: Reflections on the Iran-Iraq War," *Middle East Journal* 43, no. 2 (1989): 230–245; Joyce Battle, "Shaking Hands with Saddam Hussein: The U.S. Tilts toward Iraq, 1980–1983," National Security Archive Electronic Briefing Book No. 82, George Washington University National Security Archive, https://nsarchive2. gwu.edu//NSAEBB/NSAEBB82/index.htm; Alexandra T. Evans and A. Bradley Potter, "When Do Leaders Change Course? Theories of Success and the American Withdrawal from Beirut, 1983–1984," *Texas National Security Review* 2, no. 2 (February 2019): 1–30.

71. Ted Galen Carpenter, "U.S. Aid to Anti-Communist Rebels: The 'Reagan Doctrine' and its Pitfalls," Cato Policy Analysis #74, Cato Institute, https://www.cato.org/publi cations/policy-analysis/us-aid-anticommunist-rebels-reagan-doctrine-its-pitfa

lls; James M. Scott, "Reagan's Doctrine? The Formulation of an American Foreign Policy Strategy," *Presidential Studies Quarterly* 26, no. 4 (1996): 1047–1061; Chester Pach, "The Reagan Doctrine: Principle, Pragmatism, and Policy," *Presidential Studies Quarterly* 36, no. 1 (2006): 75–88; Michael McFaul, "Rethinking the 'Reagan Doctrine' in Angola," *International Security* 14, no. 3 (1989): 99–135; Raymond W. Copson and Richard P. Cronin, "The 'Reagan Doctrine' and Its Prospects," *Survival* 29, no. 1 (1987): 40–55.

72. Lynn E. Davis, "Lessons of the INF Treaty," *Foreign Affairs* 66, no. 4 (1988): 720–734; Herring, *From Colony to Superpower*, 868–871; Andrew E. Busch, "Ronald Reagan and the Defeat of the Soviet Empire," *Presidential Studies Quarterly* 27, no. 3 (1997): 451–466; Arnold Horelick, "U.S.-Soviet Relations: The Return of Arms Control," *Foreign Affairs* 63, no. 3 (1984): 511–537.

73. Herring, *From Colony to Superpower*, 893–908; Joshua R. Itzkowitz Shifrinson, "Deal or No Deal? The End of the Cold War and the U.S. Offer to Limit NATO Expansion," *International Security* 40, no. 4 (2016): 7–44; Svetlana Savranskaya and Thomas Blanton, "A Different October Revolution: Dismantling the Iron Curtain in Eastern Europe," *National Security Archive Electronic Briefing Book No. 290*, George Washington University National Security Archive, October 9, 2009, https://nsarchi ve2.gwu.edu/NSAEBB/NSAEBB290/index.htm; Thomas Blanton and Svetlana Savranskaya, "The Fall of the Berlin Wall, 25th Anniversary," *National Security Archive Electronic Briefing Book No. 490*, George Washington University National Security Archive, November 9, 2014, https://nsarchive2.gwu.edu/NSAEBB/NSAEBB490/.

Chapter 4 Appendix

Table A4.1 List of US Military Interventions with Duration and Fatalities, 1946–1989

Start Year	Name	Duration (Days)	US Battle Deaths	State B Battle Deaths	Total Battle Deaths	US Total Deaths	State B Total Deaths
1946	Turkish Strait Crisis	61	0	0	0	0	0
1946	Airspace Violations in Yugoslavia	10	15	0	15	15	0
1947	Uruguay Presidential Inauguration	1	0	0	0	0	0
1948	Greek Civil War	596	1	50000	50000	1	100000
1948	Arab-Israeli Conflict Evacuation		0	0	0	1	0
1948	Berlin Airlift	286	0	0	0	31	0
1949	Yugoslavia Split from Eastern Bloc	857	0	75	75	0	75
1950	Korean War	1123	34000	1006000	1257000	36835	1606000
1951	US Protection of Taiwan	319	0	376	376	0	376
1953	Air interdictions with China & Russia	51	16	21	37	16	21
1953	Aircraft Interception Russia	3	0	0	0	0	0
1953	First Taiwanese Strait Crisis	323	0	0	0	1	393
1954	Cathay Pacific Douglas DC-4 Shootdown	4	0	0	0	0	0
1954	Guatemala Coup D'état	68	0	0	0	0	0
1954	Threat to North Korea	1	0	0	0	0	0
1955	Chinese Air Battle	1	0	3	1.5	0	3
1955	Military Advisors to Vietnam	3461	406			406	

(continued)

Table A4.1 Continued

Start Year	Name	Duration (Days)	US Battle Deaths	State B Battle Deaths	Total Battle Deaths	US Total Deaths	State B Total Deaths
1956	Search & Rescue in East China Sea	2	16	0	16	16	0
1956	Suez Crisis	5	0	999	999	0	999
1957	Skirmish over Chinese Air Space	2	0	0	0	0	0
1958	Second Taiwan Strait Crisis	150	0	440	900	0	1118
1958	Tension with Iraq	277	0	0	0	0	0
1958	Operation Blue Bat	161	0	6000	6000	0	6000
1958	Air Incidents with North Korea	32	0	0	0	0	0
1958	Berlin Corridor Issue	322	0	0	0	0	0
1958	Accidental Violations of Soviet Airspace	90	17	0	17	17	0
1959	Rescue Operations During Cuban Crisis	365	0	0	0	0	0
1960	Bay of Pigs Invasion	5	122	2176	2298	122	2176
1960	Congo Crisis	1252	0	0	0	0	0
1960	Downing of US Spy Planes in Russia	695	4	0	0	4	0
1961	Dominican Republic Intervention	166	0	0	0	0	0
1961	Berlin Crisis	95	0	0	0	0	0
1961	Checkpoint Charlie Standoff	1	0	0	0	0	0
1962	Quemoy Shelling	345	0	unclear	unclear	0	unclear
1962	Cuban Missile Crisis	29	0	0	0	0	0
1962	Laos Civil War	4063	728	unclear	unclear	728	-9
1962	Support for Thai Regime	203	0	0	0	0	0
1963	Haiti—Dominican Republic Dispute	38	0	0	0	0	0

Year	Event						
1964	Cambodia Bombing Campaign	1753	4	8	6	4	N/A
1964	Operations Dragon Rouge & Dragon Noir	2	2	unclear	4	4	1500
1964	Vietnam War	311	58000	1100000	1408000	58000	2000000
1965	China/US Air Skirmishes	1041	2	0	2	2	0
1965	Operation Power Pack	512	44	1425	1469	44	2000
1965	Air Skirmish in North Korea	1	0	0	0	0	0
1966	Guatemalan Civil War		0	0	0	0	0
1967	Stanleyville Mutiny	31	0				
1967	Six Day War Rescue	9	63	0	63	63	0
1967	Sea of Japan Bumpings	2	0	0	0	0	0
1968	Buzzing of US Navy in Egypt	1	0	0	0	0	0
1968	Seizure of USS *Pueblo*	335	1	0	1	1	0
1969	Chinese Fishing Boat Provocation	16	0	0	0	0	0
1969	Shooting Down of US Plane, N Korea	3	31	0	31	31	0
1970	Cambodia Campaign in Vietnam War	61					
1970	Armenia detention	21	0	0	0	0	0
1970	Jordanian Crisis/Black September	16	0	0	0	0	4000
1971	US/Cuba Ship Seizures	306	0	0	0	0	0
1972	Bombing of Chinese lifeboats	1	0	13	1	0	13
1973	Yom Kippur War/October War	24	0	0	0	0	0
1975	Mayaguez crisis	4	18		18	41	
1975	Show of US Planes against N Korea	199	0	0	0	0	0
1976	Fishing Vessel Seizure in Cuba	4	0	0	0	0	0
1976	Evacuation of Beirut	4	0	0	0	0	0

(*continued*)

Table A4.1 Continued

Start Year	Name	Duration (Days)	US Battle Deaths	State B Battle Deaths	Total Battle Deaths	US Total Deaths	State B Total Deaths
1976	Panmunjom Tree Incident	3	2	0	2	2	0
1977	North Korea Hostilities	408	3	0	3	3	0
1978	Battle of Kolwezi	26	0	220	900	0	220
1978	US-USSR Tensions over Iran	47	0	0	0	0	0
1979	Caribbean task force	82	0	0	0	0	0
1979	Reunification Talks skirmishes	647	0	11	11	0	11
1979	Russia Torpedo Seizure	2	0	0	0	0	0
1980	Iran Hostages Rescue Mission	2	8	0	8	8	0
1980	Anorack Express Exercise	7	0	0	0	0	0
1981	Tension with Cuba over El Salvador	13	0	0	0	0	0
1981	Gulf of Sidra Incident	9	0	0	0	0	0
1981	Salvadorian Civil War	3597	3	27000	27000	3	75000
1982	Sinai Peacekeeping	128	0	0	0	248	0
1982	Greco-Turkish Tensions	473	0	0	0	0	0
1982	Contra Affair	92	0	0	0	0	0
1982	Kuril Islands Dispute	1212	0	0	0	0	0
1982	Lebanese Civil War	582	265	9797	11153	265	19000
1983	US Violation of Cuban Airspace	1	0	0	0	0	0
1983	Invasion of Grenada/Op Urgent Fury	55	19	45	64	19	69
1983	Strait of Hormuz conflict	300	0	0	0	0	0

Year	Event						
1983	AWACS Deployment	5	0	0	0	0	0
1983	Chadian Civil War	23	0	0	0	0	0
1983	US Support for Honduras	1710	0	29	29	0	29
1983	North/South Korea Skirmishes	194	0	N/A	N/A	0	2
1983	Able Archer	180	0	0	0	0	0
1984	Red Sea Minesweeping	137	0	0	0	0	0
1984	Assistance to Saudi defense	1	0	0	0	0	0
1984	Attack on Omdurman	38					
1985	Iran—Iraq War	113	0	0	0	0	0
1985	Achille Lauro Hijacking	4	1	0	0	0	0
1985	Libya-Egypt border tensions	11	0	0	0	0	0
1986	Drug seizure in Bolivia	1	0	0	0	0	0
1986	Sonic Boom event	1	0	0	0	0	0
1986	US Merchant Seizure	1	0	0	0	0	0
1986	Gulf of Sidra Incident	2	0	72	72	0	72
1986	Operation El Dorado Canyon	23	2	55	57	72	55
1987	USS Stark Incident	2	37	0	37	2	0
1987	Political Unrest in Panama	199	0	0	0	37	0
1988	Downing of Libyan Jets	2	0	2	2	0	2
1989	Andean Initiative War on Drugs		0	0	0	0	0
1989	Operation Just Cause	55	23	314	180	23	2100
1989	Philippines Coup Attempt	7	0	40	40	0	83

5

America the Unipolar Hegemon

*We live in a peaceful, prosperous time, but we can make it better. For a
new breeze is blowing, and a world refreshed by freedom seems reborn.
For in man's heart, if not in fact, the day of the dictator is over. The totalitarian era is passing, its old ideas blown away like leaves from an
ancient, lifeless tree.*[1]

George H. W. Bush, inauguration speech, January 20, 1989

A new breeze was blowing in the wake of the Cold War. The United States
stood alone as the liberal world hegemon, beginning its unipolar reign laden
with values-based missions of democratization and free market promotion.
But its unrivaled power was a double-edged sword for the progression of US
foreign policy. The United States lost its sense of purpose with the fall of the
Soviet Union. No longer driven by the acute security challenges that its Cold
War grand strategy rested upon, the post–Cold War era required a reorientation of US grand strategy. The United States needed to identify a new set of
national interests to pursue. This proved difficult.

From 1990 to 2000, the United States held to the self-proclaimed good
intentions of democratization, human rights promotion, nuclear nonproliferation, and free market expansion. Its new direction was evident in policies
like humanitarian military interventions, multilateral and post-conflict state
building operations, and a range of international free trade deals meant to
ensure regional cooperation and interdependence. Despite its increasing influence and power during this era, the United States continued to rely on
diplomacy and trade as pillars of its foreign policy, on top of its growing but
more multilateral militarism.

The new era got off to a good start. The Bush administration handled the
collapse of the Soviet Union rather effectively and supported Germany's

Dying by the Sword. Monica Duffy Toft and Sidita Kushi, Oxford University Press. © Oxford University Press 2023.
DOI: 10.1093/oso/9780197581438.003.0006

reunification shortly afterwards in 1990. America's first big military intervention in the 1990s was the quick ejection of Iraqi forces from Kuwait during the Gulf War in 1991. It was a resounding success, denoting the zenith of America's military power and multilateral influence.

But its more "principled" approach also blurred the means and aims of America's new grand strategic vision. Despite its democratic ideals, astounding power, and international respect, US leadership floundered in identifying a new coherent grand strategy in the post–Cold War era and applying it consistently and successfully across political crises. There was no unifying security threat to prioritize.

Taking office in 1993, President William J. Clinton's administration championed the resolution of nontraditional security threats. This included military interventions in distant civil wars and other human rights crises, and later anti-drug trafficking initiatives and nuclear nonproliferation efforts. Clinton also attempted to defend US economic and traditional security interests via multilateral tools, which was evident in the administration's renewed commitment to NATO, the General Agreement on Tariffs and Trade (GATT) and later the World Trade Organization (WTO), and other international economic institutions.[2]

But the Clinton administration failed to offer a coherent grand strategy, preferring to focus on domestic politics and respond to international events and crises as they occurred in an ad-hoc manner. This lack of a guiding grand strategy revealed itself in the selective application of humanitarian norms. There were relatively successful humanitarian military interventions like in the Balkans in 1999, but silence and nonintervention during the Rwandan genocide in 1994.[3] The 1993 Somalia intervention showcased the logistical flaws behind Clinton's humanitarian grand ideals, while the delayed US intervention in Bosnia in 1995 highlighted the truly reactionary nature of US interventionism during this time. A unifying grand strategy could have offered some structure and consistency to US foreign policy, allowing the world's hegemon to redefine or broaden its post–Cold War national interests in a consistent manner. If only it had one.

Nonetheless, despite the Soviet Union's demise, this era did perpetuate some of the key trends of the Cold War, including the US military presence in strategic parts of Eurasia and the containment of Iran and Iraq.[4] The United States also continued to accept new NATO members from the former Eastern bloc and preserve its interests in resource-rich Central Asia.[5] And the United States continued to push its neoliberal standards globally and support imperfect neoliberal institutions that allowed continued access to new markets and opportunities to exploit internal crises.[6]

In this chapter, we first analyze grand strategy trends during the unipolar era of US foreign policy before tracing patterns of US military interventions during the 1990s. With these larger patterns in mind, we then look at pivotal moments in which the United States employed its foreign policy vision and tools, perhaps most significantly during the 1999 NATO intervention in Kosovo.

The Unipole's New Grand Strategy?

As Charles Krauthammer wrote when the Soviet bloc collapsed, the United States found itself in its unipolar moment: "The immediate post-Cold War world is not multipolar. It is unipolar. The center of world power is the unchallenged superpower, the United States, attended by its Western allies."[7] Victory, however, also brought uncertainty for America. In the absence of a great power challenger or clears goals defined as national interests, the United States found itself without a grand strategy. The foreign policy establishment engaged in the "Kennan sweepstakes," the search for a new US grand strategy and grand strategist like George Kennan. As political scientist Colin Dueck recalls, Anthony Lake, the new national security adviser in 1993, suggested each member of the new foreign policy team had the chance to become the next Kennan by developing a new grand strategy to replace containment.[8] While no one ever won the Kennan sweepstakes by defining a single, lasting grand strategy, subsequent administrations constructed their own versions of what such a grand strategy should look like.

George H. W. Bush inherited the task of overseeing the successful conclusion of the Cold War and creating what he called "a new world order." He is considered one of the best foreign policy presidents in US history by numerous scholars, and in Joseph Nye's assessment, "like Eisenhower, he was among the most experienced men in international affairs to occupy the presidency, and this gave him excellent contextual intelligence."[9] Although a highly qualified and successful leader, Bush never presided over the creation of a new US grand strategy, nor was he interested in such an approach. When it came to grand strategy, "Bush is famous for saying 'I don't do the vision thing.'"[10] Nevertheless, Bush's diplomacy with the Soviet Union, his statecraft in bringing about the peaceful reunification of Germany within NATO, and his decision to intervene in the Gulf War with a multilateral coalition, all laid some of the foundations of a grand strategic posture in the post-Cold War era. These foundations included a unifying spirit in overcoming the adversities of the Cold War, internationalism, collective security, multilateralism, and military interventionism.

In the 1990s, the United States moved from waging predominantly unilateral interventions to waging more multilateral ones, often sanctioned by the UN. As Table 5.1 confirms, US militarism after 1990 was characterized by a dramatic increase in bilateral, multilateral, and UN-based military operations relative to unilateral operations, which had consisted of nearly 80 percent of all US interventions prior to the 1990s. The years from 1997 to 1999, however, saw the United States briefly revert to its old unilateral ways, as the UN could not reach a consensus on many humanitarian interventions that the United States and other Western actors wanted to conduct.

The Clinton administration continued to build on these internationalist foundations while designing a new grand strategy. James Boys writes,

> In his statement unveiling the grand strategy, President Clinton insisted that although the Cold War was over, American leadership remained essential. Accordingly, the administration's policy was founded on three principles: "maintaining a defense capability strong enough to underwrite our commitments credibly," American economic strength at home and abroad, and the assertion that "the best way to advance America's interests worldwide is to enlarge the community of democracies and free markets throughout the world."[11]

Table 5.1 US Military Intervention Types, 1776–2019

	Type of Intervention	#	Share
Pre-1945	Unilateral	137	78.3%
	Bilateral/Multilateral	38	21.7%
1945–1989	Unilateral	66	75.9%
	Bilateral/Multilateral	17	19.5%
	UN	4	4.6%
Post-1990	Unilateral	56	57.7%
	Bilateral/Multilateral	28	28.9%
	UN	13	13.4%

In his inauguration address in January 1993, Clinton highlighted a vision of interdependence and his expanded understanding of national
interests: "To renew America, we must meet challenges abroad as well as at
home. There is no longer a clear division between what is foreign and what
is domestic. The world economy, the world environment, the world AIDS
crisis, the world arms race: they affect us all. Today, as an older order passes,
the new world is more free but less stable. Communism's collapse has called
forth old animosities and new dangers. Clearly, America must continue to
lead the world we did so much to make."[12]

The Clinton Doctrine was dubbed by some as "Engagement and
Enlargement" after the title of the 1996 National Security Strategy.[13]
Secretary of State Warren Christopher said, "In the latest round in a
century-old debate between engagement and isolationism, the United
States chooses Engagement."[14] National Security Advisor Anthony Lake
coined the term "Democratic Enlargement" as he believed the successor
to containment must be "enlargement of the world's free community of
market democracies."[15] A key part of enlargement was the transformation
of NATO for the new world order, including the integration of three former
Soviet bloc countries and the creation of the Partnership for Peace to build
relationships with other states in Europe and the former Soviet Union.
According to Zoltan Feher, "NATO became a comprehensive forum for
East–West security cooperation during the 1990s and therefore a stable
stakeholder in global security."[16]

In pursuing engagement and enlargement, Clinton's strategy built on
Bush's foundations of military interventionism and collective security. Such
a grand strategic posture led the United States to carry out humanitarian
interventions in Somalia, Haiti, Rwanda, Bosnia, and Kosovo in the 1990s.
Critics called this "liberal interventionism" or "liberal hegemony." In political scientist Barry Posen's view, "Liberal Hegemony is a costly, wasteful, and
self-defeating grand strategy."[17] Debates around liberal interventionism and
its legacy continued throughout the 1990s and beyond.

As Figure 5.1 shows, presidents Bush and Clinton maintained similar
military intervention patterns during this era of US economic growth and
unipolarity, highlighting the importance of systematic factors, rather than
individual personalities, in making foreign policy.

US grand strategy was inconsistent and blurry during its unprecedented
power in the 1990s. The data reveals a much more interventionist America
during its era of unipolarity, but also one that enjoyed the support of its allies

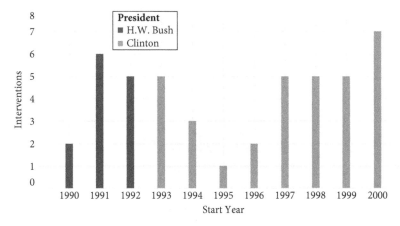

Figure 5.1. US Interventions by President, 1990–2000

and bolstered multilateral institutions to safeguard interdependencies and cooperation.

Empirical Patterns of US Interventions, 1990–2000

The post–Cold War era found the United States intervening at least once per year in different parts of the world. During the 1990s, the United States sought to protect human rights and promote democracy abroad, at least rhetorically. Thus, it is no surprise that the United States intervened in regions with a high proportion of civil wars and intrastate crises.

By the mid-1990s, the United States started to involve itself more frequently in conflicts in the Middle East, cementing its military presence in the region. This was followed by a steady rise in interventions in intrastate conflicts in sub-Saharan Africa, as illustrated in Figure 5.2. The United States undertook almost half of its military interventions within the continent of Africa during its unipolar moment, with 39 percent of them in sub-Saharan Africa and 13 percent in the Middle East and North Africa. As its involvement in the Middle East and Africa rose, US military interventions in Latin America and the Caribbean declined to their lowest numbers yet, with Haiti as an outlier.

The humanitarian military operations in the Western Balkans were infrequent outliers. These interventions occurred in the aftermath of years of US

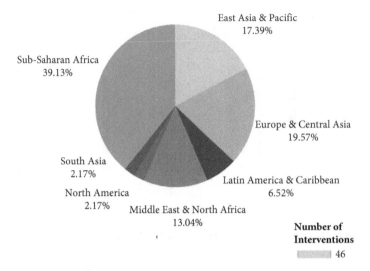

Figure 5.2. US Interventions by Region, 1990–2000

inactivity or diplomatic efforts to resolve the crises in the Balkans. Therefore, during the 1990s, military interventionism was still framed as the last resort for US foreign policy, often with dire humanitarian consequences as in the case of nonintervention in Rwanda.

Overall, the numbers of US interventions dropped from 104 cases in the previous era to 46, a 56 percent decline in intervention frequency. Yet these numbers can be misleading since the unipolar era was much shorter than earlier eras of US interventionism. In comparing eras by intervention rates per year, we see an astounding increase in the rate and hostility of US militarism in the 1990s, as Figure 5.3 highlights. In the 1990s, US intervention rates almost doubled from their Cold War levels, and hostility levels[18] remain elevated as well, despite the end of the US-Soviet rivalry that justified hyper militarism in previous decades.

Despite the high intervention rates, the United States was also reluctant to intervene during numerous ongoing genocides, such as in Rwanda and Bosnia. Thus, the United States had the luxury of selecting where to intervene, where to rescue only its own citizens, and where to stand down without sacrificing its own vital interests or security as the world hegemon.

This era reveals a paradox between US intervention frequency and power capabilities as measured by CINC. As Figure 5.4 illustrates, the United States intervened at higher rates in pursuit of less vital national interests during this

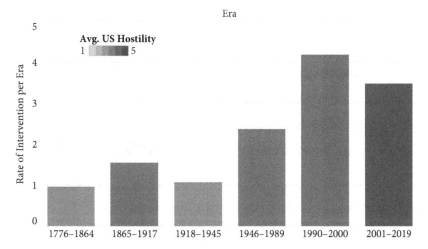

Figure 5.3. US Intervention Rates and Hostility Levels by Eras, 1990–2000

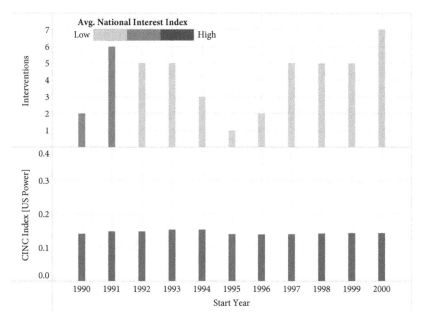

Figure 5.4. US Interventions by National Interests and Capabilities, 1990–2000

Citation: Correlates of War Project. *National Material Capabilities, 1816–2012*. Version 5. http://
www.correlatesofwar.org; J. David Singer, "Reconstructing the Correlates of War Dataset on
Material Capabilities of States, 1816–1985," *International Interactions*, 14 (1987); 115–32

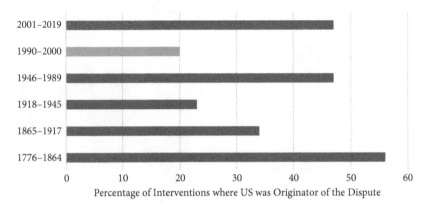

Figure 5.5. Percentage of US-Originated Disputes by Era

era. While it did not have any peer competitors, CINC also indicates that US power capabilities were lower than previous peaks, particularly right after World War I and World War II. But the United States still enjoyed global primacy across economic, political, military, and cultural sources of power, marking unipolarity for the United States, if only for a moment in time.

Without major geopolitical rivalries or clear and vital threats to homeland security, it is not surprising that the United States originated only 20 percent of its conflicts during this era—the lowest proportion out of any era—as shown on Figure 5.5. Instead, the United States responded to existing crises as a third-party actor. This pattern did not last after 2001.

The United States experienced a boom in economic prosperity in the 1990s, including drastically lower unemployment rates and a rise in international exports. GDP per capita grew exponentially through the early 1990s, peaking in 2000. These patterns of economic growth seem to correlate with greater frequency of interventionism more so than CINC power capabilities do, as shown in Figure 5.6. It is important to note that the economic prosperity and power capabilities of a country reflect different societal indicators—one reflects the growing prosperity of the average citizen, ideally, while the other reflects the much narrower indicator of military power. At times, these two measures of growth can be seen as trade-offs: does a country such as the United States invest more in domestic economic production and job growth or does it invest its money and time into building up its defense industry, which is separated from the domestic experiences of most citizens?

Despite the end of the Cold War military buildup, US military spending by the late 1990s equated to one-third of total global military spending, which

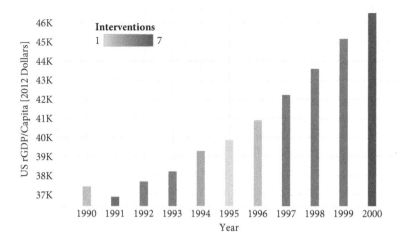

Figure 5.6. US GDP Trends and Interventions, 1990–2000

Citation: Bureau of Economic Analysis (BEA). Gross Domestic Product. *U.S. Department of Commerce, 2019.* https://www.bea.gov/data/gdp/gross-domestic-product; Loius Johnston and Samuel H. Williamson. "What Was the U.S. GDP Then?" *Measuring Worth*, 2018. https://www.mea suringworth.com/datasets/usgdp/.

can partially be explained by the economic boom that defined the era.[19] But the United States did not just rely on military and economic might; it had a wide network of values-based alliances that served as "force multipliers" across the world, helping the United States to use its political credibility and soft, cultural, and intellectual power to pursue its goals, like democratization.[20] Figure 5.7 shows that almost all target states were marked by highly autocratic regimes, with the Central African Republic in 1996 and Russia in 2000 being exceptions.

Interventions often justified to democratize target countries or defend human rights enjoyed a very high rate of initial success, as shown in Figure 5.8. Over 60 percent ended in a US victory and 6 percent in a yield by the target state. The United States' unrivaled power and normative influence made it impossible for target states to emerge victorious, signaled by the complete lack of State B victories. But short-term victories are not the full story as many of these interventions were followed by long periods of postconflict rebuilding with varying levels of success and shared sovereignty between the United States (often through NATO or the UN) and the target state, which would come to further define US foreign policy in the post-2001 era.

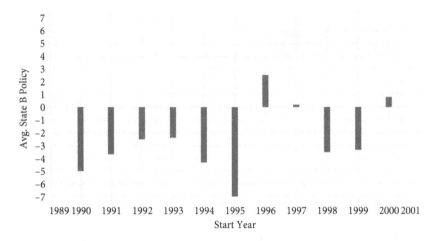

Figure 5.7. State B Democratization Scores, 1990–2000

Citation: Monty Marshall and Ted Robert Gurr, "POLITY IV Project: Political Regime Characteristics and Transitions, 1800–2017," *Center for Systemic Peace,* http://www.systemicpeace.org/polityproject.html.

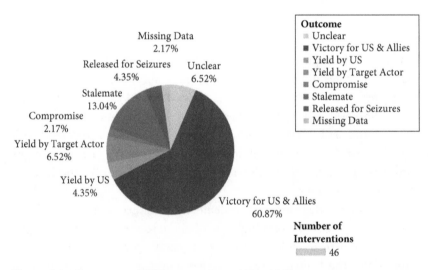

Figure 5.8. Outcomes of US Interventions, 1990–2000

Because the United States mainly acted as a third party to existing conflicts during the era, its comparative hostility levels are more balanced relative to the target state. Indeed, there are several instances in which the target states employed greater hostility against the United States, as depicted in Figure 5.9.

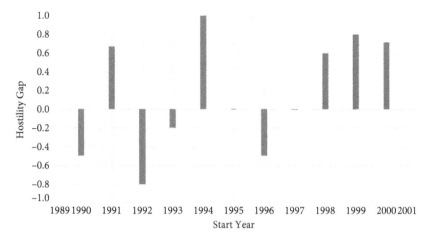

Figure 5.9. Comparative Hostility Gap between the United States and State B (US Hostility - State B Hostility Levels), 1990–2000

It should come as no surprise that the United States intervened mostly in pursuit of social protection objectives during this time. In some instances, it also toned down its hostility levels by narrowing its intervention mandates to the protection of only American citizens and properties abroad during an intrastate conflict, as in the tragic case of Rwanda in 1994. This pattern of intervention objectives displayed in Figure 5.10 represents a stark foreign policy change from the Cold War era, which prioritized the maintenance of favorable foreign regimes and policy objectives.

Ultimately, much of US foreign policy and interventionism in the 1990s relied on the rhetoric and objectives of universal human rights. Figure 5.11 traces the Physical Integrity Index and frequencies of US interventionism. The Physical Integrity Index is an additive index constructed from torture, extrajudicial killing, political imprisonment, and disappearance indicators ranging from 0 (no government respect for rights) to 8 (full government respect).[21] The graph reveals that the United States intervened in countries with extremely low levels of human rights protection.

But it is difficult to separate the negative effects of the US intervention from the humanitarian catalysts for intervention in the first place. In other words, while humanitarian objectives were widely used to justify US foreign policy choices in the 1990s, it is unclear whether US foreign policy contributed to an amelioration or further degradation of human rights within the target countries during this era.

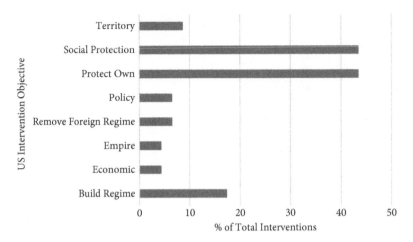

Figure 5.10. US Intervention Objectives, 1990–2000

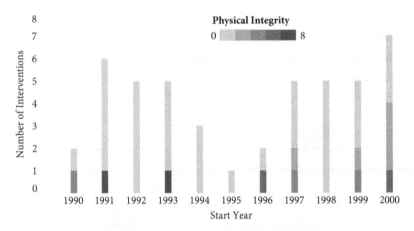

Figure 5.11. Human Rights and US Interventions, 1990–2000

Citation: David L. Cingranelli and David L. Richards, *The Cingranelli-Richards Human Rights Dataset*, *Version 2008.03.12*, http://www.humanrightsdata.org.

Historical Narratives of America the Unipolar Hegemon, 1990–2000

As the world's sole remaining superpower, the United States could use its power to promote cooperation or foment division. It could provide benign global leadership, public goods, and peace or embark upon a road of ruthless imperialism, war, and domination.[22] Unipolarity is historically rare, so few knew what to expect in 1990, and many worried about the stability and durability of a unipolar system.[23] Some even thought the United States would revert to an isolationist stance, given its behavior after World War I. But one thing was clear—the post–Cold War era brought uncertainty for America. In the absence of a great power challenger, the United States found itself without a unifying grand strategy.[24]

Within the ten short years of the era, the United States ramped up its rate of interventionism relative to all previous eras. Most of the interventions targeted the Middle East, North Africa, and sub-Saharan Africa, regions where the United States previously played a relatively minor militaristic role. Moreover, the fundamental characteristics of the interventions changed. US foreign policy was based on the inconsistent application of a murky vision that never fully formed. Unlike its former self, the unipolar America intervened predominantly within intrastate crises, usually relying on humanitarian justifications to build political will among its allies. NATO troops and planes were often sent to places of the world that previously had little to no bearing on traditional US national interests.

The Beginning of America's Perpetual Interventions in the Middle East

Prior to 1990, US policy in Iraq was based on economic and political incentives to placate Saddam Hussein's behavior, without military threats. Some critics later blamed this soft, conciliatory approach for causing the Gulf War, saying that if the Bush administration adopted a tougher approach including direct military threats the war may have been avoided.[25]

On August 2, 1990, the Iraqi army invaded and occupied neighboring Kuwait. Though the Bush administration's condemnation was swift, the United States was likely aware of Saddam's aims beforehand and may have unintentionally encouraged the invasion. One interpretation of the US diplomatic initiative prior to the Iraqi invasion of Kuwait goes as follows. On July 25, the US ambassador to Iraq, April Glaspie, met with Saddam in Baghdad, and she emphasized language from a previous cable by Secretary of State James Baker that the United States had "no opinion" on the border dispute with Kuwait.[26] Later, Glaspie was asked to deliver Bush's cable response orally, which stated that the administration "continues to desire better relations with Iraq."[27] Interpreting this statement as a signal that America would step aside, Saddam invaded Kuwait the following week. But Glaspie wasn't as directly to blame as the original narrative assumes. At the time of her meeting, the administration had yet to formulate and share a decision on how the United States would respond to an Iraqi invasion of Kuwait, partially because most US elites did not view an invasion as probable.[28]

Incredulous as the administration was of the invasion, the administration viewed the Kuwait conflict as the first real test of Bush's "new world order" promoting democracy, human rights, and the rule of law. Officials feared that if they let Saddam get away with the invasion, it would set an ominous precedent to other dictators around the world, so they stressed the need for immediate action to enforce America's new world order.[29]

After the invasion, the United States froze Iraq's and Kuwait's assets in America. The United States then enlisted the help of the United Nations to galvanize world opinion against Iraq. The UN Security Council unanimously adopted Resolution 660, which called for Iraq's withdrawal from Kuwait, and Resolution 661, which imposed severe economic sanctions against Baghdad. At the same time, reports emerged alleging that the CIA and Army Special Forces were covertly encouraging and supporting Kuwaiti resistance movements against Iraqi forces.[30] And diplomatic efforts at the UN culminated with Resolution 678 on November 29, which authorized "all necessary means"—meaning war—to remove Iraqi troops from Kuwait if Saddam failed to withdraw by January 15, 1991.

While economic and political pressure increased on Iraq, the United States and its allies prepared for the armed liberation of Kuwait. Between August and November 1990, the United States and its many coalition partners deployed over 400,000 troops to nearby Saudi Arabia as part of Operation Desert Shield and were thus prepared for military action when Saddam did not meet the January 15 deadline set by the UN.[31]

With all diplomatic efforts failing to convince Saddam to withdraw from Kuwait, Operation Desert Storm officially began on January 16. Phase one included an air campaign targeting Iraqi command and control centers in Kuwait and Iraq in addition to its air bases and nuclear and chemical weapons facilities. On February 24 (day thirty-nine of the war), the second phase of the campaign began, which took only 100 hours to complete. Phase two involved a ground campaign with Marine forces invading Kuwait from Saudi Arabia and forcing Iraqi troops back to the border. On February 27, the US-led coalition forces entered Kuwait City, liberating the country and declaring a ceasefire the next day.[32] By the end of the operation, the United States had deployed 532,000 troops, 1,800 aircraft, and 120 ships, on top of the many military resources deployed by its allies.[33]

The Bush administration made the conscious decision not to pursue Iraqi troops into their own territory or attempt to overthrow Saddam's regime, believing instead that a weakened army and internal revolutions would destabilize his government.[34] But this prediction proved incorrect, and Saddam cracked down on the civilian population with a vengeance to maintain power.

The Gulf War showcased American military superiority and reinvigorated a fighting force that was demoralized by Vietnam. The United States, however, also incurred substantial battle deaths, with 1,948 people dying across all military service branches. Yet these numbers were eclipsed by the deaths incurred by Iraqi forces and by civilians. Iraqi forces suffered 50,000 to 100,000 deaths, while an estimated 100,000 to 200,000 civilians died.[35] In the end, the Gulf War did not have the long-term stabilizing effects that the Bush administration desired. Murtaza Hussain also notes that the Gulf War was the first militant enforcement of liberal and democratic peace in the post–Cold War era. According to Hussain, "As a power that believes its values are universal, the United States seems to be unable to view illiberal states as completely legitimate, making it extremely difficult, if not impossible, to pursue good-faith diplomacy with them . . . This 'liberal intolerance' of political difference has helped fuel bloody proxy conflicts that may have been avoided had the United States been more willing, at least on principle, to accept the sovereignty of its rivals."[36]

After the war ended, Saddam's violent campaign against Iraq's civilian population prompted the United States to maintain a military presence in the area for the remainder of the decade. But unlike the original operation that enjoyed massive international support and UN approval, future US operations in Iraq, especially in the late 1990s, did not garner the same amount of multilateral support.

The United States waged its first clear humanitarian military intervention to protect the Kurdish civilian population in northern Iraq, after Baghdad violently suppressed an internal revolt.[37] By April 1991, there was an urgent humanitarian crisis with more than 1.5 million Kurdish Iraqis taking refuge in the bordering areas between Turkey and Iraq. The US military intervention aimed to rescue over one million Kurdish refugees, create a safe environment in northern Iraq, and then return Kurdish refugees to their homes. The United States and its allies relied on air power to deliver needed supplies including water, food, and medicine, and built temporary camps in the border areas to shelter refugees. To provide a secure environment, the United States and its allies deployed ground forces in northern Iraq and established a no-fly zone and a no-drive zone to prevent Iraqi air forces from crossing the 36th parallel. The United States also reconstructed damaged electrical plants and water distribution systems to help refugees return home. Up until the invasion of Iraq in 2003, the United States and its coalition continued to try to prevent further Iraqi aggression against the Kurds, warning and targeting Iraq's antiaircraft missile sites.[38]

In September 1992, the United States and its allies created another no-fly zone south of Iraq's 32nd parallel to halt Saddam's targeting of the Shi'a minority population and to force the government to comply with the ceasefire resolution.[39] In addition to continued American military involvement in Iraq for decades to come, the Gulf War paved the way for an established US presence in other parts of the Middle East. Continuing US troop presence was welcomed in Saudi Arabia, and the Navy's Fifth Fleet and stationed on-shore in Bahrain. Military cooperation with the United Arab Emirates and Oman also increased following the Gulf War.[40]

Thus, the United States started the 1990s on a high note with the fall of the Soviet Union and the victory in the Gulf War creating a sense of confidence in America's cultural and military supremacy and in its ability to enforce its new world order. At first, the Bush administration hoped to resolve the dispute through diplomatic and economic channels, but when sanctions and diplomacy failed to force Saddam out of Kuwait, it ushered in a preference for the quick and decisive nature of military force, one that would carry through to his successor. New security cooperation agreements, troop deployments, eager allies, and no-fly zones in the Middle East normalized the notion of a US military presence in far-off regions to protect foreign lives and promote global peace.

Humanitarian Interventions in Somalia, Haiti, but not Rwanda

In the 1990s, the United States' drive to democratize the world went hand in hand with the new phenomenon of humanitarian military interventions. It also often overlapped with regime change operations that went beyond humanitarian protection and stopping aggression. The United States began to

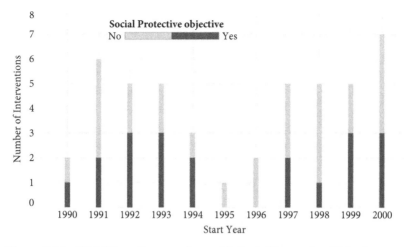

Figure 5.12. US Military Interventions with Social Protection Objectives, 1990–2000

intervene within humanitarian crises. As seen in Figure 5.12, the majority of US military interventions in the 1990s included social protective objectives for the target country.

The Bush administration followed limited humanitarian objectives. Even in the aftermath of the Gulf War, Bush refused to oust Saddam Hussein despite his grave human rights record. Bush even refused to invest in robust postconflict peacebuilding structures. Instead, Bush held to a limited doctrine of national interests and a more limited view of when to intervene on behalf of human rights.

But Bush inconsistently applied this limited doctrine in the case of Somalia in 1993, an intervention ending in disaster due to mission creep, despite good intentions. In April 1992, the UN Security Council voted to establish a humanitarian operation in Somalia, where a drought had increased political competition between warlords and ultimately created a humanitarian disaster with widespread starvation, forced displacement, and violence against civilians. But the small contingent of UN peacekeepers did not have the resources or the mandate to protect supplies or force political change on the ground. In the last few weeks of his presidency, Bush sent 25,000 US troops to assist the peacekeepers and provide food and medical assistance with the idea that they would eventually be replaced by UN forces.[41]

By the time Clinton took office, American public opinion on US involvement in Somalia had soured, compelling Clinton to immediately seek a way out. The US intervention in Somalia culminated in the October 1993 clash in Mogadishu when 18 American troops were killed and 78 wounded. Soon after, Clinton announced that American troops would depart and no longer pursue the capture of Somalia's most notorious warlord, Mohammad Farah Aideed.[42]

Still, Clinton believed in "assertive humanitarianism" and robust democratization of nations around the world. As many of Clinton's cabinet appointees were members of Carter's administration, they often pushed for more military deployments to defend human rights. But the Clinton administration's policy towards humanitarian crises was reactive. Clinton was not willing to risk American lives or spend more American money on these humanitarian missions—he simply wanted liberal hegemony on the cheap.[43]

The loss of the eighteen troops in Somalia also caused the Clinton administration to recalculate its willingness to use the military to protect human rights. After Somalia, Clinton set guidelines governing American support of humanitarian interventions worldwide, deciding that the United States would only commit troops if US interests were threatened or the crisis posed significant danger to international peace and security or human rights.[44] It's likely that Somalia prevented the Clinton administration from intervening to stop the genocide in Rwanda, where there was little national interest or international pressure to act.

Clinton's next challenge came in Haiti, where a military coup led by Lieutenant General Raoul Cedras overthrew the country's first democratically elected president, Jean-Bertrand Aristide, in 1991. Cedras and his militia conducted a brutal campaign to eliminate opposition, and gruesome images of massacres were broadcast worldwide. Forceful in his desire to restore democracy and end suffering, Clinton and the United Nations sent a 220-strong peacekeeping force on the USS *Harlan County*. However, the ship was turned around upon entry to Port-au-Prince by protestors, providing a significant blow to American credibility.

Undeterred, the United States continued to push the United Nations to take stronger action against the regime. On July 31, 1994, the UN Security Council passed Resolution 940, allowing the American-led multinational coalition to use "all means necessary" to remove the military leadership in Haiti.[45] But due to a last-minute diplomatic breakthrough under the threat of force, a deal was brokered to transfer power back to Aristide. The planned military operation with 25,000 troops readied for invasion was shifted to a peacekeeping mission. US troops landed peacefully in Haiti, and Aristide returned to the country on October 15, 1994.[46] Given Haiti's military weakness and strategic location, the almost-humanitarian intervention was relatively low-risk for US forces and there were also geopolitical risks beyond humanitarianism to consider.

Amid the turmoil and indecision over military operations in Somalia and Haiti, the Rwandan genocide was rapidly killing hundreds of thousands of Tutsis and moderate Hutu citizens. Paralyzed by its embarrassments after the incidents in Somalia and with the USS *Harlan County*, the Clinton administration chose not to intervene in Rwanda, instead focusing solely on getting Americans out of the troubled country. The speed of the murder of civilians on the ground also presented with vast logistical challenges, amongst other factors that muted possible intervention. As the US Ambassador to the UN Madeline Albright later stated, the outcomes of previous peacekeeping efforts affect future decisions; "When people want to know why we didn't do something in Rwanda, they all play together."[47]

The United States did, however, intervene in Rwanda after the genocide ended. On July 22, 1994, Clinton announced Operation Support Hope, pledging $250 million in aid and humanitarian relief to the almost one million refugees in nearby Zaire. The operation was run through the White House's national security advisor, in conjunction with the Defense Department, US Agency for International Development, and chairman of the Joint Chiefs of Staff—with the State Department notably absent. The US military airlifted food, provided access to clean water, and rebuilt basic infrastructure for the thousands of refugees.[48]

While the military interventions in Clinton's first term were defined by their humanitarian nature, national interest began to play a greater role as his presidency continued, and the president was much less eager to deploy troops overseas. Clinton ultimately decided to intervene in the Balkans in the late-1990s, albeit hesitantly, because public pressure to do so became so immense after the massacre in Srebrenica. He also feared the United States would look weak if it failed to intervene in Europe, a continent of much greater strategic interest and normative ties with the United States than Africa. But military action in the Balkans (both in the first conflict and in the war in Kosovo that followed in 1999) was limited to airstrikes and NATO-led bombing campaigns, as Clinton was still skeptical of putting boots on the ground in a foreign conflict that did not directly implicate American national or economic security. In the cases of Bosnia and Kosovo, the United States first tried to employ multilateral mechanisms like sanctions and arms embargoes in lieu of military action, but in both cases ultimately capitulated to a limited usage of force.

Crisis Event: Humanitarian Interventions in the Balkans

As cracks started to appear in the Soviet Union, the former state of Yugoslavia also began to fracture, marking the start of a long series of wars that would force millions to flee their homes and leave over 140,000 people dead throughout the Balkans by 2000.[49] The United States was initially hesitant to intervene in civil wars that it believed were driven by ancient ethnic and religious hatreds in the Balkans, but it supported NATO blockades to enforce UN sanctions on Yugoslavia, both by sea and by air via a no-fly zone starting in 1992.[50]

As a candidate, Clinton criticized the Bush administration's inaction in the Bosnian war, but he changed his tune once in office, choosing to continue the trend of US noninterventionism in the Balkan wars. The United States mostly limited itself to providing humanitarian relief. It airlifted food and supplies, supplied Bosnian Muslims with arms, and supported European diplomatic efforts, but refused to take military action. Until his departure from government in 1993, Chairman of the Joint Chiefs of Staff Colin Powell was firm that the United States did not have significant interest in the conflict and would thus not allow American intervention in Bosnia.[51] In addition, neither Congress nor the public supported committing US troops to the region, despite public knowledge of the ongoing humanitarian atrocities. The Clinton administration tried instead to contain the problem, hoping public attention would be soon diverted elsewhere.[52] It tried to downplay the atrocities committed in Bosnia as just another Balkans civil war enflamed by "ancient hatreds," until the pressure to "do something" became too intense and action was necessary.[53]

The international community's hand was forced after the Serbian massacre of 8,000 Bosnian Muslim civilian men and boys at Srebrenica in July 1995. Srebrenica was meant to be a "safe zone" for Bosnian Muslims, guarded by UN peacekeepers. Thus, the horrifying massacre was both an embarrassment and a horrible failure for the international community. After the United States and its allies failed to stop the horrors of Srebrenica, the United States and NATO decided the status quo could not hold, launching a "peace enforcement" operation to break the Serbian siege of Sarajevo. Almost

300 NATO aircraft undertook a bombing campaign targeting Serb storage depots, armories, repair facilities, and command and control nodes. By September 1995, nearly all Serb command headquarters and major defense posts were destroyed, indicating the effectiveness of air power.[54]

Later, the United States engineered a diplomatic breakthrough with the Dayton Accords in 1996, though the agreement was considered imperfect by all parties. Richard Holbrooke, the chief US negotiator, leveraged the incessant NATO bombing campaign to force the Bosnian Serbs to capitulate, thus ending the war. But Holbrooke was not satisfied with just a ceasefire—he wanted an agreement that would create a "unified, democratic, multiethnic, and tolerant Bosnia."[55] Though a laudable goal, its ambition and top-down approach made the agreement difficult to enforce and placed too many demands on the international community that subsequently went unfulfilled. Moreover, the ethnic divisions created by the agreement continue to prescribe an ethnicity-obsessed policy approach to managing the Balkans.

Left out of the Dayton Accords, the ethnic Albanian-majority territory of Kosovo descended into intrastate violence in 1997, when the Serbian state cracked down on ethnic Albanian Kosovar separatists and also targeted civilian populations in an ethnic cleansing campaign.[56] The Serbian strongman Slobodan Milošević's ethnic cleansing policies led to the expulsion of 1.5 million ethnic Albanians from Kosovo, the rape of more than 20,000 women, and the murder of more than 10,000 civilians.[57] But even after the failure to stop the Srebrenica genocide, the US government again hesitated to intervene in Kosovo. It was only in 1999, after many years of lukewarm diplomacy and after Secretary of State Madeline Albright convinced Clinton of the severity of the humanitarian crisis, that the United States and NATO undertook a bombing campaign—without UN approval—against Serbia. The Kosovo intervention became a precedent-setting case of humanitarian military intervention—it was the first time since the founding of the UN that a group of states, led by the United States, acted outside of international and domestic institutions to breach another state's sovereignty on solely humanitarian grounds.

While Clinton initially promised the American public that ground troops would not be sent to the conflict, Serbian targets proved resistant to NATO bombing. Clinton publicly affirmed in April 1999 that "all options were on the table" regarding military force.[58] However, the superiority of American air technology—including stealth bombers and precision-guided munitions that cost the United States an estimated $2.3 billion—forced a NATO victory, with some deeming it the latest "revolution in military affairs."[59] Though this new technology was hailed for its effectiveness and precision, between 489 and 529 civilians died in NATO's bombing campaign.[60] NATO's intervention did help force Serbia out of Kosovo, potentially stopping further ethnic cleansing and humanitarian atrocities. After a decade of NATO and European Union supervision, Kosovo declared unilateral independence from Serbia with US and EU support in 2008.

In the case of the Kosovo crisis, it is also important to note that it took years for the United States to consider the human rights abuses as worthy of military intervention. In other words, the United States relied on its military as a last resort when employing them toward humanitarian objectives in the Balkans. As neorealist John Mearsheimer stated at the time, "Most realists are offshore balancers, and most of us do not see any such threat emerging because of Kosovo."[61] Charles Krauthammer further denounced an intervention in Kosovo as liberal, amateurish policymaking, "righteous self-delusion" and "impossibly moralistic and universal."[62]

Without clear national interests stemming from involvement in the Balkans, the United States relied on passive attempts to negotiate with Slobodan Milosevic, which produced multiple failed ceasefires for the Kosovo "civil war." In March 1998, when General Wesley Clark warned of trouble in Kosovo, Vice Chairman of the Joint Chiefs of Staff Joseph Ralston responded, "Look, Wes, we've got a lot on our plates back here . . . We can't deal with any more problems."[63] At least until May 1998, there was little attention devoted to Kosovo's troubles in Washington. Even by the summer, when Alexander Vershbow, US Ambassador to NATO, wrote a memo pushing for a Dayton-style solution for Kosovo (with US troops leading an international peacekeeping force), he had no supporters in the White House.[64] Even by December 1998, US Major General Dennis Reimer, the Army chief of staff, responded to a warning of impending war from Clark with, "But we don't want to fight there."[65] As Republican Senator William Cohen confirmed during a postintervention interview, the majority of US policymakers and congressional members were reluctant to send even a small peacekeeping force to Kosovo in 1998.[66] Thus, it would be a mistake to assume the United States was especially trigger-happy in its precedent-setting humanitarian intervention in 1999.

But as the perception of the Kosovo crisis moved away from an ethnic and religious civil war and into the realm of a potential genocide like the one in Bosnia, the United States finally put the option of military intervention on the table.[67] Its normative credibility and values-based military institutions were now on the line. This transformation, however, was accelerated when US Ambassador William Walker witnessed the aftermath of the Raçak massacre in northern Kosovo, which killed 45 civilians. Walker subsequently held a press conference,[68] declaring Serbian security forces committed crimes against humanity on ethnic Albanian civilians.[69]

Before Walker's accounts, the United States and NATO relied on threats of force, failing to enforce them time and time again, in hopes that continued negotiations would entice Milošević to back down. In fact, until the day of the Raçak massacre, Western actors discussed and negotiated on Kosovo with the assumption that the direct use of force would not be needed, nor would it be warranted given the supposed nature of the conflict and the unwillingness to build a state in the aftermath of regime change. The United States did not want to act as the de-facto military for the Kosovo Liberation Army (KLA), a group perceived to be equally as violent as its Serbian counterparts. But Walker's testimony and international urging pushed the United States toward a militaristic response to end the human rights abuses in Kosovo and preserve the values and credibility of the NATO alliance. Thus, while the Kosovo intervention remains a strong example of the US usage of force abroad, it also showcases the importance of diplomacy in framing international events and the political significance of values-driven institutions for the United States after the Cold War.

Protecting American Lives and Hints of the War on Terror

The Clinton administration also conducted more limited military interventions to protect and defend American lives abroad. In fact, as Figure 5.10 showed, protecting American lives and property was the most frequent objective of US interventions during this era, alongside social protection. The US military protected or evacuated Americans from conflict zones and enhanced security at embassies worldwide. The military evacuated Americans from Liberia and the Central African Republic in 1996, Sierra Leone in 1997, Albania in 1997, and Guinea-Bissau in 1998.[70] In these cases, military power was used in defense of American citizens in-country rather than in pursuit of geopolitical or ideological goals.

The objective of protecting American lives also began to extend to counterterrorism operations. In fact, Clinton's first military action to defend

Americans overseas came with the bombing of the Iraqi intelligence center in June 1993 in retaliation for Iraq's sponsorship of a plot to assassinate former president Bush three months earlier. The strike was intended to deter Saddam from continuing to support such anti-American activities. At the time, US officials also believed Iraq backed the 1993 bombings of the World Trade Center, though this connection was later disproven.[71]

By 1998, the United States had fully internalized its militaristic leadership role and clothed it in the narrative of American exceptionalism and liberal values. When discussing a possible US strike to curb Saddam's weapons program in February 1998, US Secretary of State Madeleine Albright said, "It is the threat of the use of force [against Iraq] and our line-up there that is going to put force behind the diplomacy. But if we have to use force, it is because we are America; we are the indispensable nation. We stand tall and we see further than other countries into the future, and we see the danger here to all of us."[72]

In addition to sending a message to Saddam regarding terrorism and weapons of mass destruction, the United States also responded forcefully to several terrorist attacks by nonstate actors. Clinton responded "perfunctorily" with airstrikes in response to the terrorist attacks on the World Trade Center, bombing of the Khobar Towers in Saudi Arabia in 1993, and attacks against US embassies in Tanzania and Kenya in 1998.[73] Small numbers of US troops were deployed to East Africa after the 1998 bombings to boost security around the sites, help with recovery, and provide medical assistance. The United States also responded with force after learning that the embassy attacks were claimed by Al-Qaeda, bombing suspected Al-Qaeda camps in Sudan and Afghanistan as part of Operation Infinite Reach.[74] America's commitment to countering terrorism was solidified in 1998 with Clinton's Presidential Decision Directive 62. Titled "Combatting Terrorism," the document identified combatting terrorism as a top national security priority and set objectives and milestones to guide government agencies in cooperating on rooting out terrorism, actively fighting it, and preparing the homeland for a potential attack.[75]

However, Al-Qaeda's 2000 bombing of the USS *Cole* in the Gulf of Aden, killing 39 American servicemembers, indicates such efforts did not go far enough. Clinton deployed a small number of US forces to Yemen immediately after the bombing "solely for the purpose of assisting in on-site security" and to find the perpetrators, though these troops were equipped for combat.[76] A total of 3,000 American military and civilian personnel were sent to Aden to investigate the bombing.[77] Clinton also responded with airstrikes on the eve of the 2000 presidential election.[78]

By the end of Clinton's second term, the country was closing its chapter on NATO-led humanitarian military interventions and beginning to look inward to protect its own national security. Bad actors like Saddam Hussein and rogue terrorist groups posed legitimate security threats. Sporadic airstrikes were used as early responses to terrorism—though ground forces were not usually considered—and the military conducted multiple operations to evacuate US personnel from embassies in troubled countries abroad.

The United States was becoming increasingly comfortable in relying on military tools as a first line of defense and attack, and this was justified because America saw itself as a benign global police force that often intervened within ongoing international disputes. For example, the American response to the attacks in Kenya and Tanzania was forceful—diplomatic, economic, or cultural efforts were not considered when dealing with terrorist groups—and the United States bombed terrorist camps in Sudan and Afghanistan to send the message that it was committed to defending its citizens. Unlike military action in the early 1990s, by the end of the century, American usage of force was confined to swift airstrikes and bombing campaigns, allowing the United States to display what it believed was its technological superiority without endangering its own ground troops.

Conclusion

The unipolar moment in the 1990s brought forth a more interventionist US foreign policy, with higher rates of intervention. The United States continued to rely on militarism even though it enjoyed economic and cultural domination as well. The 1990s also introduced the US-led phenomenon of humanitarian military interventionism, spearheaded after the Gulf War during efforts to protect the Kurdish population in Iraq. But in the case of the Gulf War, the Bush administration refused to seek regime change in Baghdad, a limitation that would begin to fade in the next decade. The United States still hesitated to rely on military tools as a first resort, as illustrated in its reluctance to involve its military in intrastate crises in Rwanda, Bosnia, Kosovo, and other locations with questionable strategic significance. Instead, US political elites chose to wield diplomatic and economic statecraft for years prior to a military intervention in cases of foreign civil wars, sometimes to the detriment of the international humanitarian response.

Moreover, in cases where the United States ultimately intervened using military might in the 1990s, it usually did so under multilateral mandates via the UN or NATO, as in the cases of Bosnia and Kosovo, respectively. During these multilateral military operations, the United States involved itself for longer spans of time because it chose to undertake post-conflict rebuilding and monitoring duties as well. For example, the NATO intervention in Bosnia stands as the longest US military intervention, lasting over 4,000 days (see Table A5.1 in the appendix for a full list).

Through multilateral structures and US normative leadership, the era of unipolarity did include some checks on America's rising military engagements. Even through institutions such as NATO were forged for Cold War balancing, the United States chose to adapt these institutions as a way to maintain its alliance networks and bolster its soft power across the transatlantic sphere, hence limiting its own power within the multilateral arrangements. The United States relied on transatlantic alliance networks for resource-pooling, financial burden-sharing, and force multipliers. The networks enhanced the United States' normative influence and political credibility, cementing it as not only a military superpower but a cultural superpower as well. This meant that while the United States was growing in power, extending its influence, and expanding its military, might many other powers chose to bandwagon with it, rather than actively counter its hegemony.

This changed in 2001. After the September 11, 2001, terrorist attacks on US soil, American foreign policy veered down a different path, moving away from a multilateral approach to a staunchly unilateral "you are with us, or you are with the terrorists" mindset.[79] This alienated US allies and decreased the soft power and credibility it garnered in the 1990s. Political elites also began to see the role of force in a different light. Prior to 2001, the use of force was seen as a last resort, or at least considered only after some degree of diplomatic or economic statecraft were attempted. But in the post-9/11 era, the usage of force became the first line of defense for many of the threats facing the United States, collectively grouped under the Global War on Terror.

The next chapter will examine the contemporary era of US foreign policy, from 2001 until the present day, highlighting the trends that may spell disaster for the future of American power and international peace and security. Taking the lessons learned from previous eras, we will offer a set of recommendations for US foreign policy in the decades to come, calling for military restraint, reengagement with old allies and engagement with new ones, and deep involvement within global institutions to minimize the need for military force abroad.

Notes

1. "President George H. W. Bush's first inauguration speech: Full text," AOL, January 20th, 1989, https://www.aol.com/article/news/2017/01/19/president-george-h-w-bushs-first-inauguration-speech-full-te/21658319/#.
2. James D. Boys, *Clinton's Grand Strategy: U.S. Foreign Policy in a Post-Cold War World* (London: Bloomsbury Academic, 2015), 266, 271–272; Colin Dueck, *Reluctant Crusaders: Power, Culture, and Change in American Grand Strategy* (Princeton, NJ: Princeton University Press, 2006).
3. Dueck, *Reluctant Crusaders*, 114, 138–143.
4. The exception being the drawdown of 200,000 troops in the area. See, Cavanna, "U.S. Grand Strategy," 10.
5. Bastiaan van Apeldoorn and Naná de Graaff, *American Grand Strategy and Corporate Elite Networks* (Abingdon-on-Thames: Routledge, 2015), 119–121.
6. van Apeldoorn and de Graaff, *American Grand Strategy and Corporate Elite Networks*; Dueck, *Reluctant Crusaders*, 114, 138–143.
7. Charles Krauthammer, "The Unipolar Moment," *Foreign Affairs*, 70, no. 1, (1990/91), 23–33, 23.
8. Christopher Hemmer, *American Pendulum: Recurring Debates in U.S. Grand Strategy* (Ithaca, NY: Cornell University Press, 2015).
9. Joseph Nye, *Presidential Leadership and the Creation of the American Era* (Princeton, NJ: Princeton University Press, 2013), 55–56.
10. Nye, *Presidential Leadership and the Creation of the American Era*, 57.
11. James D. Boys, *Clinton's Grand Strategy: U.S. Foreign Policy in a Post-Cold War World* (London: Bloomsbury Academic, 2015), 104.
12. "President Bill Clinton's first inauguration speech: Full text," Yale Law School, January 20, 1993. https://avalon.law.yale.edu/20th_century/clinton1.asp.
13. William J. Clinton, *A National Security Strategy of Engagement and Enlargement*, The White House, February 1996, http://nssarchive.us/wp-content/uploads/2020/04/1996.pdf.
14. Warren Christopher, "'Building Peace in the Middle East,'" *U.S. Department of State Dispatch* 4, no. 39 (September 27, 1993).
15. Anthony Lake, "From Containment to Enlargement," Johns Hopkins University, School of Advanced International Studies, Washington DC. September 21, 1993, https://www.mtholyoke.edu/acad/intrel/lakedoc.html.

16. Zoltan Feher, "NATO's New Place in the European Security Architecture," *Bard Journal of Social Sciences* IX, no. I (Fall): 46–63, 59. https://www.researchgate.net/publication/341447962_NATO's_New_Place_in_European_Security_Architecture.

17. Barry Posen, *Restraint. A New Foundation for U.S. Grand Strategy* (Ithaca, NY: Cornell University Press, 2014), 65.

18. We measure hostility levels by the following scale: (1) No Usage of Force; (2) A Threat of Force; (3) A Show of Force; (4) A Usage of Force; and (5) War.

19. John Dumbrell, "America in the 1990s: Searching for Purpose," in *US Foreign Policy*, 2nd ed., edited by Michael Cox and Doug Stokes (Oxford: Oxford University Press, 2012), 100, doi: 10.1093/hepl/9780199585816.003.0005.

20. Hal Brands, *Making the Unipolar Moment: U.S. Foreign Policy and the Rise of the Post-Cold War Order* (Ithaca, NY: Cornell University Press, 2016), accessed June 3, 2021, http://www.jstor.org/stable/10.7591/j.ctt20d89k9.

21. For more details on this measure, see David L. Cingranelli and David L. Richards, *The Cingranelli-Richards Human Rights Dataset, Version 2008.03.12*, http://www.humanrightsdata.org.

22. John Ikenberry, ed., *America Unrivalled: The Future of the Balance of Power* (Ithaca, NY: Cornell University Press, 2002); John G. Ikenberry, Michael Mastanduno, and William Wohlforth, "Introduction: Unipolarity, State Behavior, and Systemic Consequences," *World Politics* 61, no. 1 (2009): 1–27; Nuno Monteiro, *Theory of Unipolar Politics* (Cambridge: Cambridge University Press, 2014); William Wohlforth, "Nuno Monteiro. 'Unrest Assured: Why Unipolarity is Not Peaceful.' Reviewed by William C. Wohlforth," *H-Diplo ISSF Article Review* 8 (2012): 1–5.

23. Charles Krauthammer, "The Unipolar Moment," *Foreign Affairs* 70, no. 1 (1990): 23–33; Christopher Layne, "The Unipolar Illusion: Why New Great Powers Will Rise," *International Security* 17, no. 4 (1993): 5–51.

24. Barry Posen and Andrew Ross, "Competing Visions for U.S. Grand Strategy," *International Security* 21, no. 3 (1996): 5–53.

25. Michael R. Gordon, "Pentagon Objected to Bush's Message to Iraq," *The New York Times*, October 25, 1992, https://www.nytimes.com/1992/10/25/world/pentagon-objected-to-bush-s-message-to-iraq.html.

26. Gordon, "Pentagon Objected to Bush's Message to Iraq."

27. Gordon, "Pentagon Objected to Bush's Message to Iraq."

28. David Kenner, "Why one U.S. diplomat didn't cause the Gulf War," *Foreign Policy* (January 2011), https://foreignpolicy.com/2011/01/06/why-one-u-s-diplomat-didnt-cause-the-gulf-war/.

29. Hal Brands, "George Bush and the Gulf War of 1991," Presidential Studies Quarterly, 34: 118.

30. Michael Wines, "U.S. Is Said to Quietly Encourage A Kuwaiti Resistance Movement," *The New York Times*, September 1, 1990, https://timesmachine.nytimes.com/timesmachine/1990/09/01/067890.html?pageNumber=4.

31. Herring, *From Colony to Superpower*, 930.

32. Joseph Englehardt, "Desert Shield and Desert Storm: A Chronology and Troop List for the 1990–1991 Persian Gulf Crisis," *Strategic Studies Institute Special Report*, March 25, 1991.

33. See Table A5.2 in the appendix for a detailed list of troop deployments during Operation Desert Storm.

34. Herring, *From Colony to Superpower,* 930.

35. John G. Heidenrich, "The Gulf War: How Many Iraqis Died?" *Foreign Policy*, (1993): 90, 117–124; Anne Leland, "American War and Military Operations Casualties: Lists and Statistics," Congressional Research Service, November 15th, 2012, 13.

36. Murtaza Hussain, "Post-Cold War U.S. Foreign Policy Has Been a Near Total Failure. Two New Books Look at Why," *The Intercept*, October 21, 2018, https://theintercept. com/2018/10/21/us-foreign-policy-after-cold-war-books/.

37. The initiative for Operation Provide Comfort arose from the UK-led Operation Safe Haven. Gordon W. Rudd, *Humanitarian Intervention, Assisting the Iraqi Kurds in Operation Provide Comfort 1991* (St. Louis: Government Publication Office, 2004).

38. Kerim Yildiz, *The Future of Kurdistan: The Iraqi Dilemma,* (London: Palgrave Macmillan, 2012), 21.

39. Salazar Torreon and Plagakis, "Instances of Use of United States Armed Forces Abroad, 1798–2018," 47.

40. Steven M. Wright, *The United States and Persian Gulf Security: The Foundations of the War on Terror*, 1st ed., Durham Middle East Monographs (Reading: Ithaca Press, 2007), 4.

41. Herring, *From Colony to Superpower,* 928.

42. *Restoring Hope: the Real Lessons of Somalia for the Future of Intervention* (Washington, DC: The U.S. Institute Of Peace, 1994), 12.

43. Colin Dueck, "Hegemony on the Cheap: Liberal Internationalism from Wilson to Bush," *World Policy Journal* 20, no. 4 (2003): 1–11, accessed June 3, 2020, http://www. jstor.org/stable/40209884.

44. Herring, *From Colony to Superpower,* 925, http://www.dawsonera.com/depp/reader/ protected/external/AbstractView/S9780199723430.

45. John R. Ballard, *Upholding Democracy: The United States Military Campaign in Haiti, 1994–1997* (Westport, CT: Praeger, 1998), 86.

46. Philippe R. Girard, *Clinton in Haiti: The 1994 U.S. Intervention in Haiti,* (New York: Palgrave Macmillan, 2004).

47. "Madeleine K. Albright Oral History," Miller Center, October 27, 2016, https://mille rcenter.org/the-presidency/presidential-oral-histories/madeleine-k-albright-oral-history.

48. John Lange, "Civilian-Military Cooperation and Humanitarian Assistance: Lessons from Rwanda," *Parameters* 28, no. 2 (1998): 106–122.

49. "Transitional Justice in the Former Yugoslavia," *International Center for Transitional Justice* (2009), https://www.ictj.org/publication/transitional-justice-former-yug oslavia.

50. "NATO's Role in Relation to the Conflict in Kosovo," NATO, July 15, 1999, http://www.nato.int/kosovo/history.htm.

51. Herring, *From Colony to Superpower*, 929.

52. Ivo H. Daalder, *Getting to Dayton: The Making of America's Bosnia Policy* (Washington, DC: Brookings Institution Press, 2000).

53. Rasmus Sinding Søndergaard, "Bill Clinton's 'Democratic Enlargement' and the Securitisation of Democracy Promotion," *Diplomacy & Statecraft* 26, no. 3 (July 3, 2015): 534–551, https://doi.org/10.1080/09592296.2015.1067529.

54. Swanee Hunt, *Worlds Apart: Bosnian Lessons for Global Security* (Durham, NC: Duke University Press, 2011), 90.

55. Derek H. Chollet and Samantha Power, eds., *The Unquiet American: Richard Holbrooke in the World*, 1st ed. (New York: Public Affairs, 2011), 206.

56. "Under Orders: War Crimes in Kosovo," *Human Rights Watch*, October 26, 2001, https://www.hrw.org/report/2001/10/26/under-orders/war-crimes-kosovo.

57. Michael Mandelbaum, "A Perfect Failure: NATO's War Against Yugoslavia," *Foreign Affairs* 78, no. 5 (2009): 2–8; see http://www.kosovomemorybook.org/ for a detailed list of the victims of the Kosovo Crisis in 1999.

58. David Halberstam, *War in a Time of Peace: Bush, Clinton and the Generals* (New York: Simon & Schuster, 2002).

59. Herring, *From Colony to Superpower*, 934.

60. "Civilian Deaths in the NATO Air Campaign—The Crisis in Kosovo," *Human Rights Watch*, accessed April 27, 2020, https://www.hrw.org/reports/2000/nato/Natbm 200-01.htm.

61. Judith Miller, "Grand Strategy: Round and Round on U.S. Interests; Kosovo Rekindles a Debate, Dormant for Nearly a Decade, of America's Global Role," *The New York Times*, April 24, 1999, http://www.nytimes.com/1999/04/24/arts/grand-strategy-round-round-us-interests-kosovo-rekindles-debate-dormant-for.html?pagewan ted=all&src=pm.

62. Charles Krauthammer, "The Clinton Doctrine," *CNN*, March 29, 1999, http://edition. cnn.com/ALLPOLITICS/time/1999/03/29/doctrine.html

63. Wesley K. Clark, *Waging Modern War: Bosnia, Kosovo, and the Future of Combat* (New York: Public Affairs, 2001), 109.

64. John F. Harris, *The Survivor: Bill Clinton in the White House* (New York: Random House, 2005), 362.

65. Clark, *Waging Modern War*, 165.

66. William Cohen, Frontline Interview, *PBS*, 2000, http://www.pbs.org/wgbh/pages/frontline/shows/kosovo/interviews/cohen.html.

67. Sidita Kushi. "Selective Humanitarians: How Region & Perception Drive Military Interventions in Domestic Crises," *International Relations* (2022). doi: 10.1177/00471178221104344.

68. Kosovo Verification Mission: "Special Report: Massacre of civilians in Racak," Organization for Security and Cooperation in Europe (OSCE), January 17, 1999.

69. William Walker, Frontline Interview, *PBS*, 2000, http://www.pbs.org/wgbh/pages/frontline/shows/kosovo/interviews/walker.html.

70. Salazar Torreon and Plagakis, "Instances of Use of United States Armed Forces Abroad, 1798–2018," 47.

71. Thomas L. Friedman, "Raid on Baghdad: An Assessment; The Missile Message," *The New York Times*, June 28, 1993, https://www.nytimes.com/1993/06/28/world/raid-on-baghdad-an-assessment-the-missile-message.html.

72. "Secretary of State Madeleine K. Albright Interview on NBC-TV 'The Today Show' with Matt Lauer," February 19, 1998, https://1997-2001.state.gov/statements/1998/980219a.html.

73. Herring, *From Colony to Superpower*, 936.

74. John Deutch, "When to Strike Back," *The New York Times*, August 22, 1998, https://www.nytimes.com/1998/08/22/opinion/when-to-strike-back.html.

75. "Declassified Documents concerning Presidential Decision Directive 62 (PDD-62)," *Clinton Digital Library*, accessed May 5, 2020, https://clinton.presidentiallibraries.us/items/show/16200.

76. William Clinton, "Letter to Congressional Leaders Reporting on the Deployment of United States Forces in Response to the Attack on the U.S.S. Cole," *Weekly Compilation of Presidential Documents* 36, no. 42 (2000): 2482.

77. John F. Burns, "Yemen, an Edgy Place, Faces Flood of Americans," *The New York Times*, October 21, 2000, https://www.nytimes.com/2000/10/21/world/yemen-an-edgy-place-faces-flood-of-americans.html.

78. Herring, *From Colony to Superpower*, 936.

79. George W. Bush. 2001. President Declares "Freedom at War with Fear," Address to a Joint Session of Congress and the American People, White House Archives, September 20. https://georgewbush-whitehouse.archives.gov/news/releases/2001/09/20010920-8.html.

Chapter 5 Appendix

Table A5.1 List of US Military Interventions with Duration and Fatalities, 1990–2000

Start Year	Name	Duration (Days)	US Battle Deaths	State B Battle Deaths	Avg. Total Battle Deaths	US Total Deaths	State B Total Deaths
1990	Operation Desert Shield	207	0	0	0	0	0
1990	Operation Sharp Edge	179	0	0	0	0	0
1991	Attack on USS *La Salle*	1	0	0	0	0	0
1991	Operation Desert Storm	43	383	75000	75000	1948	75000
1991	Operations Southern Watch, Vigilant Warrior, Provide Comfort, Northern Watch	3858	0	12	12	0	175
1991	Canadian Fishing Boats	1	0	0	0	0	0
1991	DRC Troops Airlift	3	0	0	0	0	0
1991	Operation Eastern Exit	10	0	0	0	0	0
1992	NATO Intervention in Yugoslavia	1540	0	0	0	0	150000
1992	Air Skirmish in Peru	1	1	0	1	1	0
1992	Embassy Evacuation in Sierra Leone	1	0	0	0	0	0
1992	Operation Provide Relief	112	0	0	0	0	0
1992	Operation Restore Hope	157	43	6,000–10,000	10000	43	10000
1993	NPT Threats by N Korea	21	0	0	0	0	0
1993	PRK Tension	2128	1	0	0	1	0
1993	NATO Intervention in Bosnia	4296	12	25	37	12	7000
1993	UN Resolution 842	2082	0	0	0	0	0
1993	UNOSOM II	733	43	25750	25793	43	300000
1994	Operation Support Hope	71	0	0	0	0	0
1994	Operation Uphold Democracy	194	0	0	0	0	0

Year	Operation					
1994	Operation Support Hope	60	0	0	0	0
1995	Third Taiwan Strait Crisis	100	0	0	0	0
1996	Embassy Evacuation NEO Central African Republic	11	0	0	0	0
1996	Operation Assured Response NEO	73	0	5	5	5
1997	Citizen Protection Operation	1	0	0	0	0
1997	Operation Silver Wake NEO	14	0	0	0	0
1997	Operation Southern Watch	72	0	0	0	0
1997	Evacuating US citizens	92	0	0	0	0
1997	Operation Nobel Obelisk NEO	2				
1998	Operation Infinite Reach in Afghanistan	1	0	0	0	0
1998	Evacuation (NEO) in Guinea-Bissau	6	0	0	0	0
1998	Operation Resolute Response	25	0	0	0	0
1998	Liberian Civil Wars	1	0	0	0	4
1998	Operation Infinite Reach in Sudan	1	0	1	1	1
1999	East Timorese Crisis	1166	0	0	0	0
1999	Taiwan Strait Skirmishes	441	0	0	0	0
1999	Korean Peninsula Hostilities	89	0	20	20	20
1999	Kosovo Intervention	78	0	750	750	1500
1999	Vargas Tragedy	20	0	0	0	20000
2000	Bering Strait Probes	61	0	0	0	0
2000	Russian ship carries illegal Iraqi oil	89	0	0	0	0
2000	Kosovo Border	43	0	0	0	0
2000	Phiblex 2000	3	0	0	0	0
2000	Counterterrorism mission in Yemen	3	17	17	17	17
2000	UN Mission in Ethiopia and Eritrea	2954	N/A	8	8	N/A
2000	IMATT in Sierra Leone	—	0	0	0	0

Table A5.2 Table of Military Deployments during Operation Desert Storm

Country	Number of Troops	Military assets and equipment
United States	532,000	2,000 tanks, 1800 fixed wing aircraft, 120 ships
Afghanistan	300 Mujahidin	—
Argentina	450	2 frigates
Australia	—	1 guided missile frigate, 1 destroyer, 1 supply ship
Bahrain	3500	—
Bangladesh	2,000	—
Belgium	—	2 minesweepers 1 squadron of fighters based in Turkey
Canada	1700	2 destroyers, CF-18 Squadron
Czechoslovakia	200 chemical defense unit, 150 medical personnel	—
Denmark	—	1 corvette
Egypt	40,000	4,000 tanks
France	20,000	14 ships, 75 aircraft, 350 tanks,
Germany	—	1 squadron of fighters
Greece	—	1 frigate
Hungary	40 medical team	—
Honduras	150	—
Italy	—	4 ships, 8 Tornado fighters, 1 squadron of fighters
Kuwait	7,000 Kuwait armed forces and 4,500	35 combat aircraft
Morocco	2,000	—
Netherlands	—	Two frigates, 18 F-16s
Niger	480	—
Norway	—	1 Coast Guard Cutter and military supply ship
New Zealand	—	2 C-130
Oman	25,000	75 tanks, 12 patrol ships, 50 combat aircrafts
Pakistan	10,000	—
Poland	Medical team	2 ships
Qatar	7,000	24 tanks, 9 coastal vessels, and 19 combat aircraft
Saudi Arabia	Army: 38,000 National Guard: 56,000 Air Force: 1600	550 tanks, 180 combat aircrafts, 8 frigates
Spain	—	2 corvettes, and 1 destroyer.

Table A5.2 Continued

Country	Number of Troops	Military assets and equipment
Syria	21,000+2,000 in UAE	300 armored vehicles
Turkey	—	2 frigates
United Arab Emirates	40,000+1500 in Air Force	200 tanks, 80 combat aircraft, and 15 ships
United Kingdom	42,000	16 ships and 58 aircraft.
Iraq	545,000	4550, armored vehicles 2880, artillery 3257

Sources: Military Intervention Project Case Studies. Key sources used include but not limited to:

Stephen Daggett, "Costs of Major U.S. Wars," *Congressional Research Service*, June 29, 2010; Joseph Englehardt, "Desert Shield and Desert Storm: A Chronology and Troop List for the 1990–1991 Persian Gulf Crisis," *Strategic Studies Institute Special Report*, March 25, 1991; John G. Heidenrich, "The Gulf War: How Many Iraqis Died?" *Foreign Policy*, (1993): 90, 117–124; Salazar Torreon and Barbara, "Instances of Use of United States Armed Forces Abroad, 1798–2017,"; Anne Leland, "American War and Military Operations Casualties: Lists and Statistics," Congressional Research Service, November 15th, 2012, p.13.

Table A5.3 US and Coalition Military Forces Deployed, April–July 1991

Countries	Number of Troops Deployed
United States Total	12,316
• US Army	6,119
• US Air Force	3,588
• US Marine Corps	1,875
• US Navy	734
Australia	75
Belgium	150
Canada	120
France	2141
Germany	221
Italy	1183
Luxembourg	43
Netherlands	1,020
Portugal	19
Spain	602
Turkey	1,160
United Kingdom	4,192
Total	**23,242**

Source: Gordon W. Rudd, *Humanitarian Intervention: Assisting the Iraqi Kurds in Operation Provide Comfort 1991*, St. Louis: Government Publication Office, 2004, p.226.

6

America the Unleashed

*America is united. The freedom-loving nations of the world stand by
our side. This will be a monumental struggle of good versus evil. But
good will prevail.*[1]

George W. Bush, September 12, 2001

While the unipolar moment sparked a more interventionist United States,
the post-9/11 era ushered in a significant foreign policy reorientation from
"diplomacy first, and force as a last resort," to "military force first." The sword
came first. This period saw the rise of defense budgets and special operations
and the waning of State Department funds, influence, and diplomatic capacity. While the United States promoted multilateralism in the 1990s, it now
staunchly promoted unilateral foreign policy to safeguard its security in "the
struggle of good versus evil."[2] The United States increasingly perceived the
world to be full of evil, irrational states and nonstate actors plotting America's
downfall.

The "Bush Doctrine," formalized in the National Security Strategy of
September 2002, considered terrorists as hostile states, especially fearful that
Islamist movements could obtain nuclear weapons.[3] And the terrorists could
be anywhere—hiding in states such as Iran and Pakistan, or making their way
to the Western world to hurt American citizens and their ways of life. With
such broad and blurry threat perceptions, the Bush Doctrine pushed for preemptive wars in the Middle East and North Africa and unilateral practices
of rampant militarism to keep America safe from a vague, all-encompassing
enemy.[4]

The United States overestimated its military capabilities during the era,
while disregarding other tools of statecraft. Wishful thinking about what its
military superiority could achieve led the United States to embark on military

Dying by the Sword. Monica Duffy Toft and Sidita Kushi, Oxford University Press. © Oxford University Press 2023.
DOI: 10.1093/oso/9780197581438.003.0007

operations that garnered early successes against non-state actors and weaker states, but then failed to consolidate effective post-war strategies and gain local and ally support, worsening the security situation for everyone. Such patterns left the United States mired in the "endless wars" that have come to define the era. Americans are considerably less satisfied with the United States' position in the world than they were at the start of 2001.[5]

This chapter traces America's pathway toward kinetic diplomacy and its implications for future US power, prosperity, and international security. With an incoherent grand strategy, the United States cannot win its most important foreign policy battles with military might alone. The chapter begins with an overview of US grand strategy during the post-9/11 era, followed by an empirical and historical analysis of US foreign policy and military interventions. We also discuss the evolution of US military technology, particularly drone warfare.

Grand Strategy: Liberal Interventionism without the Liberal

The George W. Bush administration inherited the grand strategy of "liberal interventionism" from its predecessors. In the early days, it looked like the main changes arising from the new Bush administration would amount to less multilateralism and collective security than in the George H. W. Bush and Clinton eras. But Al-Qaeda's terrorist attacks on September 11, 2001, were game-changers in shaping the new administration's grand strategy. In the wake of the first armed attack on the US mainland since the War of 1812, the Bush administration developed a new US grand strategy defined by the War on Terror.

In some ways, the liberal interventionist strategy of the 1990s continued and expanded into the new grand strategy. On one hand, it was motivated by liberal ideals (spreading freedom, democracy, and rule of law), it relied heavily on military intervention, and it sought to maintain US global hegemony. In fact, the liberal ideological underpinnings of the Bush grand strategy were termed neo-Wilsonianism. On the other hand, the grand strategy of the War on Terror broke with the past as it was more unapologetically unilateral than multilateral and it had spillover effects beyond security and the war on terror (Bush withdrew from the Kyoto Protocol to reduce climate change, for example), it depended less on collective security (the UN and NATO are only "used" when deemed helpful), and it perceived military might as a first line of policymaking.

Before he became president, Bush already made clear his prioritization of military might over diplomacy, saying in 1999: "In the defense of our nation, a president must be a clear-eyed realist. There are limits to the smiles and scowls of diplomacy. Armies and missiles are not stopped by stiff notes of condemnation. They are held in check by strength and purpose and the promise of swift punishment."[6] Thus, the balance between diplomacy and militarism that US policy was so carefully calibrating in the 1990s now tipped away from diplomacy, creating a grand strategy that used almost exclusively military tools.

While building the new grand strategy, the Bush administration found the doctrines of deterrence and defense insufficient for the changed security environment, so it added the doctrine of preemptive war. In Walter Russel Mead's assessment, "Historians are likely to agree that nothing in the record of the Bush administration is as significant as its decision to describe the struggle that began on September 11 as a . . . 'war on terror,' and nothing in its prosecution of that war to date is as significant as its decision to make the invasion of Iraq the centerpiece of its international strategy after smashing Al Qaeda's bases and sanctuaries in Afghanistan."[7] The subsequent wars in Afghanistan and Iraq exemplify the new grand strategy and the new doctrine of preemption. In 2005, Mead warned of the risks of alienating US allies and argued that the Bush administration should emphasize the continuities between the Cold War strategy of containment and the War on Terror: "Articulating our grand strategy in terms of containment stresses our firm and inflexible resolve to win this war, and it also stresses that we intend to use flexible, appropriate, and pragmatic strategies to fight it."[8]

But the Bush administration did not apply a pragmatic, flexible approach to the post-9/11 era. Instead, it fixated on ideological battles and disproportionately bolstered the military's influence in foreign policymaking. The lack of flexibility and pragmatism led to failure in the wars in Iraq and Afghanistan, forcing Bush to slightly alter course in his second term by allowing multilateralism and collective security to play greater roles once again. But with the Bush administration preoccupied with the broader Middle East as the two asymmetric wars became endless and unwinnable, it largely neglected the rapidly advancing rise of China as a great power competitor.

President Barack Obama took office in the midst of a devastating global financial crisis, one that forced the world to question the stability and merits of the post-World War II neoliberal order and US economic and cultural leadership. Until 2007, the War on Terror occurred in the backdrop of strong US economic growth, reflected in rising GDP per capita. But the Great Recession starting in 2007 reversed this progress, as seen in Figure 6.1. From 2007 to 2012, domestic politics predominantly focused on buffering the economic losses and financial devastation—perhaps contextualizing the lower levels of US intervention during the recession.

As part of his campaign, Obama promised to break with the military-first grand strategy under Bush and to end the wars in Afghanistan and Iraq. "The message Obama telegraphed in speeches and interviews was clear: He would not end up like the second President Bush—a president who became tragically overextended in the Middle East, whose decisions filled the wards of Walter Reed with grievously wounded soldiers, who was helpless to stop the obliteration of his reputation, even when he recalibrated his policies in his second term."[9]

Obama acquired some soft power in his first term by serving as the world's lender of last resort during the financial crisis and by engaging with the UN and other international institutions much more than the previous administration. The Obama administration, however, failed to put US grand strategy on a new course, even though it relied more on soft power and smart power.

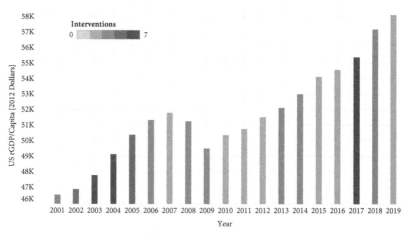

Figure 6.1. US GDP Trends and Interventions, 2001–2019

Citation: Bureau of Economic Analysis (BEA). Gross Domestic Product. *U.S. Department of Commerce, 2019.* https://www.bea.gov/data/gdp/gross-domestic-product; Louis Johnston and Samuel H. Williamson. "What Was the U.S. GDP Then?" *Measuring Worth,* 2018. https://www.measuringworth.com/datasets/usgdp/.

The militarism of the Bush grand strategy continued to impact policy, and the wars in Afghanistan and Iraq raged on without achievable victories in sight. Obama even oversaw the development of a covert drone warfare program, which critics characterize as morally inhumane and legally extraterritorial. The covert nature of the drone warfare masks the true scale of US militarism during the Obama era. But to be fair, Obama also started to shift US grand strategy toward retrenchment.

During his tenure, Obama guided the United States away from its expansive international leadership role in order to focus on the country's domestic challenges, including healthcare and inequality. Thus, beyond the economic downturn, another reason for the lower levels of US interventionism from 2007 to 2011 could be the more restrained Obama administration. Unlike in previous era when presidential administrations did not appear to significantly alter intervention patterns, the post-9/11 era showcases noticeable variations in intervention frequencies, as seen in Figure 6.2. It is important to emphasize, however, that while the Obama administration engaged in fewer traditional military missions and state building projects, America's drone warfare programs are inherently underestimated due to limited data and the covert nature of many missions.[10]

Obama saw the need to reduce America's strategic preoccupation with the broader Middle East and Europe and initiated the "pivot" to rebalance US military posture toward the Asia-Pacific where China's influence was growing. According to Michael Green, "After an emboldened China began

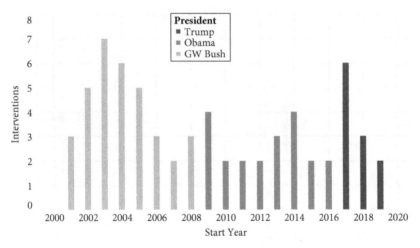

Figure 6.2. US Interventions by President, 2001–2019

throwing its weight around, the administration announced its 'rebalance' to Asia with new military deployments."[11] Nonetheless, the Pivot was not implemented successfully, and it remained only a partial (and still military-focused) balancing strategy. Even the architect of the pivot, Kurt Campbell, acknowledged these criticisms, writing that "one of the most significant critiques of the Pivot is that it lacks resources and follow-through . . . some of these criticisms are sound."[12]

Obama failed to fundamentally change relations with Russia, when the so-called reset fell through, and Moscow became more assertive and aggressive than before. The military interventionist course of the Bush grand strategy also lived on in Obama interventions in Libya, Yemen, and Syria, which continued to pit the United States against Russia and make the broader Middle East a priority despite the administration's earlier better judgment.

It is not surprising that Obama did not develop a clear grand strategy, as the president was not interested in such an approach. His guiding idea in foreign policy was to not do anything "stupid,"[13] saying that "I don't really even need George Kennan right now."[14] Instead, he pursued a more pragmatic foreign policy agenda, saying: "You take the victories where you can. You make things a little bit better rather than a little bit worse. And that's in no way a concession to this idea that America is withdrawing or there's not much we can do. It's just a realistic assessment of how the world works.[15]

The result of this pragmatic gradualism was an America that continued to be militaristic and bogged down in numerous wars in the broader Middle East (including Afghanistan, Iraq, Libya, Yemen, and Syria), but one that was also inconsistently retrenching from its international leadership role in alliances and multilateral organizations. At the end of the Obama administration, US grand strategy was in disarray, leaving room for the antiestablishment, populist Donald J. Trump to take the reins of US foreign policy as president.

Trump campaigned on an "America First" narrative, championing the approach of "peace through strength." He campaigned on foreign policy ideas that more closely resemble elements of the ideal grand strategy of the so-called realist or restraint camp, including an end to the liberal interventionist grand strategy, an end to the wars in the broader Middle East, a loosening of US commitments to alliances and multilateralism, a general retrenchment from America's costly hegemonic leadership role, and a balancing effort against China.[16]

But due to his erratic leadership style and the all-encompassing and un-relenting chaos of his administration, many of these goals were not realized, and those that were proved detrimental to US power and leadership. Trump continued to rely on militarism and marginalized diplomacy, and he failed to end the unwinnable wars in the broader Middle East. Trump was, how-ever, effective in guiding US grand strategy toward retrenchment, with the United States increasingly abandoning its global leadership role and deeply questioning its alliance commitments. Trump also recognized the dangerous strategic challenge posed by China and reoriented US grand strategy toward a real balancing posture (even though the focus was controversially on the trade arena).[17] Nevertheless, the US withdrawal from its international lead-ership role and the weakening of its alliance ties decimated America's norma-tive power and turned many countries and citizens around the world against US hegemony. This only makes balancing against China more difficult.

The era of unilateralism and the abdication of US global leadership may be coming to an end with Joe Biden's election. But it is too soon to tell whether the Biden administration will be able to fix the damage caused by previous administrations, limit US militarism (given Biden's more in-terventionist record), and truly end the endless wars. Crucially, US grand strategy continues to suffer from serious internal inconsistencies in the face of grave challenges to US power and security, from China's rise to Russia's resurgence to Iran's hostile posture to COVID-19 to climate change.[18] None of these challenges will be resolved by American military might alone.

As Figure 6.3 reveals, the United States dramatically increased its mil-itarism in the early 2000s, and it was intervening at higher frequencies in disputes with much lower levels of national interests. At the same time of such military adventurism, US power capabilities stagnated relative to other states, according to CINC.

As Figure 6.4 further reveals, the United States fully focused on noncontiguous military interventions starting in the 1980s, expanding its role as a global hegemon in a hypermilitaristic way. But America's eager-ness to unleash its military on global populations may repel other interna-tional actors, creating unneeded rivalries and hampering global solutions to twenty-first century problems that are defined by their cross-border interdependencies.

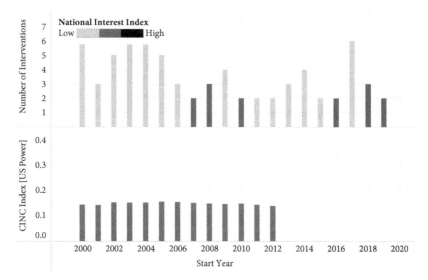

Figure 6.3. US Interventions by National Interests and Capabilities, 2000–2019

Citation: Correlates of War Project. *National Material Capabilities, 1816–2012.* Version 6. http://www.correlatesofwar.org; J. David Singer, "Reconstructing the Correlates of War Dataset on Material Capabilities of States, 1816–1985," *International Interactions* 14 (1987); 115–132

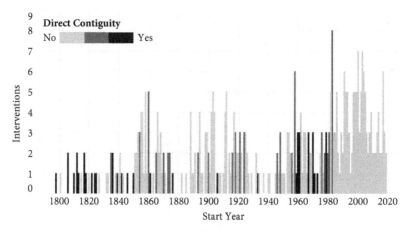

Figure 6.4. Contiguity of US Military Interventions across all years, 1776–2019

Citation: Correlates of War Project. Direct Contiguity Data, 1816–2016. Version 3.2. http://correlatesofwar.org.

Empirical Patterns of US Interventions, 2001–Present

The post-9/11 world looked very different from the unipolar world that was left behind. Before 2001, the United States frequently involved itself internationally, but usually within multilateral mandates limited by their "benign" missions of democratization, human rights promotion, and economic expansion. After 9/11, US foreign policy shifted to preventative military attacks against a vague global enemy—terrorists. Unfortunately, preventative foreign policy often amounts to waging unprovoked and unregulated military conflict, enflaming local resentments and insurgent groups.

US military interventions in all parts of the world rose after 9/11, particularly in 2002 and 2003. While most of the interventions occurred in the Middle East, North Africa, and sub-Saharan Africa due to the supposed latent terrorist threats emanating from those regions, other regions were not immune to US violence. As Figure 6.5 reveals, the United States intervened all around the world during this period, with Europe being the only relative exception.

While the United States intervened 46 times in the previous era, it intervened 66 times in the post-2001 era. The rate of intervention per year, however, is lower during the post-9/11 era, partially because the United States relied on drone warfare and smaller, unconventional operations that

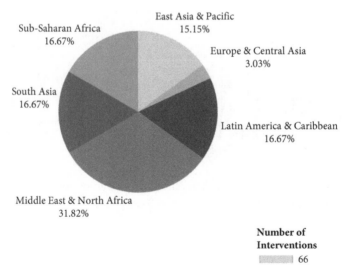

Figure 6.5. US Interventions by Region, 2001–2019

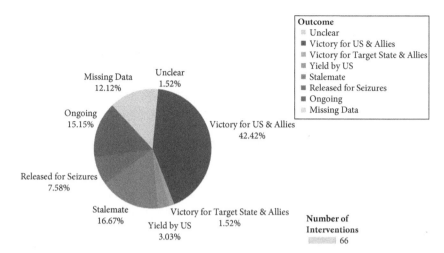

Figure 6.6. Outcomes of US Interventions, 2001–2019

are less transparent and harder to track. Unfortunately, as seen in Figure 6.3, the United States experienced higher intervention frequencies when lower levels of interest were at stake, and much lower intervention frequency when vital interests were at stake. These patterns do not bode well for aspirations for a prudent, rational, and optimized foreign policy and doctrine on the usage of force.

Despite these less-than-optimal power dynamics, the direct outcome of interventions against global terrorism appeared favorable, with the United States achieving about 42 percent of its political, military, and policy objectives during its disputes, as seen in Figure 6.6.

But in comparison to other eras of US militarism, the 42 percent success rate is one of the lowest, better only than the Cold War era, as Figure 6.7 reveals.

In the post-9/11 world, the United States was able to overcome the target states' defenses and capture their main cities, claiming quick military victories. Unfortunately, such traditional military victories did not readily translate to ultimate victories in the War on Terror. While the US military succeeded in installing new governments, it failed to capture the hearts and minds of local populations. The military campaigns bred more resentment on the ground, which bolstered local support for insurgent groups and ultimately created more long-term security threats for the United States.

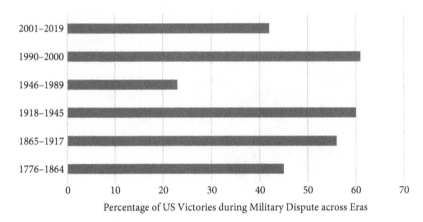

Figure 6.7. Percentage of US Military Victories across Eras, 1776–2019

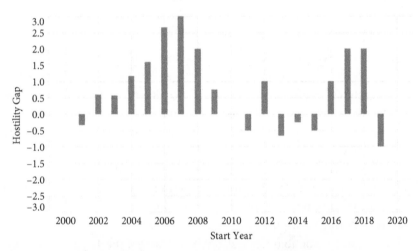

Figure 6.8. Comparative Hostility Levels (US Hostility – State B Hostility Levels), 2001–2019

America's disproportionate usage of force further increased global resentment. As Figure 6.8 reveals, US hostility levels were usually over three hostility levels above those of target states, especially from 2001 to 2008. While the target states did not respond in almost half of the cases, the United States relied on raids and nuclear alerts for the majority of its actions. The United States toned down its hostilities from 2009 until 2015, only to ramp them back up in recent years. But even the Obama years were not truly peaceful, as

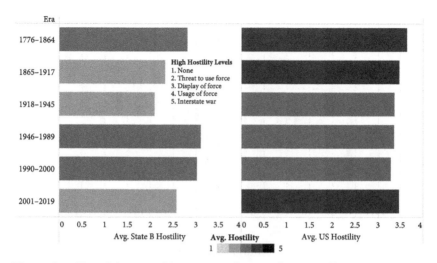

Figure 6.9. United States and State B Hostility Levels across all Eras, 1776–2019

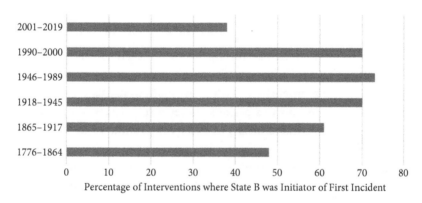

Figure 6.10. Percentage of Interventions where State B was Incident Initiator, all Eras

the United States' drone warfare programs began to replace some of the more conventional military tools of the past.

As Figure 6.9 shows, the United States relied on higher levels of hostility in the post-2001 era than prior eras.

Figure 6.10 also shows that the post-2001 era is the one with the fewest disputes initiated by another state (38 percent). Unlike prior eras, it was the United States that sparked much of the interventions and disputes that defined the era, not an outside party.

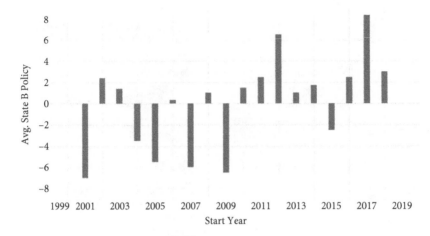

Figure 6.11. State B Democratization Scores, 2001–2019

Citation: Monty Marshall and Ted Robert Gurr, "POLITY IV Project: Political Regime Characteristics and Transitions, 1800–2017," *Center for Systemic Peace,* http://www.systemicpeace. org/polityproject.html.

Something else that changed during this era—the United States intervened in more democracies. Unlike graphics from previous eras, Figure 6.11 shows that a much higher proportion of US target states were closer to democratic governance than in previous periods. Nevertheless, levels of democratization did not seem to matter nearly as much to the United States as it had in the past. The War on Terror meant making the world safer for democracy through the eradication of a grave and evil security threat running rampant across borders, not necessarily through direct and sustained democratic reforms.

As per Figure 6.12, it appears that the primary objectives of these hostile US interventions within semidemocratic target states were to build and maintain favorable regimes to US interests, protect minority groups, and defend American diplomats and property. The protection of America's own diplomats and property was commonplace during the Bush administration, whereas social protection interventions rose in frequency during the Obama years. The human rights context was generally abysmal, but it is hard to say whether the United States intervened partly due to human rights abuses or the interventions themselves prompted these human rights abuses. Another perspective is that the United States intervened in countries seen as security threats, which generally possess many characteristics of failed states.

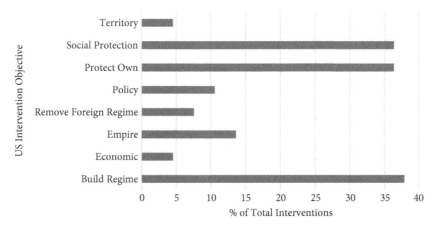

Figure 6.12. US Intervention Objectives, 2000–2019

Drone Warfare

The empirical picture of the post-9/11 world is not complete without addressing the evolution of drone warfare as a tool of US foreign policy. Since 9/11, the United States almost exclusively has used armed unmanned aerial vehicles, or drones, to fight militants in countries such as Pakistan, Somalia, and Yemen. Indeed, drones are the face of US counterterrorism policy.

Especially under Obama, the United States avoided boots on the ground and nation building in lieu of drone strikes. In his first term alone, Obama launched more than six times as many drones strikes as Bush did throughout his eight years in office, all while keeping the CIA-run drone program immune from Congressional or judicial oversight.[19] By 2012, the US Air Force was recruiting more drone pilots than traditional aircraft pilots. What's more, between 2012 and 2014 the Air Force planned to add over 2,500 pilots and support staff to the drone program, which is twice the number of diplomats the State Department hired in the same two-year period.[20] In other words, not only are drone strikes set to replace more traditional military strikes, but they may also act as replacements for nonmilitary foreign policy tools.

The Bureau of Investigative Journalism's latest database on drone strikes (according to the figures available in June 2021) lists at least 14,041 confirmed strikes since January 2002, producing 8,858 to 16,901 total kills.[21] About 910 to 2,200 of these were civilian deaths, and 283 to 454 of them were children.

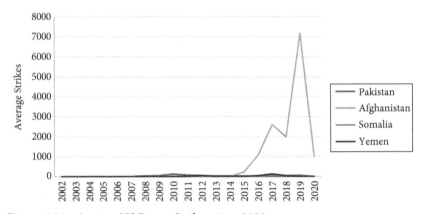

Figure 6.13. Average US Drone Strikes since 2002

Citation: Drone Warfare Database, Bureau of Investigative Journalism. https://www.thebureauinves
tigates.com/projects/drone-war.

Under the Trump administration, the drone program doubled down on its
secrecy. The lack of transparency makes it even more difficult to confirm the
program's efficacy and scope.

As Figure 6.13 reveals, most drone strikes were conducted in Afghanistan
since 2015, eclipsing other US drone programs across the Middle East and
North Africa, with an average total of 14,081 drone strikes from 2015 until
2020, killing about 7,000 people, including 150 children.

When Afghanistan is excluded, as in Figure 6.14, we can see that US drone
warfare peaked in Pakistan in 2010, Yemen in 2017, and Somalia in 2019. It
is important to note that only confirmed US air strikes are included, while
the database itself also lists many instances of possible US drone strikes and
other special operations, which are yet to be confirmed. Therefore, these
numbers are most likely significant underestimations, especially in the case
of the more recent drone programs in Yemen.

According to administration officials, drone strikes are not only efficient,
but may even be morally necessary. Drones reduce or eliminate the number
of casualties incurred by the intervener. By lowering the risk of US casualties,
their deployment abroad is also less constrained by bureaucratic delays or
public opinion. While drone strikes may be more efficient than traditional
missions, Figures 6.15 and 6.16 show that they still produce tragic civilian
and child deaths in Afghanistan and Pakistan, adding hundreds of civilian
deaths per year (which are most likely underestimations given limited data
on the ground).

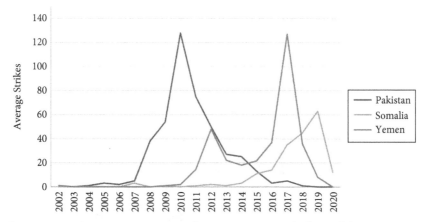

Figure 6.14. Average US Drone Strikes Since 2002, Excluding Afghanistan

Citation: Drone Warfare Database, Bureau of Investigative Journalism. https://www.thebureauinves
tigates.com/projects/drone-war.

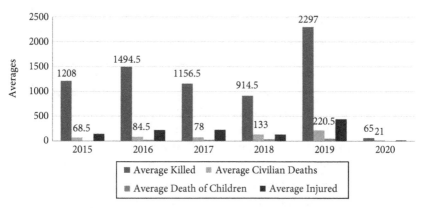

Figure 6.15. Human Cost of Drone Strikes in Afghanistan, 2015–2020

Citation: Drone Warfare Database, Bureau of Investigative Journalism. https://www.thebureauinves
tigates.com/projects/drone-war.

Proponents also argue that drone strikes are effective for killing "high
value targets," good for degrading the structures of terrorist organizations,
and safer than the alternative of deploying ground troops or manned aerial
missions.[22] Yet the effects of drones are hard to assess given the lack of transparency, remoteness of the attacks, politized nature of domestic debates, and
vague measures of effectiveness—leading to minimal empirical evidence
about the costs and benefits.

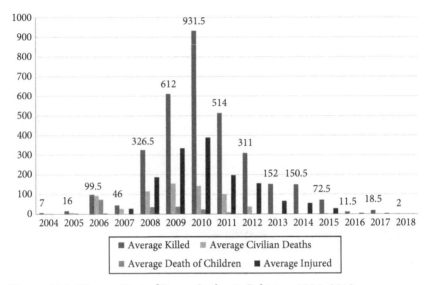

Figure 6.16. Human Cost of Drone Strikes in Pakistan, 2004–2018

Citation: Drone Warfare Database, Bureau of Investigative Journalism. https://www.thebureauinves tigates.com/projects/drone-war.

Critics argue that drone strikes create blowback. In other words, instead of reducing terrorist threats, drone attacks increase anti-American sentiments and terrorism by providing terrorist groups with new recruits. Indeed, the Atlantic Council argues that the use of drones in Yemen, especially, is short-sighted as it leads to anti-American radicalization and threatens US security interests, not to mention the civilian casualties in the country.[23] Drone strikes can destroy the stability and legitimacy of local governments, leaving the United States with few capable partners in the fight against terrorism. As Michael Boyle said, "American counterterrorism policy operates at cross-purposes: it provides a steady flow of arms and financial resources to governments whose legitimacy it systematically undermines by conducting unilateral drone strikes on their territory."[24] By taking the risk of personnel loss out of military interventions, US foreign policymakers may increasingly rely on a quick usage of force to resolve security crises instead of putting time, effort, and funds into nuanced diplomatic negotiations. In other words, the US may be acting recklessly, not heeding the warning about "dying by the sword" and not thinking through the second and third effects on US national security.

While drone attacks may achieve short-term goals at lower costs, such as killing terrorist leaders or supporting other states' antiterrorism programs, it is unlikely that they can truly harm key US adversaries when required. Their role is likely to become more limited as counter-drone efforts increase and other states acquire their own drones, decreasing US air supremacy. But there is no current consensus on the costs and benefits of America's drone policy, as some scholars believe US drone programs seem to be mitigating security risks in places like Pakistan at lower human and financial costs without major blow-back.[25] There is, however, consensus on the lack of systematic evidence on the impact of drones on US foreign policy.[26] Ultimately, drone policy reflects one of the newest methods of US military intervention across the world, and needs to be accurately represented, analyzed, and debated.

Historical Narratives of America the Unleashed, 2001–Present

Despite its widely perceived failings, the Bush era did develop some important milestones, such as the Proliferation Security Initiative, many new free trade agreements, a historically large program to address the global HIV/AIDS epidemic, and the dismantlement of Libya's weapons of mass destruction program.[27] Most significantly, the Bush administration formed a strategic partnership with India and reoriented American assets toward China. Nonetheless, the Bush administration will ultimately be remembered by the fatal flaws of America's Global War on Terror in Afghanistan, Iraq, Somalia, Yemen, and beyond, and its threatening rhetoric against the so-called axis of evil nations, which made both Iran and North Korea more eager to develop their own nuclear weapons programs to defend against the United States' global regime change ambitions.

In particular, the wars in Afghanistan, Iraq, and Syria along with lesser-known operations in sub-Saharan Africa exemplify the post-9/11 trends in US foreign policy of long-lasting regime change wars, military might over diplomacy, expansive operations against the specter of terrorism, and the rise of new special missions.

The War in Afghanistan

On September 11, 2001, the United States suffered the deadliest terror attack in its history. Members of al-Qaeda hijacked four commercial planes, crashing two jets into the World Trade Center towers in New York and one into the Pentagon in Arlington, VA.[28] Almost 3,000 people died within the span of a few hours, and another 1,000 were injured. The attack caused more than $10 billion in damage.[29] Prior to 9/11, the United States mostly fought hostile governments and sometimes hostile insurgent pro- or antigovernment groups, not hostile peoples and identities. It kept its homeland safe from other nation-states and empires, not from the ill-defined, all-encompassing threat of terrorists who could originate from and hide out in any country, including within the United States itself. The collective trauma of the day and the lingering fears of an all-permeating evil that left no country safe came to define US foreign policymaking for decades to come. This was the beginning of the Global War on Terror.

The unprecedented attacks vaulted President George W. Bush into a foreign policy crisis like no other and altered his understanding of the world and the United States' role in it. As a presidential candidate, Bush ran on a platform of retrenchment and investment in domestic programs. But 9/11 forced him to dramatically recalibrate his previously restrained foreign policy vision. On September 18, Congress passed the Authorization for Use of Military Force (AUMF), giving the US military the green light to fight the orchestrators of the 9/11 attacks. Over the years, however, the AUMF would grant permission for the United States to chase down potential terrorist threats all around the world. While the United States did not seek a multilateral UN resolution authorizing the use of force at the time, most international actors saw America's initial response as a legitimate case of self-defense against Al-Qaeda.[30] But this international support did not last long.

In Afghanistan, the United States' righteous cause was aided by the Taliban's long history of human rights repression. Since its 1996 victory in Afghanistan's civil war, the Taliban ruled over the country as an Islamic Emirate. The Taliban rejected US requests to extradite the leaders of Al-Qaeda in the aftermath of the 9/11 attacks, justifying itself on the grounds that Al-Qaeda had not yet claimed responsibility for the attacks. In the context of the deadly terrorist strike on the US homeland, such a refusal was believed to necessitate a direct US response—the complete removal of the Taliban from power. Regime change would also support humanitarian objectives, according to political elites at the time.

On October 7, the United States and United Kingdom invaded Afghanistan to remove the Taliban from power and dismantle Al-Qaeda. The United States formed a coalition of approximately 15,000 Northern Alliance fighters (primarily Tajik and Uzbek), 500 Western special operation forces, several thousand Western infantry troops (including US Marines), and later thousands of Pashtun soldiers. The US coalition fought against approximately 50,000 to 60,000 Taliban soldiers as well as several thousand Al-Qaeda fighters. This first US war against terror garnered large international support as it was seen as a just war of self-defense. Thus, while the United States led the operation, NATO allies and countries such as Australia played key roles alongside US forces in the Western coalition, boosting the United States' credibility and maintaining its normative image and leadership role.[31]

The initial bombing campaign proved quite successful with the Taliban losing control of large parts of the country by November. By December, the United States bombed Tora Bora in Eastern Afghanistan, and ousted the Taliban. There were 2,500 US troops in Afghanistan at the time. An international diplomatic campaign complemented US military operations, and ultimately established the UN-recognized government under Hamid Karzai by the end of 2001. This new government allied with US forces and contributed significant troops to the war for years to come. Yet coordination required significant capacity building and information-sharing, an endeavor that would be ineffectively implemented in the years to come.

Despite its initial success, US military might was not enough to keep the Taliban at bay or to build the capacities and loyalties of the new Afghani state and society. Even though it was heavily outnumbered and outgunned by US coalition forces, the Taliban reorganized in early 2002 and launched an insurgency campaign in response to a streak of US tactical victories. The Taliban used wanton violence against the US military and Afghan citizens to undermine the legitimacy of the Western-imposed Afghan government and the presence of foreign forces. The Taliban's insurgency and spoiler tactics were successful in regaining control of areas of Afghanistan. Despite its initial military victory in Afghanistan, by the end of Bush's presidency, there were 36,000 US troops in the country.[32] The war that began with a strong and swift US victory raged on almost a decade later, with no clear end in sight.

During the Obama years, the US military pivoted to strategies of state building and political operations to counter Taliban victories. Yet despite the strategic shift and campaign promises to reduce the US military presence in Afghanistan, Obama increased the number of US troops in Afghanistan, and by 2011 there were more than 100,000 troops in the country.[33] The United States achieved a significant tactical victory in May 2011 when Al-Qaeda's leader, Osama bin Laden, was assassinated by the United States in Pakistan. Yet by this point, the United States was waging a

Global War on Terror that was far from over, which saw the deployment of US forces in multiple regions, including in the Philippines, Sahara, Horn of Africa, Central America, and Central Asia.[34] The United States government legitimized these new and growing interventions through the vagueness of the original 2001 AUMF. But international support for the expanded mandate was waning fast.

In 2012, NATO forces announced their withdrawal from Afghanistan, and by 2014 the last British military base in the Helmand province was transferred to the Afghan military. NATO maintained some capacity in the country, providing support to domestic Afghan counterterrorism operations. Yet by 2015, the United States relaunched its military operations in Afghanistan, working in coordination with NATO on counterterrorism initiatives. Nonetheless, by the end of Obama's presidency, it looked as if America's slow withdrawal from Afghanistan was in progress, with the number of US troops levels in Afghanistan dwindling down to 9,000.[35] But these lower troops levels were deceiving since the United States was relying on drone warfare during this time, which obscured some of its involvement in Afghanistan.

In 2017, shortly after his inauguration, Trump shocked his supporters and critics alike by announcing an increase in troops in Afghanistan by 50 percent. Like his predecessor, Trump campaigned on withdrawing from Afghanistan, which had now become the longest US war.[36] But once again, US involvement in Afghanistan continued to grow. At this stage of the war, US forces focused on destroying sources of Taliban financing and supporting Afghan troops throughout the country. But there was severe blowback to the United States' increased troops levels, with the Taliban expanding its use of terror against civilians.[37]

It wasn't until February 2019 that communication between the United States and the Taliban began to gain traction, resulting in the first set of peace talks between the two parties. US special envoy, Zalmay Khalilzad, and a top Taliban official, Mullah Abdul Ghani Baradar, focused the discussion on the United States withdrawing its troops in exchange for the Taliban pledging to block international terrorist groups from operating on Afghan soil. After a year of dialogue that waxed and waned, each party's representative signed an agreement on February 29, 2020. Despite some initial optimism, the agreement did not include a ceasefire, and immediately following its signing the Taliban attacked US positions in Afghanistan. The United States responded in kind with aerial strikes, continuing its longest war despite the short-lived hope of a diplomatic compromise.[38]

As of fiscal year 2019, 2,372 US military personnel and 2,372 private contractors were killed in Afghanistan. More than 65,000 people in the Afghan military perished in battle.[39] In total deaths, including nonbattle casualties, the United States lost over 7,000 people while Afghanistan lost over 100,000.[40] The financial costs were quite extreme as well, totaling $975 billion, with the maximum number of US troops in Afghanistan peaking under Obama at more than 100,000.[41]

With the Biden administration's withdrawal of the US military from its longest war, fears of continued Taliban support for nonstate armed groups and the outbreak of a new civil war run rampant in US policy circles.[42] In other words, after two decades of costly military occupation and operations, the United States managed to leave Afghanistan on the brink of collapse.

Pivotal Event: The Iraq War

While the Afghanistan war began the contemporary trends in US foreign policy, the protracted war in Iraq cemented the view of the United States as an aggressor following militaristic doctrines. The previous decade's victory against Saddam Hussein pushed Iraqi forces out of Kuwait and imposed stringent requirements restricting Iraq's military ambitions. The United States and the United Kingdom implemented a strict no-fly zone in the North and South of Iraq to protect populations previously vulnerable to Saddam's aggression. The UN also placed multiple economic sanctions on the country and required mandatory weapon inspections to ensure compliance. Patrolling Iraq's territory led to occasional clashes between Iraqi and US forces, but it wasn't until the passage of the Iraqi Liberation Act in 1998, which appropriated $97 million for democratization efforts in the country, that the full removal of the Iraqi government became a more accepted view in the United States.[43] Later that year, Iraq refused to comply with UN requirements by harassing and interfering with inspections. The United States responded unilaterally by bombing Iraqi military and weapons production infrastructure, prompting lambaste from the international community.

Following the terror attacks of 9/11, the Bush administration viewed Iraq as a much greater security threat than ever before, tying Iraq's political dynamics to the ongoing war in Afghanistan. Senior advisors and officials produced information alleging the Iraqi regime was making weapons of mass destruction (WMD) and maintaining ties with Al-Qaeda. The United

States seemed increasingly keen on forcefully deposing Iraq's leader through a military intervention by manipulating the public's fears of potential nuclear attack by a terrorist group like Al-Qaeda. Despite a lack of evidence on the ground, US public opinion was gradually molded to reflect the administration's interest in a regime change war in Iraq, all while the United States continued to fight in Afghanistan.

On October 16, 2002, Congress passed the joint Iraq Resolution, authorizing the use of military force against Saddam's regime in Iraq.[44] This gave Bush the green light he wanted to initiate the war in Iraq. Up to this point, however, weapons, security, and intelligence experts disagreed with the official US conclusions regarding Iraq's WMD programs and connections to Al-Qaeda. In early 2003, the United States attempted to garner multilateral support for its regime change war, pushing for a UN Security Council resolution to use of force in Iraq. But facing opposition and vetoes from France and Russia, the United States and its coalition members, Britain, Italy, Poland, Spain, Denmark, Italy, Japan, and Australia, withdrew the resolution. The façade of multilateralism, collective security, and liberal norms crumbled, and in the post-9/11 era the United States was no stranger to embracing unilateralism despite the staggering loss to its international image.

On March 20, 2003, the US-led coalition invaded Iraq to depose of Saddam Hussein. The United States deployed more than 100,000 soldiers stationed in Kuwait,[45] with the size and technological advancement of coalition troops swiftly defeating the weakened and poorly organized Iraqi military. By May, Bush announced the end of major combat operations in front of a triumphal mission accomplished banner, and US troops found Saddam near the city of Tikrit in December. Thus, it took less than a year for the United States to declare military victory in Iraq, but as in the case of Afghanistan, this fast military win did not translate into a long-term victory. The United States formed the Coalition Provisional Authority as a transitional government to create democratic institutions in Iraq, which was dissolved following free elections that elected Nouri al-Maliki as prime minister in June 2004. Around the time the new government was inaugurated, US forces began engaging with insurgent troops in Iraq.

The United States successfully invaded Iraq, toppled its existing government, occupied the country, and sponsored a new government, prompting a wave of local resentment. Making matters worse, the new al-Maliki government enacted policies marginalizing Iraq's Sunni majority. Insurgent groups began emerging throughout the country as a form of rebellion against the new government and continued US presence. By 2006, sectarian divisions escalated into a de facto civil war requiring US troops to remain in the country to protect Iraqi government forces. In 2007, Bush announced a surge of 21,500 troops into Iraq and expanded security and reconstruction programs costing $1.2 billion.[46] But around the same time, many coalition members began withdrawing their militaries from the country, sensing that another endless war was to follow.

They were partially right. The United States military remained engaged in Iraq for years to come as it combatted insurgent groups throughout the country. But unlike the case of Afghanistan, in 2009 Obama announced that US combat missions in Iraq would end in August 2010 with a force of 50,000 troops to remain until 2011 to train Iraqi soldiers.[47] Despite better training and resources for the local troops, the withdrawal of US troops left a significant power vacuum in a country beset by sectarian fighting (another legacy of US occupation). The Iraqi government proved unable to pacify internal unrest. Thus, the US operation in Iraq had no long-term victories to speak of. Indeed, the legacy of the Iraq War is the rise of another threat to US security and the region: the Islamic State. In 2014, Sunni extremists established the so-called Islamic State (IS), which spread into Syria and destabilized the whole Middle East and beyond.

In all, the Iraq War proved to be a disastrous foreign policy blunder for the United States. Between 2003 and 2010, 4,491 US service members were killed in action and an estimated $1.2 trillion dollars were spent.[48] Even more devastating, 185,000 to 208,000 Iraqis were killed.[49] The United States paid huge human and financial costs only to further enflame regional insurgencies and help give rise to IS, which would push the United States to embroil itself in Syria too. The war in Iraq also demoted the United States from its liberal high horse in both Western and non-Western spheres. Iraq destroyed the goodwill and political credibility that defined the post–Cold War era for US foreign policy. Now unhindered and often unwanted by international collective institutions, the United States set off on its own military adventures, fueled by its bloated military budget.

The Syrian Civil War

After Iraq, the United States was compelled to intervene next door in Syria not only because of an ongoing civil war but also because the Islamic State

(IS) expanded from Iraq to Syria, threatening regional security. The Syrian conflict began following popular protests against the Ba'athist regime led by Bashar al-Assad. The state's brutal repression of students' anti-government graffiti in Dara'a coupled with pro-democratic movements in North Africa the previous year brought forth large anti-government protests in cities across the country. No longer able to stem the protests through political concessions, Assad directed the Syrian Army to suppress government resistance in April 2011. Soon after, the opposition took up arms, organizing itself as the Free Syrian Army (FSA).[50] Keen on supporting the opposition but weary of another Middle Eastern quagmire, the Obama administration first supported the FSA with nonlethal aid, including food, water, and delivery trucks.[51]

In August 2011, as the humanitarian situation worsened, Obama said Assad must "step aside" and froze Syrian government assets.[52] The following year, Obama announced that if Assad's forces used chemical weapons, it would constitute a "red line," prompting military intervention by the United States.[53] But in 2013, when US intelligence concluded that Assad had indeed used chemical weapons against his own citizens, Obama did not intervene, a decision which was widely criticized as detrimental to America's image.[54]

As fighting escalated between Assad's army and the FSA, the international community failed to reach a meaningful ceasefire agreement. By late 2012, the Syrian conflict unraveled into an all-out war with the Assad government shelling whole cities and rebels using hybrid warfare to weaken and demoralize the Syrian army. At this time, the CIA and several Arab nations decided to militarily supply and train FSA fighters under Operation Timber Sycamore.[55] Instead of relying on a full-blown, transparent, and traditional military operation or gradual diplomatic tools, the United States choose to spearhead a CIA operation as its first on-the-ground involvement in Syria. Weapons were transferred through Jordan's ports and shuttled into Syria by CIA operatives. CIA operatives were also tasked with training Syrian rebels. But with such direct US involvement, the civil war escalated into an international battleground and proxy conflict. Before long, the success of Operation Timber Sycamore was hampered by Russian shelling of rebel strongholds.[56] As fighting continued to consume the far reaches of the country, more third-party states became involved in the conflict.

By 2014, the Syrian opposition began to fracture along multiple lines, complicating any US foreign policy options. The major schism was along religious lines and among jihadist groups including Jahbat al-Nusra, Ahrar al-Sham, and Jaysh al-Islam. Unfortunately, many of these groups benefitted from the US military assistance provided to opposition forces.[57] Thus, similar to previous operations in Iraq and Afghanistan, US policy in Syria inadvertently bolstered the threat of terrorism, instead of limiting it. In the same year, IS, born out of the political vacuum and instability the United States left behind in Iraq, exploited the instability in Syria and swept through the country's northeast. IS's brutal tactics were globally televised and condemned by governments worldwide.

It was only when Syria's civil war turned into an undisputable terrorist playground that Obama announced the United States had started an aggressive air campaign against IS in September 2014.[58] Although Obama sought to restrain US militarism at the beginning of his presidency, his involvement in Syria served as yet another example of breaching his original promise. Over the next five years, the US-led coalition against IS conducted airstrikes on approximately 17,000 targets in Syria.[59] In 2015, fifty US ground troops first moved into Syria, but as US involvement in the war increased, the troop count swelled to roughly 2,000. These soldiers were tasked with organizing and recruiting Syrian Kurdish and Arab soldiers to push IS out of Syria.[60]

With Assad's regime increasingly threatened by the FSA and US involvement, Assad officially requested military aid from the Russian government. By 2015, Russia's military began an air assault on rebel-held positions in western Syria. Russia followed the US playbook and sent military advisors to assist the Syrian Army's efforts against opposition strongholds and IS-held areas in the east.[61] Iran also came to Assad's aid, coordinating with its network of proxy groups in the region, namely Hezbollah, to fight against the FSA.[62] Therefore, the United States' involvement in Syria catalyzed a greater proxy conflict between regional powers in Syria.

The multiparty war created a massive humanitarian catastrophe. "Syria's precipitous decline in well-being [was] unparalleled in the world, even when compared to countries similarly experiencing war, protests, and disasters."[63] The destruction of vital infrastructure and the indiscriminate bombing of civilians forced millions to flee Syria.[64] The exodus led to a refugee crisis that engulfed Turkey and the rest of Europe. By the end of 2015, foreign nations with a stake in the Syrian conflict agreed to meet in Vienna for talks on how to resolve the civil war. Despite the mounting pressure to alleviate both the human suffering and the geopolitical burdens, the talks were largely unsuccessful. The Obama administration maintained its position that peace was contingent on Assad's removal from power, while Russia and Iran refused to debate regime change, focusing instead on how to tackle IS, a mutual enemy for all.[65]

The United States did, in fact, focus its attention on dismantling the IS terror network, especially following deadly terror attacks in Europe and the United States linked to the group in 2015. Obama deployed special operation forces to assist the Kurdish People's Protection Units (YPG) and continued a heavy bombing campaign against IS.[66] By 2016, US support for the YPG proved effective, and the YPG managed to liberate cities controlled by IS. However, the US-YPG relationship was immediately condemned by Turkey, a NATO ally and important US strategic partner, who viewed the YPG as an offshoot of the Kurdistan Worker's Party (PKK). In 2017, a senior State Department official described the United States' relationship with the YPG as "temporary, transactional, and tactical." But also in 2017, Trump expanded US support to the YPG by sending an additional 400 US Marines for training and logistical support.[67]

Despite increased US support, Syrian, Russian, and Iranian forces continued to crush the remaining opposition forces in western Syria. In April 2018, the Assad regime launched a suspected chemical attack on the town of Duoma. A week later, Trump, after vowing to keep America out of further conflict in the Middle East, retaliated with missile strikes against Syrian military bases. It was the first direct US attack on the Syrian government in the war.[68]

In December 2018, Trump surprised both domestic and international audiences alike by announcing the withdrawal of US forces in Syria. This shock announcement increased tensions within the US government and prompted the resignation of Defense Secretary James Mattis. Despite YPG requests for a continued US presence in the area, the United States planned to reduce troop numbers from 2,000 to around 200 by Fall 2020, appearing to abandon its Kurdish allies without notice. Prominent Republicans and Democrats expressed concern, saying the United States was turning its back on the YPG after their sacrifices against IS. In response to domestic backlash, Trump promised the United States would maintain a presence in Syria to prevent the resurgence of IS.[69]

The United States achieved a major tactical victory over IS in the Barisha Raid in 2019, which saw the death of IS's leader, Abu Bakr al-Baghdadi. But this win came after almost a decade of violence and horrors in Syria. The Syrian Civil War is one of the deadliest conflicts of the twenty-first century. According to the Syrian Observatory for Human Rights, almost 400,000 have been killed in Syria since the start of the war (although MIP fatality estimates are higher).[70] The war has internally displaced almost seven million people and created 6.6 million refugees.[71] Yet the US response to the humanitarian and geopolitical components of the crisis remains muted compared to Russia's continued militaristic and soft engagement in the region. Both US presidents, Obama and Trump, were weary of getting involved in another Middle East quagmire, and although both ultimately agreed to conduct air strikes and to provide military support, their delays and inaction are criticized given the scale of humanitarian need in Syria and Russia's and Iran's increasing power in the region. The presidents' involvement in Syria continued the string of interlinked, convoluted wars in the Middle East that meld counterterrorism, regime change, and humanitarian objectives together, but they all appear to have no clear endgame in sight, beyond calls for more or less military might.

Searching for the Lord's Resistance Army

Operation Observant Compass in Central Africa remains an underexplored yet important special operation for US foreign policy in the post-9/11 era, especially given the new interventionist trend of relying exclusively on special forces in sub-Saharan Africa. The operation targeted the Lord's Resistance Army (LRA), a violent nonstate actor operating throughout a swath of Central Africa since the 1980s. LRA's leader, Joseph Kony, attained international notoriety for the organization's use of child soldiers, kidnapping, and the campaign's longevity and resiliency. From 2005 to 2007, Uganda's armed forces pushed the LRA out of the country and into the Democratic Republic of the Congo, decreasing the LRA's capacity to carry out offensive operations. While it was left with only 200 fighters, it continued to recruit in the Democratic Republic of the Congo, Central African Republic, Sudan, and South Sudan. Several regional efforts attempted to defeat the LRA, with the most recent regional alignment including Uganda, the Democratic Republic of the Congo, Central African Republic, and South Sudan joining under the auspices of the African Union.[72]

At the height of the LRA's campaign, the United States provided significant humanitarian aid (hundreds of millions of dollars) to Uganda, and later began funding peacekeeping operations in 2009.[73] After unanimously passing in the House and Senate, Obama signed the Lord's Resistance Army Disarmament and Northern Uganda Recovery Act into law in May 2010.[74] The United States moved beyond humanitarian aid to military strategy. The first 100 US special forces began staging in Entebbe in October 2011. Until this first deployment of special forces, the United States only supported the Ugandan military with training and equipment, not unlike many other American partnerships.[75]

Toward the end of Operation Observant Compass, American operations morphed into gray-zone warfare. The United States conducted messaging and tactical influence operations using leaflets and provided logistical and intelligence support. American troops were also actively going on patrols with regional task force partners. Instead of engaging in direct combat, the advisers guided the regional task force patrols, instructing them on tactical operations in real-time.

Operation Observant Compass cost $780 million by the time it ended in March 2017. This equates to $3.9 million per LRA member. Although the operation lasted six years, at no point did American troops appear to number above 300 personnel.[76] US Africa Command considered Operation Observant Compass a success because it reduced the LRA to roughly 100 fighters and killed or captured four of its top five leaders (all except Kony).[77] But the United States also generally abandoned legal, economic, and diplomatic tools in favor of search and destroy operations in Central Africa. A more balanced strategy could have directly targeted the LRA's capacity to wage war, such as reducing their illicit funding sources like ivory poaching even via nonmilitaristic, diplomatic incentives. Also, the United States (and the UN) needed to train Uganda's defense forces and other partners in human rights and civil affairs, not only direct military action, to help ameliorate the human rights conditions that contributed to the LRA's success.

Operation Observant Compass represents an instance where the United States prioritized and normalized the usage of special forces as standard practice, which is worrisome given the unique challenges of conducting gray-zone military operations that are difficult to review and scrutinize domestically. Beyond the lack of transparency, such military missions increase military expenditures, further perpetuating the incentive to rely on military might as a line of first defense against terrorists, unfavorable regimes, and even small, little-known militant groups like the LRA.

Conclusion

It could be argued that the United States has amassed enough power to adopt a more "adventurous" foreign policy, because it can afford to make mistakes (such as the wars in Afghanistan and Iraq) while remaining more powerful than its competitors. But of course, military involvements also kill US citizens and foreign nationals, raise federal spending on defense and increase the national debt, and harm US soft power among its friends and foes alike. These US military occupations also create path dependencies and harmful incentives since target countries ultimately depend on US military support to maintain their fragile new governments and ward off worse actors such as the Taliban in Afghanistan. US interventions can aggravate existing security threats and create new ones that have not been anticipated or fully thought through.

As it stands, the United States has an expansive military budget but shriveling foreign aid and diplomatic budgets, speaking to the dominance of the Pentagon, rather than the State Department, in foreign policymaking. What does the future hold for US power, influence, and foreign policy? Should the United States pull back its international engagements, or expand them even more? Where and when? What types of foreign policy tools should the United States rely upon in the twenty-first century? Should it act unilaterally or multilaterally? The last chapter examines these questions, taking into account the historical data on US militarism and the lessons learned from previous eras of US foreign policy.

Notes

1. "Remarks by the President in Photo Opportunity with the National Security Team," The White House Archives, September 12, 2001, https://georgewbush-whitehouse. archives.gov/news/releases/2001/09/20010912-4.html.
2. "Remarks by the President in Photo Opportunity with the National Security Team."
3. John L. Gaddis, *Surprise, Security, and the American Experience* (Cambridge, MA: Harvard University Press, 2004), 30–31.
4. Andrew J. Bacevich, *American Empire: The Realities and Consequences of U.S. Diplomacy* (Cambridge, MA: Harvard University Press, 2002); Michael Mann, *Incoherent Empire* (London: Verso, 2002).
5. See the date here: "US Position in the World," *Gallup*, 2021. https://news.gallup.com/poll/116350/position-world.aspx

6. Governor George W. Bush, "A Distinctly American Internationalism," Ronald Reagan Presidential Library, Simi Valley, California, November 19, 1999, https://www.globals ecurity.org/wmd/library/news/usa/1999/991119-bush-foreignpolicy.htm.

7. Walter Russel Mead, *Power, Terror, Peace, and War: America's Grand Strategy in a World at Risk* (New York: Vintage Books, 2005), 110.

8. Mead, *Power, Terror, Peace, and War,* 171.

9. Goldberg, "The Obama Doctrine," 6

10. Hal Brands, *American Grand Strategy in the Age of Trump* (Washington, DC: Brookings Institution Press, 2018), 55.

11. Michael Green, "The Legacy of Obama's Pivot to Asia," *Foreign Policy* (September 3, 2016), http://foreignpolicy.com/2016/09/03/the-legacy-of-obamas-pivot-to-asia/.

12. Kurt M. Campbell, *The Pivot: The Future of American Statecraft in Asia* (New York: Twelve, 2016), 26.

13. Goldberg, "The Obama Doctrine."

14. Quoted in Graham Allison and Niall Ferguson, "Why the U.S. President Needs a Council of Historians," *The Atlantic,* September 2016, https://www.theatlantic.com/magazine/archive/2016/09/dont-know-much-about-history/492746/.

15. Elias Groll, "Obama's Foreign Policy Summed Up in One Quote," *Foreign Policy* (February 9, 2015), https://foreignpolicy.com/2015/02/09/obamas-foreign-policy-summed-up-in-one-quote/.

16. Zoltan Feher, "Neorealist Trump: A New Grand Strategy?" *The Fletcher Forum of World Affairs,* March 4, 2014, http://www.fletcherforum.org/home/2017/3/4/neoreal ist-trump-a-new-grand-strategy.

17. Zoltan Feher, "Does the Trump Administration Have a Strategy for Asia? Thoughts Ahead of the Trump-Xi Summit," *The Fletcher Forum of World Affairs,* April 6, 2017, http://www.fletcherforum.org/home/2017/4/6/does-the-trump-administration-have-a-strategy-for-asia-thoughts-ahead-of-the-trump-xi-summit.

18. Zoltan Feher, "How Can the World Escape Captivity? *Realpolitik* and Cooperation in the Age of COVID-19," *eCCO Magazine,* May 15, 2020, http://www.eccom.info/index.php/business-communication/global-business-global-affairs/214-how-can-the-world-escape-captivity.

19. Michael J. Boyle, "The costs and consequences of drone warfare," *International Affairs* 89, no. 1 (2013): 1–29.

20. Ann Wright, "Killer Drones and the Militalization of U.S. Foreign Policy," *The Foreign Service Journal*, June 2017, http://www.afsa.org/killer-drones-and-militarization-us-foreign-policy.

21. Drone Warfare Database, Bureau of Investigative Journalism, 2018, https://www.thebureauinvestigates.com/projects/drone-war.

22. Boyle, "The Costs and Consequences of Drone Warfare."

23. "U.S. Yemen Counterterrorism and Drone Policy Shortsighted, Undermines U.S. National Security Interests," *States News Service*, October 9, 2014.

24. Boyle, "The Costs and Consequences of Drone Warfare," 3

25. Aqil Shah, "Do U.S. Drone Strikes Cause Blowback? Evidence from Pakistan and Beyond," *International Security* 42, no. 4 (2018): 47–84.

26. Boyle, "The Costs and Consequences of Drone Warfare."

27. Cavanna, "U.S. Grand Strategy."

28. The fourth plane downed in rural Pennsylvania after passengers thwarted the terrorists' fatal intentions.

29. Matthew J. Morgan, "The Impact of 9/11 on Politics and War: The Day that Changed Everything?" *Palgrave Macmillan*, July 15, 2009.

30. Ben Smith and Arabella Thorp, "The Legal Basis for the Invasion of Afghanistan," *House of Commons Library, International Affairs and Defence Section*, February 26, 2010.

31. Michael O'Hanlon, "A Flawed Masterpiece: Assessing the Afghan Campaign," *Foreign Affairs* 81, no. 3 (2002), accessed April 1, 2019, https://www.brookings.edu/wp-cont ent/uploads/2016/06/20020501.pdf.

32. Danielle Kurtzleben, "CHART: How The U.S. Troop Levels In Afghanistan Have Changed Under Obama," *National Public Radio (NPR)*, July 6, 2016, https://www.npr. org/2016/07/06/484979294/chart-how-the-u-s-troop-levels-in-afghanistan-have-changed-under-obama.

33. Kurtzleben, "CHART: How The U.S. Troop Levels In Afghanistan Have Changed Under Obama."

34. Linda Robinson, Patrick B. Johnston, and Gillian S. Oak, U.S. Special Operation Forces in the Philippines, 2001–2014," *RAND Corporation*, 2016, https://www. rand.org/content/dam/rand/pubs/research_reports/RR1200/RR1236/RAND_RR1 236.pdf.

35. Kurtzleben, "CHART: How The U.S. Troop Levels In Afghanistan Have Changed Under Obama."

36. See Table A6.1 in the appendix of the chapter for detailed numbers on operation duration and fatalities.

37. "Timeline of U.S. War in Afghanistan," Council on Foreign Relations, last updated March 2020, https://www.cfr.org/timeline/us-war-afghanistan.

38. "Timeline of U.S. War in Afghanistan," Council on Foreign Relations.

39. "Casualty Status," *U.S. Department of Defense*, Oct. 5, 2020; Neta C. Crawford, *Update on the Human Costs of War for Afghanistan and Pakistan, 2001 to mid-2016* (Providence, RI: Watson Institute, Brown University, 2016), accessed April 3, 2019, https://watson.brown.edu/costsofwar/files/cow/imce/papers/2016/War%20in%20 Afghanistan%20and%20Pakistan%20UPDATE_FINAL_corrected%20date.pdf.

40. See Table A6.1 in the appendix for MIP data on operation fatalities.

41. Neta Crawford, "Cost of War: United States Budgetary Costs of the Post-9/11 Wars Through FY2019: $5.9 Trillion Spent and Obligated," *Brown University Watson Institute*, November 14, 2018, https://watson.brown.edu/costsofwar/files/cow/imce/ papers/2018/Crawford_Costs%20of%20War%20Estimates%20Through%20FY2 019.pdf.

42. Kevin Liptak, Natasha Bertrand, Jeremy Herb, Zachary Cohen, and Oren Liebermann, "A 'Gut Decision': Inside Biden's Defense of Afghanistan Withdrawal Amid Warnings of Country's Collapse," *CNN Politics*, July 2, 2021, https://www.cnn.com/2021/07/02/ politics/afghanistan-biden-withdrawal-security/index.html.

43. "H.R. 4655—Iraqi Liberation Act of 1998," 105th Congress (1997–1998), US House of Representatives, October 31, 1998, https://www.congress.gov/bill/105th-congress/house-bill/4655.

44. "Authorization for the Use of Military Force Against Iraq Resolution of 2002," 107th Congress (2001–2002), US House of Representatives, October 16, 2002, https://www.congress.gov/bill/107th-congress/house-joint-resolution/114.

45. "U.S. Has 100,000 Troops in Kuwait," *CNN*, February 18, 2003, https://www.cnn.com/2003/WORLD/meast/02/18/sprj.irq.deployment/index.html.

46. Heidi Peters, "Department of Defense Contractor and Troop Levels in Afghanistan and Iraq: 2007–2020," *Congressional Research Service,* updated February 22, 2021, https://sgp.fas.org/crs/natsec/R44116.pdf.

47. Peters, "Department of Defense Contractor and Troop Levels in Afghanistan and Iraq: 2007–2020."

48. Neta Crawford, "U.S. Costs of Wars Through 2014: $4.4 Trillion and Counting; Summary of Costs for the U.S. Wars in Iraq, Afghanistan, and Pakistan," *Boston University*, June 25, 2014, https://watson.brown.edu/costsofwar/files/cow/imce/papers/2014/US%20Costs%20of%20Wars%20through%202014.pdf.

49. "Documented Civilian Deaths from Conflict," *Iraq Body Count*, accessed April 5, 2022, https://www.iraqbodycount.org.

50. Zachary Laub, "Syria's Civil War: The Descent into Horror," *Council on Foreign Relations*, March 17, 2021, https://www.cfr.org/article/syrias-civil-war.

51. Elise Labott, "Obama Authorized Covert Support for Syrian Rebels, Sources Say," *CNN*, August 1, 2012, https://www.cnn.com/2012/08/01/us/syria-rebels-us-aid/index.html.

52. Kirit Radia, "Obama Calls on Syria's Assad to Step Down, Freezes Assets," *ABC News*, August 18, 2011, https://abcnews.go.com/International/obama-calls-syrias-assad-step-freezes-assets/story?id=14330428.

53. Wyn Bowen, Jeffrey W. Knopf, and Matthew Moran, "The Obama Administration and Syrian Chemical Weapons: Deterrence, Compellence, and the Limits of the 'Resolve plus Bombs' Formula," *Security Studies* 29, no. 5 (2020): 797–831, DOI: 10.1080/09636412.2020.1859130.

54. Joby Warrick, *Red Line: The Unraveling of Syria and America's Race to Destroy the Most Dangerous Arsenal in the World. New York: Doubleday* (New York: Doubleday, 2021).

55. Mark Mazzetti, Adam Goldman, and Michael Schmidt, "Behind the Sudden Death of a $1 Billion Secret CIA War in Syria," *The New York Times*, August 2, 2017, https://www.nytimes.com/2017/08/02/world/middleeast/cia-syria-rebel-arm-train-trump.html.

56. Operation Timber Sycamore is estimated to have cost $1 billion. The program was unsuccessful as Russian bombing eliminated gains made by rebel groups. Moreover, the sale of weapons and training is believed to have flooded the regions black market with weapons and possibly armed extremist groups that initially fought for the overthrow of Assad such as al-Qaeda's splinter group, Jabhat al-Nusra. Mazzetti, Goldman, and Schmidt, "Behind the Sudden Death of a $1 Billion Secret CIA War in Syria."

57. Mazzetti, Goldman, and Schmidt, "Behind the Sudden Death of a $1 Billion Secret CIA War in Syria."

58. "Operation Inherent Resolve; Targeted Operations to Defeat ISIS," US Department of Defense May 2017, https://dod.defense.gov/OIR/.

59. "Operation Inherent Resolve; Targeted Operations to Defeat ISIS," US Department of Defense.

60. "Combined Joint Task Force; Operation Inherent Resolve," *United States Military*, Published July 2017, https://www.inherentresolve.mil/Portals/14/Documents/Miss ion/HISTORY_17OCT2014-JUL2017.pdf?ver=2017-07-22-095806-793.

61. Mariya Petkova, "What Has Russia Gained from Five Years of Fighting in Syria?" *al Jazeera*, October 1, 2020, https://www.aljazeera.com/features/2020/10/1/what-has-russia-gained-from-five-years-of-fighting-in-syria.

62. Navvar Saba, "Factbox: Iranian Influence and Presence in Syria," *Atlantic Council*, November 5, 2020, https://www.atlanticcouncil.org/blogs/menasource/factbox-iran ian-influence-and-presence-in-syria/.

63. F. Cheung, A. Kube, L. Tay et al., "The Impact of the Syrian Conflict on Population Well-Being," *Nature Communications* 11 (2020): 3899, https://doi.org/10.1038/s41 467-020-17369-0.

64. Cheung, Kube, Tay et al., "The Impact of the Syrian Conflict on Population Well-Being."

65. "Russia Says Syria Peace Talks Fail to Agree on Fate of President Assad," *Reuters*, October 30, 2015, https://www.reuters.com/article/uk-mideast-crisis-russia-lavrov/ russia-says-syria-peace-talks-fail-to-agree-on-fate-of-president-assad-idUKKC N0SO2G720151030.

66. Mark Thompson, "Why More Airstrikes Won't Beat ISIS," *TIME Magazine*, November 17, 2015, https://time.com/4116888/paris-attacks-isis-strategy/.

67. Amanda Sloat, "The US Played Down Turkey's Concerns about Syrian Kurdish Forces. That Couldn't Last," *Brookings Institute*, October 9, 2019, https://www.brooki ngs.edu/blog/order-from-chaos/2019/10/09/the-us-played-down-turkeys-conce rns-about-syrian-kurdish-forces-that-couldnt-last/.

68. Michael Crowley and Andrew Restuccia, "Trump Strikes Syria," *Politico*, April 14, 2018, https://www.politico.com/story/2018/04/13/trump-syria-strikes-523051.

69. Alex Johnson, "U.S. to Leave about 200 Troops in Syria, White House Says," *NBC News*, February 21, 2019, https://www.nbcnews.com/news/us-news/u-s-leave-about-200-troops-syria-white-house-says-n974356.

70. "Syria Death Toll Tops 380,000 in Almost Nine-Year War: Monitor," *France24*, April 1, 2020, https://www.france24.com/en/20200104-syria-death-toll-tops-380-000-in-almost-nine-year-war-monitor.

71. "Syria Emergency," UN Refugee Agency (UNHCR), https://www.unhcr.org/en-us/ syria-emergency.html.

72. James J. F. Forest, "U.S. Military Deployments to Africa: Lessons from the Hunt for Joseph Kony and the Lord's Resistance Army," *Joint Special Operations University*, August 2014. https://apps.dtic.mil/dtic/tr/fulltext/u2/a617136.pdf.

73. Alexis Arieff and Lauren Ploch, "The Lord's Resistance Army: The U.S. Response," *Congressional Research Service*, May 15, 2014, https://pdfs.semanticscholar.org/21f5/552d22cc5abaaa4c08f6aa16641d56a06e93.pdf?_ga=2.61102956.1134487768.1588945989-636046872.1588945989.

74. Barack Obama, "Letter from the President to the Speaker of the House of Representatives and the President Pro Tempore of the Senate Regarding the Lord's Resistance Army," October 14, 2011, https://obamawhitehouse.archives.gov/the-press-office/2011/10/14/letter-president-speaker-house-representatives-and-president-pro-tempore.

75. Obama, "Letter from the President to the Speaker of the House of Representatives and the President Pro Tempore of the Senate Regarding the Lord's Resistance Army"; Jeffrey Gettleman and Eric Schmitt, "U.S. Aided a Failed Plan to Rout Ugandan Rebels," *The New York Times*, February 6, 2009, https://www.nytimes.com/2009/02/07/world/africa/07congo.html; Jolle Demmers and Lauren Gould, "An Assemblage Approach to Liquid Warfare: AFRICOM and the 'Hunt' for Joseph Kony," *Security Dialogue* 49, no. 5 (October 1, 2018): 364–381, https://doi.org/10.1177/0967010618777890.

76. Arieff, Ploch, "The Lord's Resistance Army: The U.S. Response."

77. "U.S. Forces Transition Counter-LRA Mission to Broader Security and Stability Activities," *United States Africa Command*, March 29, 2017, https://twitter.com/USAfricaCommand/status/847133591314272259.

Chapter 6 Appendix

Table A6.1 List of US Military Interventions with Duration and Fatalities, 2001–2019

Start Year	Name	Duration (Days)	US Battle Deaths	State B Battle Deaths	Avg. Total Battle Deaths	US Total Deaths	State B Total Deaths
2001	Hainan Island Incident	102	0	1	1	0	1
2001	China/Taiwan Dispute	1	0	0	0	0	0
2001	War in Afghanistan	7268	2372	69500	139192	7092	235100
2002	Freedom Eagle; Enduring Freedom, Philippines	350	1	3	4	12	4
2002	Colombia Special Forces Deployment	ongoing	0	0	0	0	0
2002	Operation Enduring Freedom—Horn of Africa	ongoing	0	0	0	19	0
2002	US Assistance to Pakistan	ongoing					
2002	Evacuation Mission in Cote d'Ivoire	1	0	0	0	0	0
2003	Indonesia Freedom of Navigation Operation	1	0	0	0	0	0
2003	PRK withdraws from NPT	215	0	0	0	0	0
2003	Hood Event against Turkish soldiers	2	0	0	0	0	0
2003	Operation Iraqi Freedom	3196	4491	34630	39121	4491	196500
2003	Detention of US Service members in Iran	3	0	0	0	0	0
2003	Joint Task Force Liberia	69	0	1787	1.787	0	3787
2003	Operation Enduring Freedom—Horn of Africa ongoing		0	0	0	2	0
2004	Fortification of Kwangju	216	0	0	0	0	0
2004	Operation Secure Tomorrow	100	0	0	0	0	4080

(continued)

Table A6.1 Continued

Start Year	Name	Duration (Days)	US Battle Deaths	State B Battle Deaths	Avg. Total Battle Deaths	US Total Deaths	State B Total Deaths
2004	Iran Border Fortification	3203	0	0	0	0	0
2004	Violations of Iranian Airspace	135	0	0	0	0	0
2004	Syria Border Clash	1	0	0	0	0	0
2004	Operation Enduring Freedom—Horn of Africa	ongoing	0	0	0	3	0
2005	Counterterrorism mission in Yemen	ongoing	1	-9	-9	1	15
2005	Iraqi Border Clashes	99	9	100	109	9	100
2005	Pakistan Earthquake Response	175	0	0	0	0	0
2005	Pakistan drone strikes	1	0	2	2	0	2
2005	Drone Strikes in Waziristan	95	0	11	11	0	33
2006	Israel-Hezbollah War/July War	15	0	0	0	0	0
2006	Drone strikes in Pakistan	1510	0	1444	1444	0	1998
2006	Support of AMISOM	453	0	10	10	0	8500
2007	Erbil Raid	179	0	0	0	0	0
2007	Detaining Iranian Nationals	2	0	0	0	0	0
2008	Abu Kamal Raid	1	0	1	1	0	12
2008	Airspace violation in Pakistan	1	0	19	19	0	19
2008	Waziristan Drone Strikes	410	0	32+	32+	0	-9
2009	Naval Skirmish	11	0	0	0	0	0

2009	Korean Sea Hostilities	705	0	0	2	0	0
2009	Al-Majalah Cruise Missile Strikes	1	0	14	14	0	55
2009	Trespassing Drone in Iran	1	0	0	0	0	0
2010	Venezuela Airspace Violation	1	0	0	0	0	0
2010	Border clash in Pakistan	1	0	2	2	0	2
2011	Operation Odyssey Dawn	227	0	N/A	N/A	0	66
2011	Operation Observant Compass	1358	0	4	4	0	4
2012	Philippines Typhoon Relief	13	0	0	0	0	0
2012	Hostage Rescue Mission in Somalia	1	0	9	9	0	9
2013	Syrian Civil War/Counter IS	ongoing	0	0	0	3	0
2013	Burundi Airlift	21	0	N/A	N/A	0	N/A
2013	Operation Juniper Shield	ongoing	4	21	30	4	21
2014	Ukraine Military Assistance	ongoing	0	10500	10500	0	13850
2014	Operation Inherent Resolve	ongoing	75	80000	80075	89	80000
2014	US involvement in Syrian Civil War	1868	5	200000	200000	5	500000
2014	Operation United Assistance	288	0	0	0	0	11310
2015	Operation Freedom Sentinel	ongoing	91	N/A	N/A	91	N/A
2015	Boko Haram	1564	0	N/A	N/A	0	N/A
2016	Hurricane Matthew Relief	17	0	0	0	0	0
2016	Cruise Missile Strikes in Yemen	1	0	0	0	0	0
2017	Hurricane Maria Relief	76	0	0	0	0	0
2017	Operation Continuing Promise	62	0	0	0	0	0
2017	Peru Flooding Relief	19	0	0	0	0	0

(continued)

Table A6.1 Continued

Start Year	Name	Duration (Days)	US Battle Deaths	State B Battle Deaths	Avg. Total Battle Deaths	US Total Deaths	State B Total Deaths
2017	Joint Task Force Hurricane Relief in DR	29	0	0	0	0	0
2017	Stella Daisy Uruguay Search and Rescue	5	0	0	0	0	0
2017	Sri Lanka Humanitarian Assistance	6	0	0	0	0	0
2018	Thai Cave Rescue	13	0	0	0	0	2
2018	Venezuelan Refugees Humanitarian mission	8	0	0	0	0	0
2018	Operation Enduring Promise	68	0	0	0	0	0
2019	Baghdad Embassy Protection	2	0	0	0	0	0
2019	Oil tanker attacks response in Saudi Arabia ongoing		0	0	0	0	0

Note: Missing duration figures denote that the dispute is still ongoing as of December 31, 2019.

7

America the Lost?

> *We choose hope over fear. We see the future not as something out of
> our control, but as something we can shape for the better through con-
> certed and collective effort. We reject fatalism or cynicism when it
> comes to human affairs. We choose to work for the world as it should
> be, as our children deserve it to be.*[1]
> Barack Obama, address to the United Nations, September 24, 2014

Since its early years, the United States considered itself to be exceptional,
both domestically and in foreign affairs. A force for good; an exemplar for
the world. This American exceptionalism drove the young country to expand
westward within the continent, spreading its ideology and economic system;
then proclaiming itself the benign steward of the Western hemisphere and,
after World War II, the globe.[2] Thus, since its founding the United States has
viewed itself as uniquely good: a nation of pious and prosperous peoples anx-
ious that others emulate its great example. The US Civil War ushered in great
changes in US thinking about technology and war, because advances in rail
communications, coal-powered steam engines in locomotives and ships,
and the telegraph rapidly increased the speed and density of global trade and
communications networks. The US tradition of isolationism, of inward expansion, eroded. By World War I, US exceptionalism was poised for a major
update: military intervention. The world would never be the same.

Despite its growing expansionism overseas after the US Civil War, the
United States refused to perceive itself as an imperialist power and largely
ignored the harmful consequences of its military adventurism, even when
its militarism starkly contradicted America's self-image of restraint, democracy, and rule of law. These contradictions between America's self-image and
its impact on those it sought to benefit by its interventions have intensified

Dying by the Sword. Monica Duffy Toft and Sidita Kushi, Oxford University Press. © Oxford University Press 2023.
DOI: 10.1093/oso/9780197581438.003.0008

painfully in the twenty-first century. Most Americans remain unaware of just how often the United States has resorted to the use of force—just how often the United States has drawn its sword from its sheath—and unaware both that this use of violence as a first resort has been increasing over time, and that it has tarnished a once enviable global reputation.

In the name of "freedom" and democracy, the United States displaced and wiped out much of the indigenous American Indian nations in its Frontier Wars from the 1700s until the early 1900s.[3] It occupied much of Latin America and overthrew left-leaning leaders using both military might and economic pressure throughout the 1900s, leaving a legacy of corruption, dependence, dictatorship—and unrecognized resentment by Latin America's peoples—in its wake. During the Cold War, US foreign policy relied on covert operations and proxy wars to prevent what it believed to be communist expansion and the dictatorship that inevitably followed a communist takeover. But this militaristic impulse often accomplished the opposite by installing cruel and corrupt dictators.

Tragically, US anticommunist foreign policies during the Cold War mainly injured nonwhite populations; echoing US policies back home in ways that were antithetical to human rights and democracy.[4] Since anticolonial struggles were often influenced by communist parties, it wasn't long before anticommunist sentiment in the United States was used to justify domestic racism alongside military interventions in Latin America, the Caribbean, and Asia. For example, J. Edgar Hoover used his position in the Federal Bureau of Investigation to "raise alarm over the alleged propensity of African American leaders toward communism." He said that communists had "done a vast amount of evil damage by carrying doctrines of race revolt and the poison of Bolshevism to the Negroes."[5]

Even George Kennan's perceptions of the Soviet Union were influenced by his sense of a global racial (and sexist!) hierarchy. He was repelled by "most Third World Peoples," writing in 1938 that the United States should be turned into a "benevolent despotism" of upper-class white males, excluding women, immigrants, and blacks.[6] There are thus clear connections between anticommunism as an aggressive US foreign policy and racism at home and abroad.

In the post–Cold War era, starting during its "unipolar moment", the United States continued its regime change wars in the name of democracy and human rights, despite the end of the US-Soviet rivalry. It expanded its definition of national interest to perhaps the most vague and dangerous goal—freedom—to the detriment of establishing core objectives and indicators of mission success in specific interventions. Unlike the Woodrow Wilson era, when "freedom" meant allowing those liberated to choose their own destiny, the post–Cold War US understanding of "freedom" incorporated the unreasonable expectation that those liberated from tyranny would necessarily choose to emulate all aspects of US- or European-style democracy; and when they didn't manifest, postwar "nation building," led by the sword, must follow.

Though lacking the same existential security threats as during the Cold War, today US foreign policy remains militaristic, and the US continues to allow its once formidable diplomatic assets to wither away. Despite its overall power and potential, America appears lost. Its bloated defense budgets perpetuate blurry, broadened visions of national interests to pursue across all corners of the world, while special interest groups within the defense industry continue to push the Iron Triangle into greater military expansion and engagement abroad. More disturbing still, US militarism has continued to prioritize technologies that can kill at ever greater distances with impugnity, thus avoiding messy national debates about the appropriate or effective use of lethal armed force abroad in the service of US national interests.

When analyzing the historical data on US military interventions since the nation's founding, five lessons stand out. Policymakers should heed these lessons if they want to steer America's foreign policy toward a more effective path for US national interests. Historically, most polities who reach a level of relative power as great as that of the United States after World War II provoke countervailing alliances. The only way to prevent such alliances, which ultimately overwhelm a rising hegemon, is to act in ways that liberate and benefit more than they oppress and exploit. That's rare, but it's something the United States may have been able to manage until the twenty-first century, when its overuse of armed force and its hypocrisy and double standards began to dramatically erode its legitimacy in the eyes of global public opinion. We isolate five lessons and the policies that these lessons imply because we believe it's not too late to turn that around.

We should start with clarifying that we do not think US military preeminence is itself necessarily an obstacle to restoring the United States to its aspiration to lead. Clearly an effective military with global reach remains a critical asset for US national and security interests in rare circumstances. But an excessively aggressive America is a problem that everyone should care about. The United States' long aspiration to be an exemplar for others can backfire too: US "force-first" foreign policy may make it easier for other state actors, especially eager revisionist powers such as Russia and China, to justify their growing militarism abroad; it prioritizes global militarism and defense spending over domestic programs and economic support; and it turns the United States into a feared and increasingly resented global actor, instead of the beacon of liberty, the rule of law, and democracy that the United States aspired to be since its founding.

Five Key Lessons

After looking at the data on US interventions across eras and assessing the historical narratives of America's grand strategy, we identified five key lessons. These lessons may offer a sense of direction to contemporary US foreign policy, and perhaps most importantly, identify the dimensions in immediate need of reform.

The Countries That Are Framed as Contemporary Aggressors to the United States Are Often the Countries Most Targeted by US Military Interventions

The United States often justifies its militarism through defensive rhetoric—it must protect itself from belligerent international actors and anti-Americanism. In this interpretation, the world is out to get the United States, threatening its freedom and its way of life. But as Figure 7.1 illustrates, the countries that are often labeled as our enemies—such as China, Russia, North Korea, and Iran—are the same countries that have incurred the lion's share of US military interventions across history; which ironically has likely contributed to their modern-day patterns of international aggression. This trend should never be used to justify these countries' modern-day policies and wars but simply to connect the dots on the possible consequences of the long-term usage of force abroad by the US and all other actors.[7]

US interventions in China, for instance, account for about 10 percent of all US military interventions, and this number does not even include US interventions against multiple states at once, such as interventions against Chinese influence in East Asia. While this cannot justify the aggressive behavior of these states today, it is important to note for improved policymaking

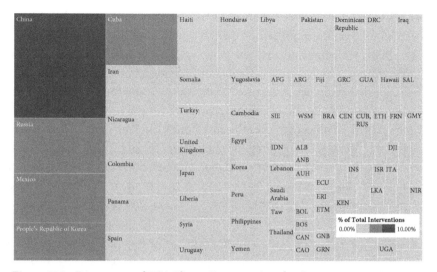

Figure 7.1. Percentage of US Military Interventions by Country, 1776–2019

Note: US interventions that targeted multiple countries are not included in this graphic. Therefore, the percentages listed here are underestimated as they do not consider US interventions that may have intervened in a different country or countries but served as proxies for another (such as interventions against Russia in Eastern Europe).

for all: any escalating US militarism against such actors may make matters worse by confirming their worst fears and pushing them to bolster their militaries, spheres of influence, and weapons programs to guard against US regime change operations and regional domination. Greater US military intervention, in this case, might worsen the existing security dilemma between the United States and its aggressors, rivals, and enemies. In other words, by living by the sword, we increase our risk of dying by it.

US Foreign Policy Objectives Shifted from Territorial Gains to Regime Change Wars in Contemporary International Politics, with New Consequences

Leaving a bloody trail across the US continent, the United States first vied for territorial and direct economic gains throughout the 1800s in North America, and in the early 1900s across the entire Western hemisphere. After the two world wars, it shifted to less tangible national objectives, such as "containment"; and after the Cold War, the US use of armed force to support the creation of favorable regimes or the removal of unfavorable ones escalated;

and came to include overlapping objectives of "social protection," and "protective" interventions on behalf of US business interests abroad. Finally, in the 1990s, we witnessed the new phenomenon of humanitarian military interventions, which were invariably well-intended, but often resulted in less than optimal outcomes. As Figure 7.2 shows, the United States relied on military intervention to pursue regime change and social protective operations more than other objectives after the end of the Cold War.

Notably, the objectives of regime change and social protection are blurry, difficult to define even in theory, and more problematic to enforce in practice. They invariably incorporate "outside-in" conceptions of legitimacy in rule (e.g., elections), and they demand above all else a centered understanding of the people the US is trying to help—people literally being tortured, abused, and oppressed by, say, a corrupt and venal dictator. Too often—perhaps invariably—the United States imagined that simply bringing down this oppressive dictator would be sufficient to achieve long-term security, prosperity, and stability; all goals consistent with broader US foreign policy and national security objectives. But without a functioning State Department, it is too easy to mistake a yearning to replace an evil dictator with a desire to emulate Western conceptions of legitimate governance, or covalent foreign policy interests. This is why so many efforts at regime change lead the United States down the path of ill-defined "forever wars" with no endgame

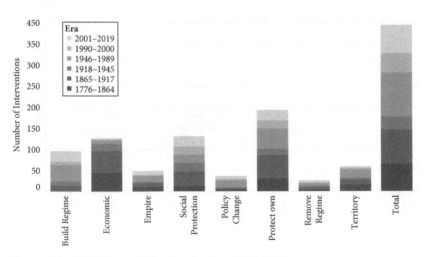

Figure 7.2. US Military Objectives by Era, 1776–2019

in sight and no clear national interests to pursue, as in Afghanistan and Iraq. And when the people being "liberated to death" object and resist Western efforts with violence, that also serves to justify greater and greater US military spending and expansion across the world through US bases, technological investment, drone programs, and the intrusion of US private military contractors into foreign wars. Violence, in the absence of great care in its use and its targets, in other words, begets violence. The Muslim Brotherhood metastasizes into Al Qaeda. Al Qaeda metastasizes into IS/IL; and on and on. Extending of the concept of national interest to include regime change by force and state building also means creating unsustainable and counterproductive demand for greater US military engagement worldwide. This risks perpetuating and prioritizing a military-industrial complex, and supports military adventurism at large. The resources lost then starve America's education infrastructure and democratic institutions, creating a feedback cycle of increasingly unrestrained militarism abroad. Today, it would be more accurate to return the Department of Defense to its former name, the War Department: US wars of "self-defense" have become US "forever wars," and they're moving further away from public and democratic scrutiny due to technological innovations, permissive legal authorizations, and increasingly lax Congressional oversight.

America's Rivals Have Deescalated Armed Disputes, While the United States Has Escalated Them Since 2001

After 9/11, the United States grew more belligerent in its global militarism while its rivals became less aggressive in response. Figure 7.3 shows that the post-9/11 era featured the lowest rates of State B-initiated incidents, with State B initiating less than 40 percent. As the figure also reveals, this represents the greatest decrease in State B-initiated incidents relative to previous eras. Previous data on US hostility levels relative to its target states also reveal a similar trend.

As the world became safer for the United States, the country grew more aggressive, not less; with higher rates of military intervention. This data should cause US foreign policy elites and citizens alike to shift their perspective. If the resort to arms is only justified when threatened with war, conquest, and occupation, then the increase in US military interventions in

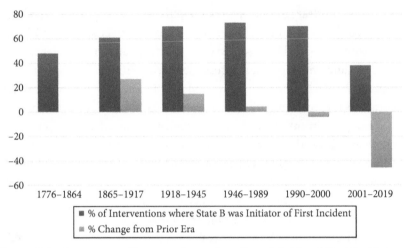

Figure 7.3. Percentage of Interventions where State B Initiated First Incident, Change across Eras, 1776–2019

the absence of such a threat harms US legitimacy and damages its reputation abroad. Given that the United States still possesses tremendous diplomatic and economic resources, it need not behave in such combative ways to defend itself. False perceptions about US security create a self-fulfilling prophecy.

Moreover, the reduction of resort to arms by US adversaries should not lead to the conclusion that hyper aggressive US military intervention has caused its adversaries to stand down. The use of cyberattacks by, for example, the Russian Federation in 2016 were not only implicated in Britain's exit from the European Union, but also a US presidential election whose Russia-supported winner was avowedly hostile to NATO. All this without firing a shot. If you can't compete with the United States in military power and global reach—and honestly, no other state in the international system can—why waste resources trying when you can gravely damage your rivals by less costly, risky, and other-than-military means? And as US legitimacy has declined, the same diplomatic power that the United States once so powerfully deployed to isolate its totalitarian rivals during the Cold War, may be deployed by others to isolate the United States should it be perceived as a bully.

The United States Now Uses Greater Military Force in Pursuit of Lesser National Interests

After greatly increasing its militarism since the 1980s, Figure 7.4 reveals that by the 2000s the United States was intervening at similar frequencies in disputes that held lower levels of national interests.

In fact, the unipolar era and the post-9/11 era are marked by the lowest levels of national interest and higher rates of intervention across all of US history. At the same time of such military adventurism, US power capabilities relative to the international system stagnated, according to CINC. Waning power coupled with growing militarism disconnected to vital national interests is a recipe for imperial overstretch—the depletion of domestic resources and economic power, decline in international goodwill and soft power, multiple international conflicts raging with no clear end, and target countries like Afghanistan left on the brink of civil war after decades-long occupations.[8]

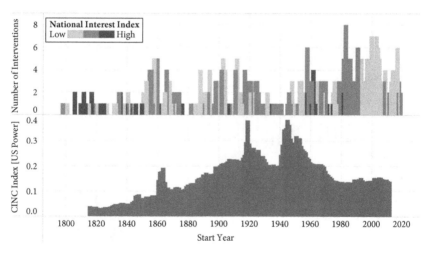

Figure 7.4. US Military Interventions across all years and CINC Power Capabilities, 1776–2019

Citation: Correlates of War Project. *National Material Capabilities, 1816–2012.* Version 6. http://www.correlatesofwar.org; J. David Singer, "Reconstructing the Correlates of War Dataset on Material Capabilities of States, 1816–1985," *International Interactions* 14 (1987): 115–132

As the United States Grew in Power, It Moved from Regional Militarism to Global Militarism, Driven by a Growing Military Budget and Fewer Restraints

As Figure 7.5 shows, it was in the 1980s that the United States embarked on fully noncontiguous military interventions, expanding its role as a global hegemon in a hypermilitaristic way.

Recent hypermilitarism does not mean the United States was dovish in the decades and centuries prior. It undertook frequent military interventions within the Western hemisphere and the Pacific before it was powerful enough to expand itself around the globe. The United States' willingness to unleash its military beyond the Western hemisphere, however, may turn other international actors away, creating new rivalries and preventing global solutions to twenty-first century problems that require transnational goodwill and cooperation.

Moreover, as the graphs also underline, America's move to a more global militarism coincides with a jump in US military expenditures, pointing to the need to reassess domestic priorities and special interests as a vital step toward reducing US militarism abroad. After all, if the United States only has

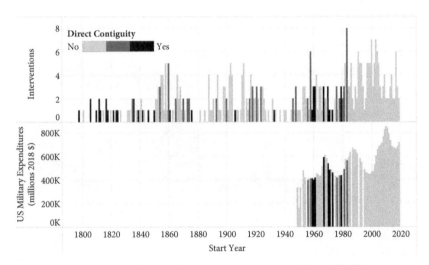

Figure 7.5. Contiguity of US Military Interventions and Overall Military Expenditures across All Years, 1776–2019

Citation: Correlates of War Project. Direct Contiguity Data, 1816-2016. Version 3.2. http://corr elatesofwar.org; Stockholm International Peace Research Institution (SIPRI). Extended Military Expenditure Database. Beta. https://www.sipri.org/databases/milex.

a hammer as defense budgets rise while diplomatic budgets diminish, then it will inevitably treat every problem in the world as a nail.

Implications for Theory and Policy

When the United States and its allies constructed a liberal world order in the aftermath of World War II, the US was the most powerful international actor of the time. The United States was spared the destruction of both world wars, but in recognition of the need to prevent a third, possibly species-ending world war, and in possession of an unmatched economy and a military with global reach, the United States established a key set of global institutions, economic rules, and shared values linked to collective security, democracy, and free trade. Its commitment to liberal principles and rules were inconsistently applied because its fear of the USSR led it to double standards and hypocrisy in the service of national security or, as was said at the time, national survival. Most odious was US support of dictatorships in Africa, Asia, and Latin America.

This liberal world order produced a wide range of success stories after the devastation of World War II. It turned mortal enemies like Germany and Japan into prosperous, democratic US allies. It ushered in a wave of democratization, especially after the end of the Cold War. And it encouraged the consolidation of European states into what would eventually become the European Union. NATO also expanded eastward—first to deter Soviet expansion and aggression, but then to maintain the liberal character and shared values and alliances of the American-led order. Indeed, with its power and influence, the United States supported and led ("hegemon" comes from the ancient Greek word for *leadership*, not tyranny) a liberal empire that others wanted to join; founded less on coercion and more on consensual trends (at least that was the growing understanding in the 1990s). Some have called it an "empire by invitation," but an empire nonetheless.[9]

Unfortunately, recent data indicate that the United States is hemorrhaging credibility as the benevolent leader of this liberal world order; a particularly worrisome trend among its allies and transatlantic partners. Global polls reveal that many countries across the Western world began to see the United States less as a promoter of freedoms and liberties, and more as a suppressor of these ideals.[10] It was defense of the liberal order that propelled extreme levels of US military expenditures and launched US military interventions—first in the Korean War, and next in Vietnam. But by the year 2000, this changed. US-led military interventions in Afghanistan, Iraq, Syria, Yemen, and so many other places were hard to justify as supporting the liberal order that brought down the Soviet Union and prevented a third world war. And many citizens of the world are now dissatisfied, as the promised gains of liberal free trade and globalization have been increasingly restricted to fewer and fewer of the world's peoples. Resentment over accelerating income inequality within and between countries has been manipulated by politicians across the democratic world; including in the United States itself. While we used to think threats to the liberal world order would come from the outside (from revisionist states such as China or Russia), today it increasingly looks like the most serious threats—indeed, a repudiation of the rule of law, the principle of majority rule, and free trade—are coming from within the order itself.

Given such trends, which grand strategic vision should the United States adopt to best confront its future challenges—continued primacy? deep engagement in the world order made in its image? or something closer to the restrainer or offshore balancing approaches?[11] Any change in American foreign policy trends will be difficult to achieve if history is any guide. Neither former presidents Barack Obama nor Donald Trump proved able to alter the course of the US security policy, even though both promised radical change. Both administrations ultimately caved to pressure to continue US primacy through militarism, albeit with different approaches and degrees of success. Importantly, each new administration begins weighed down by the legacy not only of the administration preceding it, but decades of what we believe is US foreign policy malpractice. Moreover, shifts to the political right within the United States since 2000 have only further empowered the Iron Triangle Eisenhower warned about in the 1950s. A domestic arms industry is making weapons at an unprecedented pace (and profit),[12] while the benefits of defense industrial output continue to shrink, producing fewer jobs per dollars spent relative to other sectors in the US economy.[13] If we are right, and past overuse of violence has made a present overuse of violence increasingly necessary, we should expect a politically risky gap between the revival of multidimensional US power that is called for, and the perceived need to respond to every threat to US interests with armed force.

Thus, the future of US foreign policy may continue to look very similar to its present. Even with the withdrawal from Afghanistan, the United States may remain in the Middle East as an occupying force and continue to support countries like Israel and Saudi Arabia as allies that further entangle it in the region. It may continue its counterproductive embargo of Cuba, and pursue aggressive tactics against Iran while ignoring the more dangerous Sunni-based extremism against the United States in the region. Finally, it may continue down the path of frequent special operations missions while minimizing the role of diplomacy. This would be the continuation of US "primacy" by force, rather than by example.

But "primacy" was always a shibboleth—a self-congratulatory illusion. To the extent the United States was a unipole, capable of imposing its will on any other state in the international system, the very idea of primacy obscures that US power included its reputation as a *legitimate* actor and the support of key allies, as the US led by consensus. It led, in other words, with more than the sum of its military, economic, and diplomatic parts. Beyond that, even as its main rival collapsed, its other rivals were hard at work innovating around US strengths and devoting resources to attacking its vulnerabilities.[14] US exceptionalism seems likely to continue to define US national identity. While Americans refuse to perceive their country as a bully, given America's continued aspiration to lead a democratic, liberal, and prosperous world, Americans will also believe that any harm they've caused along the way must be forgiven as "collateral." They seem to believe that America's excessive resort to the use of force must be remembered as a force of good. As the late senator Barry Goldwater once put it when he accepted the Republican Party's nomination for the presidency in 1964, "[E]xtremism in the defense of liberty is no vice."[15]

Primacists do not believe other great powers will challenge US hegemony, which removes a limit on America's global militarism. They believe US power is unrivaled, and the United States is a benign hegemon providing many economic and political benefits to other countries of the world. Plus, primacists argue that the United States can always withdraw from its global commitments if needed, without risking its power position (a claim that is currently being tested in postwar Afghanistan). When it comes to the US-China rivalry, pro-primacy advocates William Wohlforth and Stephen Brooks contend that China's rising GDP does not truly threaten the United States as it does not translate into power capabilities or global hegemony—it just means China has a big population and a big economy and that its economy will soon reach its peak growth and stagnate.[16] The United States still maintains unmatched military, technological, and innovation dominance, which translates into global power and influence.

Despite the difficulty of changing well-cemented path dependencies, a restrainer camp believes the solution to America's foreign policy woes and international backlash is for the United States to greatly reduce its global responsibilities and withdraw from most of its military commitments around the globe, even with its Western allies. They argue that the US military presence destabilizes regions like the Middle East and North Africa and undermines US security.[17] Smaller powers strive to protect themselves from US aggression by attempting to secure nuclear weapons or by attacking US allies in the region. Thus, the restrainers propose a plan in which the United States prioritizes diplomatic and economic involvement over militaristic missions.

A restrained grand strategy would rely on the deterrent power of nuclear weapons—because nuclear-armed great powers are the greatest threat to US interests and security—rather than on efforts to halt nuclear proliferation; which have pitted the United States against countries like Iran. It would also seek to withdraw most US military presence from NATO, Europe, and the Gulf, while maintaining some presence in Asia to balance against China.[18] For instance, a US policy toward the Middle East would be guided by two core interests: protecting the United States from attack and promoting the free flow of global commerce. The first step would be the drawdown of the US military in the region over the next five to ten years.

Restrainers are careful to say that the United States must still prevent the rise of hostile regional hegemons in the Persian Gulf, Northeast Asia, and Western Europe, but that doesn't mean that the United States should play the role of the hegemon itself. For instance, instead of maintaining an artificial power balance in the Middle East by supporting states such as Saudi Arabia (and thus fueling proxy conflicts as in Yemen), the United States should allow the multipolarity in the region to serve its own vital interests, permitting regional actors such Iran and Saudi Arabia to balance against each other to preclude regional domination by any other state.[19]

Political scientist Christopher Layne and others also argue the United States should end its strategy of primacy as America's hegemonic position makes countries like China work harder to counterbalance by increasing their own military might and technology. When rivals succeed, the United States loses more power, prestige, and credibility. Layne and fellow political scientist John Mearsheimer suggest the strategy of offshore balancing, a strategy in which the United States withdraws its military presence globally and relies on self-sustaining allies to balance out against rivals.[20] Critically, this position is about restraint of US power, not necessarily disarmament, retrenchment, or isolationism.

As our data illustrate, the answers to America's foreign policy dilemmas do not lie in greater military might or global domination, as the strategy of primacy would suggest.[21] International politics, or great power politics as students of structural realism prefer to identify it, is as much about status and reputation as it is about relative material power. Formally, structural or neo-realists don't deny that concerns other than relative material power matter, but in application, relative material power combined with latent capacity to fight and win wars is really all they care about. This is the main reason why so many neorealists in the 1980s failed to anticipate the collapse of the Soviet Union in 1991. The genius of the H. W. Bush administration is that in all its dealings with Moscow and the Russian Federation's first President Boris Yeltsin following the Soviet Union's collapse, Bush treated the Russians with the same respect previous presidents had treated the Soviets. This was true even as it emerged that Russia had become a shadow of its long-feared predecessor in terms of material power and global reach. But this tradition of geopolitical respect of Russia did not survive the H. W. Bush Administration. Americans began to speak of a "unipolar" moment—a perceived insult to Russia and other revisionist powers, from their perspective. This reputational insult became a pattern following H. W. Bush; and Russians complained privately that they were no longer getting the respect they believed they deserved.

As Yeltsin's successor, President Vladimir Putin pushed Russia to authoritarian kleptocracy. As a result, Russia's reputation further declined and its repeated requests to be treated with the respect due a superpower were ignored. Even before Putin had taken full control of Russia's government, this resentment came to a head in Kosovo in 1999, when Russia assumed NATO and the West would recognize Russia's traditional interests in determining the political structures in the aftermath of the Kosovo Crisis. When a US-led NATO contributed to the end of Serbian President Slobodan Milosevic's rule and his ethnic cleansing policies in Kosovo, Russia took the Western humanitarian intervention as an insult and a precedent that Russia would later co-opt as justification for its war of conquest against Ukraine. While the NATO intervention in Kosovo has generally been hailed as a successful humanitarian one, in the post-9/11 era, the United States arrogated to itself the privilege of a great power to undertake more questionable military interventions in

Iraq, Afghanistan, Libya, and Syria. Each new US intervention altered international norms and made it easier for other countries to justify their own military interventions or militaristic aspirations. If the United States can do it, so can we; *so must we.*

While primacists understand the biggest global threats as stemming from failed, rogue, or illiberal states, they do not connect US hegemony to the rise of these same threats through US regime change interventions, democratization operations, and persistent and growing military hostilities abroad. A heavy-handed, overstretched United States creates more blowback in its wake and destabilizes regions of interest by worsening the spirals of security dilemmas. A proper solution demands a decrease in US military engagements, with an attendant increase in diplomacy, intelligence sharing with allies, and deploying economic tools of statecraft.

The grand strategy of selective engagement might be the compromise required between the restraint and the liberal hegemony or primacy camps.[22] It could allow for a more realistic transition away from current US global commitments and ongoing conflicts to allow it to concentrate on matters that are primary interests. According to selective engagement, the United States should only intervene in regions that directly affect its security, leaving the United States to focus on its relationships with Europe, East Asia, and the Persian Gulf. Its main objectives would be to prevent war between great powers, prevent the rise of aggressive regional hegemons, and prevent nuclear proliferation. US goals of free trade, democratization, and human rights promotion may still be pursued but only if they do not interfere with its primary strategic interests, and only if the United States itself abides by its own laws. This is the real danger of exceptionalism in foreign policy (a problem hardly unique to the United States): it blinds the exceptional state to how its well-intended actions will be perceived by others. It renders those perceptions irrelevant. In selective engagement, the United States would maintain its existing alliance networks but withdraw its military forces from regions of the world with no capacity to hurt it militarily, ultimately reducing the US military footprint domestically (via lower defense spending) and internationally, while still promoting multilateral institutions and liberal ethos. In fact, the US withdrawal of forces from other regions of the world may be expected to significantly reduce anti-Americanism sentiments in the long-run. Territorial bases/occupations matter differently because humans are hard-wired to prioritize control of territory. With US lift capacity, this hybrid grand strategy promises to be able to advance shared US and allied interests without provoking nationalist backlash or empowering nationalist demagogues.[23]

In August 1988, after the United States mistakenly downed a commercial Iran Air flight killing 290 civilians, then-Vice President George H. W. Bush said, "I will never apologize for the United States—I don't care what the facts are . . . I'm not an apologize-for-America kind of guy."[24] The quote perfectly summarizes a defining feature of US foreign policy and leadership—the United States must only highlight and work within the exceptional components of its preferred identity, never facing up to the flaws and mistakes of its global legacy. The United States sees no double standard in asking Japan to apologize to Korea and China for genocide, or Germany to apologize to Poland for the same crime, but it has yet to make peace with its own genocides against indigenous North American tribes. It has yet to make peace with its own legacy of slavery and, after 1865, insufficient work toward eradicating race discrimination. But if the leadership and population of the United States won't apologize for its moral failings or strategic blunders, how can it expect to learn from historical mistakes, bad intentions, and flawed policies? If there is nothing to apologize for, then there is nothing to change.

American exceptionalism blinds policymakers and citizens to strategic choices that ultimately harm both the United States and the world, perpetuating path dependencies. To shift away from America's militarism, the US foreign policy community and the body politic must assess and accept past successes and failures to begin to make amends. Our work merely catalogs the frequency and intensity of US military interventions over time, but the implications of these interventions remain staggering not only for US foreign and domestic policy, but for the long-standing shared human interest in preventing another world war, and in building a world in which while maintaining space for serious differences, we find ourselves able to work together to resolve other threats to humanity, such as global warming or pandemics. It is time to apply the historical lessons and empirical findings of our study toward the innovation of fresh solutions and different paths to promote US and international security in the decades and centuries to come.

Notes

1. "Choosing Hope: President Obama's Address to the United Nations," *The White House Blog*, September 24, 2014, https://obamawhitehouse.archives.gov/realitych eck/blog/2014/09/24/choosing-hope-president-obama-s-address-united-nations.

2. For a broader debate on American Exceptionalism, see John W. Kingdon, *America the Unusual* (New York: Worth Publishers, 1999); Godfrey Hodgson, *The Myth of American Exceptionalism* (New Haven, CT: Yale University Press, 2009).

3. Jeffrey Ostler, "Genocide and American Indian History," *Oxford Research Encyclopedia of American History*, March 2, 2015, accessed July 6, 2021, https://oxfor dre.com/americanhistory/view/10.1093/acrefore/9780199329175.001.0001/acref ore-9780199329175-e-3.

4. Richard Seymour, "The Cold War, American Anticommunism and the Global 'Colour Line,'" in *Race and Racism in International Relations,* edited by Alexander Anievas, Nivi Manchanda, and Robbie Shilliam (London: Routledge, 2014), https://www.taylorfrancis.com/chapters/edit/10.4324/9781315857299-16/cold-war-ameri can-anticommunism-global-colour-line-richard-seymour.

5. Seymour, "The Cold War, American Anticommunism and the Global 'Colour Line,'" 162.

6. Seymour, "The Cold War, American Anticommunism and the Global 'Colour Line,'" 165.

7. Sidita Kushi, "Double Standards Abound, But only Russia Is to blame for Its Imperialist War in Ukraine," *EURACTIV*, April 11, 2022. https://www.euractiv.com/section/europe-s-east/opinion/double-standards-abound-but-only-russia-is-to-blame-for-its-imperialist-war-in-ukraine; Sidita Kushi, "Don't Compare Russia's War to NATO in Kosovo," *EURACTIV*, March 1, 2022. https://www.euractiv.com/section/europe-s-east/opinion/dont-compare-russias-war-to-nato-in-kosovo/.

8. Kevin Liptak, Natasha Bertrand, Jeremy Herb, Zachary Cohen, and Oren Liebermann, "A 'Gut Decision': Inside Biden's Defense of Afghanistan Withdrawal amid Warnings of Country's Collapse," *CNN Politics*, July 2, 2021, https://www.cnn.com/2021/07/02/politics/afghanistan-biden-withdrawal-security/index.html.

9. G. Lundestad, "Empire by Invitation? The United States and Western Europe, 1945–1952," *Journal of Peace Research*, 23, no. 3 (1986): 263–277, https://doi.org/10.1177/002234338602300305.

10. See polls here that offer broad public opinion on US international image and role, Richard Wile, Janell Fetterolf, and Mara Mordecai, "U.S. Image Plummets Internationally as Most Say Country Has Handled Coronavirus Badly," *Pew Research Center*, September 15, 2020, https://www.pewresearch.org/global/2020/09/15/us-image-plummets-internationally-as-most-say-country-has-handled-coronavirus-badly/.

11. Barry Posen and Andrew Ross, "Competing Visions for U.S. Grand Strategy," *International Security* 21, no. 3 (1996): 5–53.

12. Byron Callan, "Why Most of the Top 100 Saw Defense Revenue Grow," *Defense News*, August 8, 2022. https://www.defensenews.com/opinion/commentary/2022/08/08/why-most-of-the-top-100-saw-defense-revenue-grow/.

13. Costs of War Project, "Employment Impact," Watson Institute, Brown University, 2019. https://watson.brown.edu/costsofwar/costs/economic/economy/employment

14. Ivan Arreguin-Toft, "In the Digital Age, Retrenchment May Not Make America Safer," *The National Interest*, September 27, 2022. https://nationalinterest.org/blog/

techland-when-great-power-competition-meets-digital-world/digital-age-retre
nchment-may-not-make/.

15. Goldwater's 1964 Acceptance Speech. *The Washington Post*, 1964. https://www.was
hingtonpost.com/wp-srv/politics/daily/may98/goldwaterspeech.htm.

16. S. Brooks and W. Wohlforth, *World Out of Balance: International Relations and the
Challenge of American Primacy* (Princeton, NJ: Princeton University Press, 2008),
retrieved June 14, 2021. http://www.jstor.org/stable/j.ctt7sxgh.

17. Paul Pillar, et al., "A New US Paradigm for the Middle East," *Quincy Institute*, July 17,
2020. https://quincyinst.org/2020/07/17/ending-americas-misguided-policy-of-mid
dle-east-domination/?mc_cid=3cbffcdaa3&mc_eid=a904f6b0e9.

18. Barry R. Posen, *Restraint: A New Foundation for U.S. Grand Strategy* (Ithaca,
NY: Cornell University Press, 2014); Eugene Gholz, Darryl G. Press, and Harvey M.
Sapolsky, "Come Home, America: The Strategy of Restraint in the Face of Temptation,"
International Security 21, no. 4 (2017): 5–48.

19. Pillar, et al., "A New US Paradigm for the Middle East."

20. Christopher Layne, "The Unipolar Illusion: Why New Great Powers Will Rise,"
International Security 17, no. 4 (1993): 5–51; John J. Mearsheimer and Stephen
M. Walt, "The Case for Offshore Balancing," *Foreign Affairs*, July/August 2016;
Christopher Layne, "The U.S. Foreign Policy Establishment and Grand Strategy: How
American Elites Obstruct Strategic Adjustment," *International Politics* 54, no. 3
(2017): 260–275; Christopher Layne, "From Preponderance to Offshore Balancing,"
International Security 22, no. 1 (Summer, 1997): 86–124; John J. Mearsheimer, *The
Great Delusion: Liberal Dreams and International Realities* (New Haven, CT: Yale
University Press, 2018).

21. Also called liberal hegemony or deep engagement. Stephen G. Brooks, John G.
Ikenberry, and William C. Wohlforth, "Don't Come Home, America: The Case
against Retrenchment," *International Security* 37, no. 3 (2012): 7–51; Stephen
G. Brooks, John G. Ikenberry, and William C. Wohlforth, "Lean Forward: In Defense
of American Engagement," *Foreign Affairs*, 92, no. 1 (2013): 130–142, 137; John G.
Ikenberry, *Liberal Leviathan: The Origins, Crisis, and Transformation of the American
World Order* (Princeton, NJ: Princeton University Press, 2011); Joseph S. Nye, *The
Future of Power* (New York: Pacific Affairs, 2011); Robert Kagan, *The World America
Made* (New York: Alfred Knopf, 2012); Stephen G. Brooks and William C. Wohlforth,
America Abroad: The United States' Global Role in the 21st Century (New York: Oxford
University Press, 2016).

22. Robert J. Art, "Geopolitics Updated: The Strategy of Selective Engagement,"
International Security 23, no. 3 (Winter 1998–1999): 79–113; Robert J. Art, *A Grand
Strategy for America* (Ithaca, NY: Cornell University Press, 2004).

23. Monica Duffy Toft, *The Geography of Ethnic Violence: Identity, Interests, and the
Indivisibility of Territory* (Princeton, NJ: Princeton University Press, 2003); Dominic
D. P. Johnson and Monica Duffy Toft, "Grounds for War: The Evolution of Territorial
Conflict," *International Security* 38, no. 3 (2014): 7–38.

24. Marty Steinberg, "'Kinder, Gentler' and other George H.W. Bush Quotes," *CNBC*,
updated December 12, 2018, https://www.cnbc.com/2018/12/01/george-hw-bush-
quotations.html.

Index

For the benefit of digital users, indexed terms that span two pages (e.g., 52–53) may, on occasion, appear on only one of those pages.

Tables, and figures are indicated by *t* and *f* following the page number